The Heart of
Catholic Social
Teaching

The rational creatures participation
in the <u>eternal law</u>
        ↳ God's wisdom.

The Heart of
Catholic Social
Teaching

Its Origins and Contemporary Significance

David Matzko McCarthy

BrazosPress

a division of Baker Publishing Group
Grand Rapids, Michigan

© 2009 by David Matzko McCarthy

Published by Brazos Press
a division of Baker Publishing Group
P.O. Box 6287, Grand Rapids, MI 49516-6287
www.brazospress.com

Printed in the United States of America

Library of Congress Cataloging-in-Publication Data
McCarthy, David Matzko.
    The heart of Catholic social teaching : its origins and contemporary significance / David Matzko McCarthy.
        p.   cm.
    Includes bibliographical references (p.   ) and index.
    ISBN 978-1-58743-248-4 (pbk.)
    1. Christian sociology—Catholic Church. 2. Catholic Church—Doctrines. I. Title.
BX1753.M363 2009
261.8088′282—dc22
                                                                                    2008047966

In Memory of
Father James M. Forker (1932–1994)

I love this place—College, Seminary, and Grotto." So said Jim Forker, on his alma mater, in a talk the year before he died. Rev. James M. Forker, graduate of both Mount Saint Mary's College and Seminary (1960), and priest of the Diocese of Trenton, New Jersey, served the Mount as teacher and administrator for twenty-seven years. "I'm a citizen of the world but based in Bayonne," proclaimed the *New Yorker* cartoon on his office door. As an Irishman, he came by his passion for justice honestly and shared it proudly with Mount priests who had gone before him—Bishop Walsh of Maryknoll, Fr. Stanley Rother, a Central American martyr, and Msgr. Geno Baroni, HUD secretary in the Carter administration. He talked about them. You didn't have to ask. Catholic Social Teaching was his passion and his favorite course. At his death, he left a generous gift so that Catholic Social Teaching would carry on at the Mount. This book, *The Heart of Catholic Social Teaching*, would have tickled him. Four of its contributors were his friends and colleagues. How he could go on about solidarity and subsidiarity! In life he would have devoured the essays—and no doubt would have contributed one. Now he looks down on them rejoicing with pride and that Irish twinkle in his eye.

William L. Portier
Mary Ann Spearin Chair of Catholic Theology, University of Dayton
Mount St. Mary's University 1979–2003
September 29, 2008

Contents

Part Three: Justice

Part Four: Moving Forward

Introduction

*T*he *Heart of Catholic Social Teaching* emerges from an ongoing collaboration of teaching philosophy and theology. It represents more than a few years of conversation and argument about how to integrate social ethics and concerns about the common good into our courses and our own lives. In the chapters that follow, the reader will see the effects of our discussions. The contributors represent not a random collection of academics, but philosophers and theologians who talk with each other weekly, if not daily, read one another's work, attend each other's lectures, and frequently brainstorm about how best to engage students in our conversations about love and justice. We certainly do not always agree, but we are committed to common efforts to enhance the mission of our institution, Mount St. Mary's University. It is a lively and unusual place. We are happy for the opportunity to use this book in addressing our own students and, for some of us, addressing the members of our parishes. Hopefully, the book will invigorate conversations where we live and work. But we are especially pleased to reach a wider audience.

Our sense of audience draws on two important concepts in Catholic social teaching: solidarity and subsidiarity. These terms will be developed in the book, especially in chapters 7 and 8. Generally speaking, solidarity points to the interdependence and mutual responsibilities of people, locally and across the globe. Subsidiarity highlights the function of local institutions, communities, cooperatives, and networks of people who join together in common endeavors for the common good. We think about *The Heart of Catholic Social Teaching* as an exercise in thought that ought to inspire solidarity and encourage investment in subsidiary networks and groups. Some of the chapters offer specific suggestions and challenges to the reader, challenges which the authors take very seriously. We are taking up these challenges as regular habits of life—starting fair-trade networks in our parishes, making time and space for practices of hospitality, and changing our patterns of consumption and waste. If you extend the inquiry of the book through conversations with others, and if you make efforts to promote the common good through subsidiary networks, you will be connected to us, and reading the book, like our writing of it, will be a practice of solidarity.

The Heart of Catholic Social Teaching is mainly about modern Catholic social teaching. Books on Catholic social thought usually begin with Pope Leo XIII's encyclical on the condition of labor, issued in 1891. In this volume, however, we will begin with basic sources of the Christian life: scripture, worship, and membership in the church (chaps. 1–3). After these topics, we will introduce (in chapter 4) Leo XIII's encyclical, "On the Condition of Labor." The encyclical also goes by the Latin title, *Rerum Novarum* or "new things" (which are the first two words of the Latin translation of the document). An "encyclical" letter, from the Greek word for "circle," is a major teaching document of a pope that is addressed and circulated to the whole church. In *Rerum Novarum*, Pope Leo XIII deals with "revolutionary changes" of the modern era: the industrial revolution, the plight of the wage-earning poor, the *laissez faire* or hands-off approach of governments with capitalist economies, and the challenges of socialism.

From this beginning, a series of documents follow, some of which are encyclicals issued on the anniversary of *Rerum Novarum*. Pope Pius XI, for example, disseminates *Quadragesimo Anno* ("forty years") in 1931, and John Paul II issues *Centesimus Annus* ("one hundred years") in 1991. The body of Catholic social teaching also includes documents of the Second Vatican Council (Vatican II) which met between 1962 and 1965. The Council gives us a number of (conciliar) documents, and the one most often cited in relationship to social teaching is the "Pastoral Constitution of the Church in the Modern World"—*Gaudium et Spes* ("the joys and hopes"). Also included is "Justice in the World," a document written by the Synod of Bishops that was assembled by Pope Paul VI in 1971. In short, modern Catholic social teaching is based on a set of documents initiated by Pope Leo XIII's *Rerum Novarum*. The documents are available on various websites (www.vatican.va) and in published collections.[1]

Our book is divided into four parts. Within each part, the chapters will be followed by issues or texts for discussion: biblical texts, key documents in Catholic social teaching, issues like health-care reform, and proposals about how we might live differently. As noted above, the first part provides a discussion of sources—the Bible, liturgy, and the church, along with a chapter on Pope Leo XIII's teaching on the "revolutionary changes" in the modern world. Parts 2 and 3, titled "Love" and "Justice," are also organized by sources important to the modern social tradition. Both parts will indicate that love and justice, in Catholic thought, cannot be treated as entirely independent goods or spheres. You will see discussions of justice in part 2 on love, and a good bit of love in part 3 on justice. In theological terms, God's grace and righteousness are one. Nonetheless, the division between love and justice allows us to trace Augustinian themes in modern thought (on love in part 2) and the importance of Thomas Aquinas (on justice in part 3). Part 4 (with three chapters) treats topics that have become contentious in recent years: religion in public life, moral pluralism, and environmental stewardship (particularly the problem of global climate change). This last part of the book is a "sending forth" of sorts. The final chapters present hospitality as the way for Christians to engage others in a world of disagreements and indifference on matters of justice and the pursuit of truth.

Outline: Part One—Sources

Part 1 discusses the primary sources in the Christian tradition: scripture and worship. It also treats what is marked as the beginning of modern Catholic social teaching, Pope Leo XIII's "On the Condition of Labor" (1891). Each chapter of part 1, and the entire book, is followed by a discussion section and usually by proposals about what we can do in response to the ideas presented in the chapter. In other words, the themes of Catholic social thought are set in terms of everyday life.

In chapter 1, "Biblical Justice," Sr. Mary Kate Birge develops an understanding of justice in terms of our relationship to God. She reviews the Old and New Testaments, from Genesis to Jesus. She shows that biblical justice is not like the blindfolded Lady Justice depicted in courthouses across the country. God's justice is not anonymous and disinterested, but personal and full of compassion. From the Exodus to the ministry of Jesus, we know that God lifts up the lowly; Jesus gathers the outcast and announces the reign of God. In response to this chapter, we introduce a discussion on how we are called to read scripture in community, and Sr. Mary Kate guides us through a reflection on the parable of the good Samaritan in Luke 10:25–37.

Chapter 2 is titled, "The Liturgy as a Source of Formation in Catholic Social Teaching." In this chapter, Fr. James Donohue explains the formative nature of worship, particularly through sacraments of initiation, baptism, confirmation, and the Eucharist. He focuses on the word of God—scripture—in the context of these acts of worship through which we become members of the body of Christ. Fr. Donohue tells us about people who are receiving the sacraments of initiation, and we see the biblical witness (outlined in chapter 1) coming alive in their lives. In response to the chapter, the reader is invited to walk through a similar reflection on the liturgy. God's word of justice in the liturgy, we should remember, is always an offer of grace.

In chapter 3, Rodica Stoicoiu writes on the "Eucharist and Social Justice." Later in the book (in chapter 8), the term social justice will be considered in philosophical terms. We will see that "social" justice is concerned with how we—as individuals but especially in our communities—should order our lives to the common good. In her chapter, Dr. Stoicoiu heightens our awareness of what is happening to us in the celebration of the Eucharist and how we are called by God to new life. She presents the theology of God's self-giving in Jesus Christ and helps us understand the significance of our liturgical actions—not only what we do but also the silence that we so often want to fill with noise. The fundamental point of the chapter is that we are formed, through the Eucharist, into the body of Christ. The discussion that follows the chapter is a reflection on our eating habits. It is an exercise in understanding how our worship might transform our everyday lives.

In chapter 4, John Donovan introduces us to the founding document of modern Catholic social teaching, Pope Leo XIII's *Rerum Novarum*. Note the phrase "modern" Catholic social teaching. The first three chapters of the book draw from our continuity with the ancient church: scripture and worship. Chapter 5 will discuss St. Augustine (354–430), and chapter 8 attends to the thought of Thomas Aquinas (13th c.). In other words, Leo XIII does not provide a new beginning of Christian thought on social and economic life. Rather, he provides a statement of Catholic thought in the language of modern social philosophy and in relationship to specifically modern social problems. These two points will be made by Dr. Donovan. He will show how Pope Leo XIII gives us an orientation to contemporary questions by transforming the individualism of modern political theory. At stake, according to Donovan, is how we understand what it means to be human. Following the chapter, we will consider how a Christian conception of the human being shapes our understanding of property and our work (especially in terms of relationships at work).

Outline: Part Two—Love

In chapter 5, William Collinge provides a concise but rich presentation of Augustine's life and thought. Augustine's writings and his reflections on his own life are voluminous, so it is no easy task to put his life and work in clear focus. In "Saint Augustine of Hippo: Love, Community, and Politics," Dr. Collinge explains central ideas in Augustine's work and helps us understand his influence on Christian theology and contemporary social ethics. After outlining the context of Augustine's thought, Collinge explains Augustine's understanding of love and friendship as well as his theology of the church and his famous description of the two cities, earthly and heavenly.

Collinge gives us a framework to understand Augustine's call to participate in the good of the earthly city (working toward an earthly peace), with our eyes trained on an entirely different and perfect love in the city of God. Following the chapter, we will consider our call to Christian love as it is developed in the modern document, *Pastoral Constitution on the Church in the Modern World*. In chapter 6, Dr. Collinge goes further by setting Pope Benedict's encyclical on the love of God in its Augustinian context. In "A Contemporary Augustinian Approach to Love and Politics—Pope Benedict XVI's *Deus Caritas Est*," he reviews Benedict XVI's account of love and his concern to show the unity between desiring love (*eros*) and self-giving love (*agape*). From this account of love, Collinge guides us through the complicated relationships, in *Deus Caritas Est*, between the church and the society, between our vocations of Christian love and the requirements of justice. In response to the chapter on Benedict XVI, we will discuss guidelines for Christian contributions to civic life as provided by the United States Conference of Catholic Bishops in their *Forming Consciences for Faithful Citizenship*.

The questions about political life, which are raised by chapters 5 and 6, culminate in David Cloutier's chapter on "Modern Politics and Catholic Social Teaching." The reader will find a great deal of continuity with other chapters as well. Dr. Cloutier begins with the same image used by Sr. Mary Kate Birge to introduce chapter 1: the image of a blindfold on the eyes of Lady Justice. He also treats, as John Donovan does, the problem of individualism in modern political thought. Dr. Cloutier skillfully interweaves contemporary documents (by John Paul II, for example) with everyday examples and reflection on modern habits of life. He shows how Catholic social teaching makes its way between the problems of individualism and collectivism. Following this chapter, we will consider the current debate on health-care reform (which usually swings between individualism and collectivism) and how we might respond in terms of Catholic social thought and on the basis of community practices and the common good.

Outline: Part Three—Justice

Part 3 begins with chapter 8: "Natural Law—St. Thomas Aquinas and the Role of Reason in Social Order." In this chapter Joshua P. Hochschild presents a stream of Catholic thought that differs from, but complements, the chapters on scripture, worship, Augustine, and love. Dr. Hochschild introduces the topic of justice by presenting basic questions of Greek (and therefore Western) philosophy. The chapter provides a clear elucidation of Aristotle's framework of natural justice and law. In the Catholic tradition the Augustinian, scriptural, and Aristotelian stream come together in the theology of Thomas Aquinas. Hochschild explains Aquinas's social philosophy with particular emphasis on the ordering of the members of society to the common (what in the tradition is called "subsidiarity"). In the discussion that follows the chapter, we will consider two key subsidiary institutions: labor associations and the family.

The title of chapter 9, "Modern Economy and the Social Order," indicates the thematic connection with the discussion of natural law and the social order in chapter 8. The discussion that follows this chapter, for example, will discuss the exchange of goods through subsidiary institutions in the fair-trade movement. In this chapter David McCarthy shows that considerations of economic life, in Catholic social thought, set economic exchange and contracts within a broader framework of social roles and duties. Modern economic theory tends in the opposite direction. Economics is considered a free-standing realm of behavior where exchange is ruled by disinterested mechanisms. Catholic social thought, in contrast, considers economic exchange within the context of our callings in social life and in terms of the common good.

The subsequent chapter, by Kathy Dow Magnus, presents a thoroughly relational—Catholic and personalist—view of material goods and the place they ought to occupy in our lives. In this part of the book (part 3), we move from Greek philosophy and natural law back to the call of Christian discipleship. In the chapter Dr. Magnus puts us face-to-face with a gospel imperative, one that cannot be neglected in any extended discussion of social and economic life: "If you wish to be complete, go and sell your possessions and give to the poor, and you will have treasure in heaven; and come, follow Me" (Matt. 19:21). The chapter tells the story of Dorothy Day, Peter Maurin, and the Catholic worker movement, which was formed and spread in the United States in the 1930s. The Catholic worker movement, among others things, opened houses of hospitality so that Catholic workers might share life with the poor. In the words of Dorothy Day, "The mystery of poverty is that by sharing in it, making ourselves poor in giving to others, we increase our knowledge and belief in love." In response to this chapter, we will discuss whether or not hospitality to the poor is possible for ordinary families. Is such hospitality possible only for extraordinary people who live with the poor and apart from the rest of us?

Outline: Part Four—Moving Forward

We have titled the last part of our project "moving forward." Chapters 11 and 12 consider ways to sustain community and our desires to live truthfully in a context of moral and religious pluralism. Chapter 13 on the "greening" of Catholic social teaching frames our responsibilities as citizens of the earth in terms of a sacramental understanding of creation. We have placed this chapter last because it presents, in clear relief, some critical challenges of Catholic social teaching—how to sustain just social relations and how to act and to change our lives for the sake of the common good.

In Chapter 11, Richard Buck examines the conflicts and tensions that are produced for the Catholic church when faced with the rise of the modern secular state. The church and its social philosophy develop out of the medieval consensus of Christianity, so that understanding where to stand in relationship to secularism and a plurality of religions is no easy matter. Dr. Buck offers a careful treatment of *Dignitatis Humanae*, the *Declaration on Religious Freedom*, which was written at the Second Vatican Council (Vatican II) in 1965. Buck shows that religious freedom is understood not as a concession or a lesser of evils, but as a positive good that respects the inherent freedom of the human being—a freedom that is at the heart of faith and includes the call to make one's faith active in social life. Following this chapter, we will take a look at statements by John Paul II and Benedict XVI and the connections they make between freedom, nonviolence, and truth. We will also consider the fruits of dialogue between Catholics and Jews and their common social concerns.

Trudy Conway, in chapter 12, highlights a problem of moral pluralism. Too often our goals of tolerance overshadow our social concerns for living truthfully and working for the common good. In "Compassion and Hospitality," Dr. Conway proposes that hospitality is the alternative to the indifference of passive tolerance. She defines hospitality as openness and welcome to others for the sake of living truthfully. Such hospitality to the stranger and to those who are quite different from us is animated by the same compassion that moves us to love what is good. These are only definitions. In contrast, Dr. Conway shows us the meaning of hospitality by telling the story of the people of Le Chambon, a mountain village that provided Jews refuge during the Nazi occupation of France. She skillfully weaves the story with key documents in Catholic social teaching (e.g., the synod of bishops "Justice in the World," 1971). The apt reflection and response to the chapter, in the discussion following the chapter, is to tell Trudy Conway's story of hospitality. She has put hospitality in action in her work to abolish the death penalty in Maryland. Her story serves as a guide for how we might move forward in relation to other critical issues of our time.

Finally, in chapter 13 Brian Henning offers us a perspective on environmental ethics. Often books and articles on the environment will emphasize impending disaster in order to move us to action. Dr. Henning, in contrast, develops our relationship to the earth in terms of a God-centered view of creation. Our stewardship of nature is simply part of the web of relationships that constitute who we are as human beings. Theologically, Dr. Henning draws on what Catholic theology calls a sacramental orientation to creation from addresses by both John Paul II and Benedict XVI, as well as documents by the United States Conference of Catholic Bishops. In response to this chapter, the discussion shows that the problem of global warming is a problem of social ethics—a problem, as Dr. Henning argues, of our relationships. Global climate change is a challenge to how we are able to work together—personally, communally, and collectively—and to do so in a way that requires us to change, together, how we live. These are fundamental challenges of Catholic social teaching.

PART ONE

Sources

1

Biblical Justice

MARY KATHERINE BIRGE, SSJ

In twenty-first century Western society, we usually conceive of justice as a matter of being fair. That is, we believe justice means that every person ought to receive an equal amount of whatever is under discussion, no matter what his or her life circumstances may be. Every citizen is equal under the law. We often translate this to mean every citizen is the same under the law. In the United States the familiar image of a blindfolded goddess, Lady Justice, holding up the scales of justice and weighing out the "fair," the "just," or even the same amount for each petitioner under the law adorns many of our court buildings. This figure decorates not only the pediment of the U.S. Supreme Court building, but appears often in the opening sequence of television series devoted to stories about crime, punishment, and the rendering of justice according to constitutional law (for example, any one of the *Law and Order* or *CSI* episodes). In addition to this picture of blindfolded Lady Justice, the familiar sayings "equal justice under the law" and "justice is blind" also signal how the ideal of impartiality or objectivity has shaped Western society's vision of what is just. Members of our society, for the most part, presume that justice is cold and detached. Ironically, this so-called detachment protects and privileges those who least need such protecting or privileging. Such "blind" justice tends not to consider the leper and the poor, but would rather overlook their needs. To acknowledge their needs would be to acknowledge that the privileged and the disadvantaged belong to the same society. The privileged would have to acknowledge that they are inextricably bound to the poor through their common life. So they refuse their shared identity, blind themselves through objectivity and dispassion toward suffering, and practice detachment rather than mercy. In the biblical world, however, the concept of justice (sometimes called righteousness) binds every human being to relationships full of compassion.

The First Stories

In the Bible justice is based on the relationship between God and human beings and the relationship among human beings themselves. Both the vertical relationship with God and the horizontal relationship with other human beings must be in balance in order for justice or righteousness to exist. If either part of this equation is out of balance, the other is too. Only when the demands of a particular human relationship are met is the vertical relationship between God and the person in balance. And only when the demands of the divine/human relationship are being met, is the horizontal relationship between human persons in balance. The initial stories of Genesis illustrate the reason for justice based on relationship and demonstrate how injustice arises when the human being fails to meet the demands of either part of the divine-to-human or human-to-human equation.

In Genesis 1, human beings, male and female, are created in the image and in the likeness of God (Gen. 1:27). Because they bear the image of their divine creator, who is the source and summit of all justice, when human beings act with justice they reveal both the justice of God and their own fidelity to living out of that image of God in them. When they fail to act with justice, that is, to mirror the likeness of God in their dealing with one another or with God, the rightness or trueness of their relationship both with God and other human beings is affected adversely. This happens much the way a bicycle wheel loses its ability to run true when one of its spokes fails to maintain a torque to the rim proportionate to the torque of all the other spokes of the wheel. Its relationship with the other spokes and the wheel's rim is out of whack, and, as a result, the whole wheel—spokes, rim, hub, and tire—cannot attain the purpose for which it was created. So it is for us human beings.

In Genesis 3:1–24, the story of the first man and first woman and their failed relationship with God portrays the justice of God. We see first their failure to act justly toward God and one another and then, from God's subsequent actions toward them (expulsion from the garden, provision of protective clothing, and perseverance on God's part to continue in relationship with them and their offspring), we discover that the practice of mercy (along with judgment) is a constitutive element of God's justice. These actions by the first man and woman also reveal that the exercise of justice or of injustice by human beings always discloses the state of their relationship with the divine; that is, either in or out of balance. Two fundamentals must be kept in mind as we move ahead to examine more explicit calls in the Bible to practice justice. First, justice proceeds to human beings from God (of whom it is constitutive) by virtue of their creation in God's image. Second, justice is relational, and its fulfillment depends upon our meeting the demands of life lived with others and our call to be faithful to God in relation to the world.

Desert Experience

In the Old Testament there are three terms which, along with their related forms, denote the enactment or the quality of what we have named biblical justice. They are: *tsedeq* (and its feminine form *tsĕdāqāh*), *mishpāt*, and *dîn*. Each of these words and their Hebrew cognates illustrates some aspect of the notion that God is the source of justice or righteousness, that God reveals justice or righteousness, and that God expects human beings to practice it in their dealings with one another and with God. In the books of Exodus and Deuteronomy, after God has liberated the descendants of Abraham, Isaac, and Jacob from Pharoah's oppression and the burden of Egypt's injustice, the Holy One establishes through Moses a new society in which the practice of justice extends to the powerless as well as to the powerful, to the poor as well as to the wealthy, and to the outsider as well as to the insider (Exod. 12:49; 22:21–23; Deut. 25:19). In Exodus 22:26–27 we hear God charge Israel through Moses:

> If ever you take your neighbor's garment in pledge,[1] you shall restore it to him before the sun goes down; for that is his only covering, it is his mantle for his body; in what else shall he sleep? And if he cries to me, I will hear, for I am compassionate.

And similarly, in Deuteronomy 24:11–13 we hear again:

> When you make your neighbor a loan of any sort, you shall not go into his house to fetch his pledge. You shall stand outside, and the man to whom you make the loan shall bring the pledge out to you. And if he is a poor man, you shall not sleep in his pledge; when the sun goes down you shall restore to him the pledge that he may sleep in his cloak and bless you; and it shall be righteousness [*tsĕdāqāh*] to you before the LORD your God.

The practice of justice (or righteousness) that is promoted in both these examples illustrates how integral the notion of relationship is to the very nature of justice. In the example from Exodus, the exercise of justice (restoring to the poor person before night falls the cloak one has taken in pledge) entails the lender's relationship with the borrower, the lender's relationship with God, and the borrower's relationship with God. The lender has the option of with-holding the neighbor's pledge until reimbursed, as long as the poor person is not without the rudimentary shelter of a cloak at night. But when the poverty of the neighbor will cause her to be without the most basic of night shelters, the lender must return the neighbor's only shelter for the night, even without her making good on the bond. Why?

The lender is certainly worthy of being reimbursed what was lent. But the immediacy of the borrower's basic human need for night shelter, and the human misery which would ensue for the borrower were she to pass the night unprotected from the elements—these trump the lender's legitimate but de-ferrable need for material reimbursement. Torah requires such an exercise of mercy (or compassion) toward one creature by another because compassion is as elemental a component of God's justice as is the necessity to hold every creature accountable for her choices (Exod. 22:27; cf. Gen. 2:18; 3:21; 4:15). The lender has a relationship with the neighbor that is based on the divine image they both bear (Gen. 1:27). That image of God, shared by all human-ity, requires each person to imitate God. To remain in right relationship with God, to continue to live justly, the lender must apply mercy even as she seeks accountability. For, as Exodus 22:27 indicates, God is not objective or impartial where the poor and oppressed are concerned. God will hear their cries because God is compassionate as virtually every prophet taught since the kingship was established and Israel became a nation among the nations.

In the Land

With Moses in the desert, God had fashioned Israel into a society based on just relationships. When the people came into the land, God had to summon forth individuals who had remained faithful to that desert vision of justice to bid the powerful and haughty to remember what God required of them: "to act with justice" (Mic. 6:8b), especially toward those who could not demand it for themselves: the weak and the poor. In the tenth century, when David stole Bathsheba away from her husband and arranged his murder, the prophet Nathan spoke a parable of injustice to David the king (2 Sam.11–12). David, roused by the story, rightly proclaimed judgment at such an injustice done by a powerful and wealthy man to one of the weakest and least among his people. "That man is you!" was Nathan's cry (12:7), and David recognized himself, his guilt, and the ruin he had made of his relationship with God in the shambles he had made of his relationship with Bathsheba and Uriah. The king too was not above, or exempt from, the demands justice required of every human relationship in Israel. To honor the Lord God, to remain in right relationship with the Holy One, to offer right worship, each person, whether of exalted status or not, had to act with justice in everyday interactions.

The introduction of kingship and urbanization had brought radical changes to Israel. The community would need the continuous activity of prophets like Nathan to challenge those with power and wealth in Judah and Israel, and make clear to them through prophetic utterance and action that their temple offerings, sacrifices, and worship were unacceptable—were worthless before God—without their acting justly toward every member of the community. We see this connection made between right worship of God and right relationship with members of the community, to a greater or lesser degree, in the writing of almost every prophet of the Old Testament. I choose four to examine more closely how they shaped their cry for justice for the poor and the weak.

Amos prophesied in the eighth century when the northern kingdom was in its last decades of existence. He had the unenviable task of preaching to a rather wealthy and comfortable population that all was not well between them and the God whom they professed to worship. They were being judged on their practice of justice and found grievously wanting. In 5:21–24 he wrote:

> I hate, I despise your feasts, and I take no delight in your solemn assemblies.
>
> Even though you offer me your burnt offerings and cereal offerings, I will not accept them, and the peace offerings of your fatted beasts I will not look upon.
>
> Take away from me the noise of your songs; to the melody of your harps I will not listen. But let justice roll down like waters, and righteousness like an ever-flowing stream.

Amos is searing in his condemnation of worship offered without the connected and requisite practice of justice in everyday life by people who claim to worship God. It is no mere chance that in a desert clime Amos compared the necessity of acting with justice to that most essential of elements required for human life—water, and not just any kind of water, but water that was abundant, living, and unending. Earlier in his book, he already had preached:

> For three transgressions of Israel, and for four, I will not revoke the punishment; because they sell the righteous for silver, and the needy for a pair of shoes—they that trample the head of the poor into the dust of the earth, and turn aside the way of the afflicted; a man and his father go in to the same maiden so that my holy name is profaned; they lay themselves down beside every altar upon garments taken in pledge; and in the house of their God they drink the wine of those who have been fined. (2:6–8)

Those in power, who lived in security and in plenty, Amos judged fiercely, as fiercely as he had judged Israel's enemies arrayed about her (cf. 1:3–2:5). The powerful of Israel had failed to remember that the needy, the poor, the afflicted, the borrower, and the wrongly fined bear the image of God. They had ignored at their peril the injunctions of Exodus (e.g., 22:26–27) and Deuteronomy (e.g., 24:11–13) against abusing the weak and indigent. They had forgotten that God has a vested interest in the broken and the lost and will champion them every time.

Later, Jeremiah continued in the southern kingdom the work of Amos and other prophets by criticizing the uneven distribution of wealth among the citizens of Judah and linking their mistreatment of the poor with false worship. In the temple he preached:

> For if you truly amend your ways and your doings, if you truly execute justice one with another, if you do not oppress the alien, the fatherless or the widow, or shed innocent blood in this place, and if you do not go after other gods to your own hurt, then I will let you dwell in this place, in the land that I gave of old to you fathers forever. (7:5–7)

He conveyed God's abhorrence at their false worship (Jer. 7:8–11), connected their failure to live justly with their failure to worship rightly, and set before them a choice which echoed the one offered Israel in Deuteronomy 30:19–20: (1) walk in the way of the Lord—that is, "execute justice with one another"—and live, or (2) persist in the oppression of "the alien, the fatherless or the widow" and perish (viz., Jer. 5:28; 7:13–15; 9:12b–16). For their failure to heed the desires of God, Jeremiah rendered oracles of God's judgment against them as other prophets had (e.g., Amos 5:10–12) and other prophets would (e.g., Ezek. 18:25–32). Yet these same prophets, and others still, also spoke to Israel of another component of biblical justice: God's compassion.

In the midst of Babylon's final siege of Jerusalem, Jeremiah acted out a prophecy of hope he had received. At a time when it appeared to any right-thinking inhabitant of Jerusalem that God had finally and irrevocably washed the divine hands of Israel, Jeremiah bought a parcel of land. After he took great care to see that the deed was recorded and witnessed, he carefully sealed it in a clay jar and buried it, to be found at a time in the future when Israel had once more returned to live in the land (32:6–15). God's judgment of Israel was to be tempered by God's compassion and refusal to abandon this people. Ezekiel continued in this tradition of prophecy when he preached to the first wave of exiles to Babylon (597–87 BC).

Their worship of God had to include the practice of righteousness; they had to keep the God of Israel's commands to care for the weak, the poor, the widow, and the orphan in order for God to find them without reproach. Worship without the practice of justice was not worship.

> If a man is righteous and does what is lawful and right—if he does not eat upon the mountains or lift up his eyes to the idols of the house of Israel, does not defile his neighbor's wife or approach a woman in her time of impurity, does

not oppress any one, but restores to the debtor his pledge, commits no robbery, gives his bread to the hungry and covers the naked with a garment, does not lend at interest or take any increase, withholds his hand from iniquity, executes true justice between [one person and another], walks in my statues, and is careful to observe my ordinances—he is righteous, he shall surely live, says the Lord God. (Ezek. 18:5–9)

The prophet foresaw the end of Israel as God's judgment on the people (Ezek. 21:1–32). Before the final deportation (587 BC), Ezekiel had focused on Israel's failure to observe God's ordinances, evident in the Israelites' treatment of those who lived on the margins of their society. After the final destruction of Jerusalem and the temple, Ezekiel sounded a voice of hope to the exiled community about Israel's future. He envisioned a rebuilding of the land and the temple that was accompanied by a renewal of just relationship among the peoples (Ezek. 40–48), bonds consonant with the image of God they continued to bear (Gen. 1:27). At the end of the almost fifty-year exile, when Israel had returned to the land and had begun to rebuild city and temple, the prophet, known by scholars as Third Isaiah (Isa. 56–66), noticed the cost of such projects on some in the community who could least stand to bear it, and he began to preach.

He preached in order to make visible those who had become invisible, to recall for those, hell-bent on recreating worship of God to fit their own image, what folly they practiced. Third Isaiah focused on their claim to practice right worship (today we might say orthodox worship). He tied God's rejection of such worship, and so of them, to their own rejection of the poor around them (58:3–4). He reframed the demands of right worship so they might recognize that their compassionate interaction with the least able and most vulnerable among them comprised the kind of worship—the right worship—that God sought from them (58:5–10). Their relationship with God depended on their meeting the demands, the needs, of the poor, the widow, and the orphan around them.

Like the prophets who had gone before him, Third Isaiah recognized justice not as something to be measured, weighed, or apportioned equally to every member of society no matter the circumstance. To practice justice (*tsĕdāqāh*) was to follow the ordinances (*mishpāt*, viz. Deut. 24–25) given by God in Torah. In order to offer worship acceptable to God, Israel had to be in a state of right relationship with God. To be in that state of right relationship with God, they had to be in right relationship with the least and poorest among them. This balance could only be achieved by the people of Israel practicing compassion, corporately as well as individually, with every bearer of God's image (cf. Gen. 1:27). When the time came that such justice ruled in the land, prophets of the Old Testament proclaimed it would be a time of *shalōm*; it would be the reign of God. This was what Amos declared when he cried,

"Behold, the days are coming," says the LORD, "when the one plowing shall over take the reaper and the treader of grapes the one who sows the seed; the mountains shall drip sweet wine, and all the hills shall flow with it. I will restore the fortunes of my people Israel, and they shall rebuild the ruined cities and inhabit them; they shall make gardens and eat their fruit. I will plant them upon their land, and they shall never again be plucked up out of the land which I have given them." (Amos 9:13–15; cf. Joel 2:21–29; Mic. 4:1–4)

Shalōm Israel understood to be the time when God would rule at last (cf. Isa. 52:7), when God would vanquish every injustice and act of violence, when sickness and disfigurement would be healed forever, the people would never again hunger or thirst, and justice would be restored to all. It was this time of peace with justice (*shalōm*) that Jesus announced had begun in him (Luke 4:16–21). It was for this work of reshaping the world into God's hope for it that Jesus invited his disciples to join him.

Jesus, Justice, and the Reign of God

Every time Jesus performed a miracle by healing illness, by exorcizing evil spirits, or by restoring persons to this life, he was simultaneously revealing and enacting the reign of God. He was making present in an unjust and broken world the justice of God. In Mark 1:40–45 (cf. Matt. 8:2–4; Luke 5:12–16), when Jesus was in the early stages of his Galilean ministry, a leper sought him out to be healed.

Leprosy is a contagious disease, first recognizable to the human eye through skin lesions. If it remains untreated by antibiotics, the illness becomes progressively disfiguring and debilitating, eventually resulting in a person's death. In the first-century world, society protected its members the only way it knew how, by forcibly expelling from the community anyone who seemed to have even the most remote chance of being infected with leprosy (cf. Lev. 13–14; Deut. 24:8). In first-century Judea, this expulsion from human society was a death sentence. The leper would be certain of a death that would come more rapidly and be more miserable than what the leprosy itself would have inflicted. A human being could not survive long this harsh and violent world without a community with which to share the burdens and from which to receive support in the eking out of one's daily existence. These were the circumstances of the leper who begged Jesus to heal him.

By restoring the leper to health, Jesus restored him to life and restored a piece of God's justice to the world. Jesus was moved by compassion at the leper's plea. He risked his own health—physical and communal–when "he stretched out his hand and touched him" (v. 41). When Jesus practiced God's justice, and so God's compassion, he revealed something of God and something of God's hope for the world. The prophets before Jesus had denounced the rich and powerful when they ignored the plight of the weak; they had decried the conduct of the rich which increased the poor's misery, and they had called the privileged of their society to recognize the demands stemming from relationship with God for their relationship with their neighbor. Jesus's actions in this story signal that same concern: to make right the people's relationship with God by making possible the people's relationships with one another.

Every time Jesus preached a parable to his disciples and crowds gathered to hear him, he was simultaneously revealing the reign of God and inviting his listeners to join him in practicing God's reign and justice. In Matthew 20:1–16, Jesus presented a scene familiar to his listeners: a collection of day laborers, gathered in a locale, waiting for some landowner to hire them so that they might scratch out a meager day's wage by working in his vineyard. If they were workers hiring themselves out on a daily basis in first-century Judea, it meant they had become landless or, at the very least, the land which they had been working for themselves had not produced sufficiently to feed the worker and his family and also cover heavy taxes imposed by Rome and whatever local vassal-king they might owe. They were one day's wage away from having to sell themselves into slavery to make ends meet.

Jesus's vineyard owner comes five times to the marketplace to hire workers for that day. Each time he comes to hire the workers, time has moved on. Early in the morning, he has agreed to pay the first group of workers a set price for the day's work, one denarius (v. 2). With each subsequent group he hires, he agrees simply to pay "whatever is just" (v. 4). The vineyard owner's unanticipated generosity turns, and the parable's disconcerting ending hangs, on this word "just" (*dikaion* in Greek and *tsaddîq* in Hebrew). From the first to the last, each who had been hired received a wage sufficient to live on for the next day. The first group had agreed to the price. The later groups had agreed to what was "just."

The parable leads to various reversals of expectations. The most surprising reversal for the characters and listeners of the story is that all the laborers received the same amount of pay, whether they worked for an hour or a day. All received the exact amount to which the first group had agreed. The surprise in the story came because the owner did not prorate the wages of all the workers according the amount of time each had worked. Rather, he paid each worker a living wage. The amount of this wage reflected the landowner's awareness that to be in right or just relationship with God, one must be in right or just relationship with one's neighbor. Jesus was demonstrating what the law and the prophets had taught about justice—one's daily interactions with other human beings affect and reveal the state of one's relationship with God. Every time Jesus challenged notions of what constituted justice, he was revealing God's hope and desire for the kind of relationships the stories of Genesis 1–2 had disclosed, the Torah had prescribed (e.g., Exod. 12:49; 22:21–27; Deut. 25:19), and the prophets had preached (e.g., Isa. 1:12–17; 61:1–4; Mic. 6:6–8; Mal. 3:5).

Conclusion

We human beings image God and so, at our deepest and most elemental place of being, the justice we seek and the justice we give is God's. Biblical justice is not fair; that is, it is not disinterested or detached in the face of suffering. Rather, it is united to compassion. Like us, it is bound because of its relationship to the reign and justice of God. As a result, it does not treat everyone anonymously, but looks to who we are and what we need to become the human beings for whom God has longed from before history began. In other words, biblical justice will always privilege the needs of those without the basics for a dignified life over the wants of those who live in abundant prosperity. It will always be personal and relational because biblical justice derives its meaning and authority from the relationship God has established with human beings, embodied by Jesus.

Discussion

Justice, Mercy, and the Good Samaritan

Mary Kate Birge's essay on biblical justice makes clear that Christian worship and discipleship call us to the way of God's justice. But questions and problems about how to live "in Christ" emerge almost as soon as Christians gather in Christ's name. We need only to consider the letters of Paul in the New Testament. For example, in 1 Corinthians 11:17–34, Paul expresses shock and exasperation that the Christians in Corinth are divided when they share the Lord's Supper.

> [W]hen you come together as a church, I hear that there are divisions among you. . . . Indeed, there have to be factions among you, for only so will it become clear who among you are genuine. When you come together, it is not really to eat of the Lord's Supper. For when the time comes to eat, each of you goes ahead with your own supper, and one goes hungry and another becomes drunk. What! Do you not have homes to eat and drink in? Or do you show contempt for the church of God and humiliate those who have nothing? (1 Cor. 11:18–22).

This problem of humiliating the poor, along with Paul's judgments against it, is strikingly similar to the prophetic tradition outlined by Sr. Birge. The prophets speak the word of God to the people and show the intimate connection between worship and God's righteousness—which is both God's judgment and compassion.

As a matter of discussion, let us make a shift from Paul's worries about divisions in Corinth to our typical ways of reading scripture. Like the Lord's

Supper, scripture is shared during worship. In the liturgy of the word, we hear the gospel read and proclaimed and we respond with one voice (particularly through the prayers of the people and the creed). But I wonder if our habits of responding to the Bible tend toward the individualistic and might reveal divisions and factions among us. We are accustomed, as we should be, to hearing the scripture as the word of God spoken to us and in our lives. How often do we take the "for us" of salvation in Jesus Christ to be only a "for me"? Do our factions and divisions appear because we isolate ourselves in our towns or suburbs? How often do we avoid humiliating those who have nothing by simply living and worshipping far apart from them? We hear scripture as the word directed to us, and we all know that the word is not simply for our comfort. The chapter notes that God's justice is God's compassion, and we also know that God's compassion might be God's judgment on our lives. We are called to hear and "have ears"—to hear the gospel as a call to live in Christ and to live out Christ's way—to hear the word of God's justice as a call to move beyond our factions and divisions.

Sr. Mary Kate has outlined the following reflection for us.

Read through the following parable from Luke. The larger context for this parable-generating conversation between Jesus and the lawyer is the large section of the gospel which Luke uses to instruct members of his own community (AD 85–90) about how to follow Jesus as they wait for his return (9:52–19:27). Recall the basic definition of biblical justice in the chapter and the principles on which it is based. Use those as the filters through which you try to answer the basic question modern believers must raise whenever we read a biblical text: So what? So what does this text mean for me today as a follower of Jesus in the twenty-first century?

> 10:25 And behold, a lawyer stood up to put him to the test, saying, "Teacher, what shall I do to inherit eternal life?" 26 He said to him, "What is written in the law? How do you read?" 27 And he answered, "You shall love the Lord your God with all your heart, and with all your soul, and with all your strength, and with all your mind; and your neighbor as yourself." 28 And he said to him, "You have answered right; do this, and you will live." 29 But he, desiring to justify himself, said to Jesus, "And who is my neighbor?" 30 Jesus replied, "A man was going down from Jerusalem to Jericho, and he fell among robbers, who stripped him and beat him, and departed, leaving him half dead. 31 Now by chance a priest was going down that road; and when he saw him he passed by on the other side. 32 So likewise a Levite, when he came to the place and saw him, passed by on the other side. 33 But a Samaritan, as he journeyed, came to where he was; and when he saw him, he had compassion, 34 and went to him and bound up his wounds, pouring on oil and wine; then he set him on his own beast and brought him to an inn, and took care of him. 35 And the next day he took out two denarii and gave them to the innkeeper, saying, 'Take care of him; and whatever more you

spend, I will repay you when I come back.' [36] Which of these three, do you think, proved neighbor to the man who fell among the robbers?" [37] He said, "The one who showed mercy on him." And Jesus said to him, "Go and do likewise."

Below are some questions for us to ponder as we try to determine what this passage means for us today and how it might shape our own practices of biblical justice:

- What question does the lawyer first ask Jesus?
- What connections can we draw between the lawyer's answer in v. 27 to Jesus's counterquestion in v. 26 and the concept of biblical justice found in the chapter you have just read?
- Why does the lawyer ask Jesus a second question in v. 29?
- In v. 36 what question does Jesus ask the lawyer? How is this question from Jesus connected, or not connected, to the question the lawyer asks in v. 29?
- We ought to ask ourselves the same question the lawyer asked of Jesus in v. 29: "And who is my neighbor?" What are our answers? How do our answers help us respond to the initial question in this exercise: So what? So what does this passage mean for us today as followers of Jesus in the twenty-first-century?

Keep your responses to these questions in mind as we move on to a discussion of worship in the next two chapters. The parable of the good Samaritan calls us into community with the despised Samaritan (as we put ourselves in the place of the lawyer), and with those who suffer (as Jesus draws near to the leper). More importantly, perhaps, the neighbor is the one who shows compassion. Here, we might think of the good Samaritan as an image of God in Christ, the one who meets us on the roadside, attends to our wounds, and gives us respite at an inn. In liturgy (as we will see in the next two chapters), we receive the hospitality of God to live it out in our homes and communities.

2

The Liturgy as a Source of Formation in Catholic Social Teaching

Rev. James M. Donohue, CR

When I was a boy of about six or seven, I had my eye on Billy Smith's pirate ship. About eighteen inches long, with sails and plastic pirate figures, it was worth stealing—or so I thought at the time. I guess my covetousness was transparent, because it did not take too long before Mrs. Smith came to our house to recover the pirate ship. After the customary denials, I eventually wore down under the interrogation of Mrs. Smith and my mother—what chance did I have?—and retrieved the pirate ship which I had hidden in the milk box. There would be suitable punishment to come, but after Mrs. Smith left with the recovered stolen merchandise, my mother looked at me in utter frustration and asked a simple, but profound question, "Haven't you learned anything from going to church?" Reflecting upon this incident, I note that my mother did not ask me why I did not remember the seventh commandment— "You shall not steal"—or what she and my father or my teachers at Catholic school had taught me about jealousy and stealing. Instead, she appealed to the liturgy of the church which, thus far, had had seemingly little effect in my young life—at least in the case of pirate ships. She had expected more from the power of the liturgy to transform me into a disciple of Jesus: one who, to paraphrase the Old Testament prophet Micah, "acts justly, loves tenderly, and walks humbly with God" (Mic. 6:8).

Because we often think of church as separate from life, we might take for granted the influence that sacraments and liturgy exert on our lives. We know that extraordinary experiences such as a serious accident, the birth of a child, or the death of a loved one can have a profound influence upon us. Similarly, more ordinary experiences, such as friendship, achievement, pain, and work are part of each person's life and have an effect as well. Consider that day after day, and week after week, small and large groups of people gather to be influenced, changed, and conformed ever more closely to Christ. In the liturgy, we hear the word of God announce God's love for all creation and God's reign of justice and peace. In the liturgy, we listen as the homilist provides reflections upon God's word, highlighting the life and dignity of each person, the common good, service to the poor and the vulnerable, hunger and thirst for justice, solidarity with the whole human family, peacemaking, and good stewardship of God's creation. In the liturgy, we are challenged to imitate Christ in service and self-sacrifice as the community remembers the sacrifice of Jesus, who gives of himself freely and lovingly for the life of the world. In the liturgy we are reminded of who we are called to be and, gathered and transformed into his body, the church, we are sent out to be salt for the earth and light for the world.

Amid the competing ways to interpret reality, the church in its liturgy and sacraments offers an approach to human life based on Jesus, who is the Way, the Truth, and the Life (John 14:6). This approach maintains that the way to a most human and fulfilled life comes from imitating Jesus, especially in upholding the life, dignity, and equality of all human persons, in recognizing the special obligation to defend the poor and vulnerable, in understanding the need to promote the common good so that people may reach their full human potential and human dignity, and in accepting the challenge to respond in charity to human needs, while also working in justice to change structures that perpetuate poverty and inhuman conditions. As we will see, these major themes of Catholic social teaching occupy a prominent place in the church's liturgy and sacraments, providing a unique perspective for Christians to see and to live in God's created world.

In lieu of exploring how the major themes of Catholic social teaching are present in every sacramental liturgy, I propose to focus on the sacraments of initiation celebrated within a two week period of ordinary time (the parts of the liturgical year that are not focused on Advent, Christmas, Lent, or Easter). While thinking through and outlining this chapter, I presided at and participated in each of the sacraments of initiation: an infant baptism, a parish confirmation of young adults, and daily and Sunday celebrations of the Eucharist. Through an examination of these liturgical celebrations during the tenth and eleventh weeks of ordinary time, I would like to demonstrate the pervasiveness of Catholic social teaching themes within the liturgy, in its readings, prayers, and ritual action, and to comment upon the potential for these themes to assist us in interpreting experience, thus shaping the Christian's basic hermeneutic of life.

Infant Baptism

On the tenth Sunday in ordinary time, Dorothy Rose Cannon was baptized into her local Catholic parish community. Her parents are people of deep faith who are active in social ministry in their parish. They were instrumental in establishing a sister parish in the inner city and they organize the homeless shelter that the parish houses each month. Having waited many years, her parents had almost given up hope of having a child. They named her Dorothy for what she was in their lives—a gift from God. Not coincidently, Dorothy is also the name of a saintly woman who had inspired this little girl's parents for years: Dorothy Day of the Catholic worker movement.

As little Dorothy Rose's parents brought her forward for baptism, they were asked if they understood their responsibility "to bring her up to keep God's commandments as Christ taught us, by loving God and our neighbor" (no. 77).[1] After the godparents pledged their support to help the parents in their duty as Christian parents, the cross was traced on the little girl's forehead as a sign that she had been "claimed for Christ our Savior."

The baptismal readings drew out more fully what being claimed for Christ might mean for the future of this little girl. Paul's Letter to the Romans (6:3–5) reminded the gathered assembly that when we were baptized, we joined Jesus in death so that we might walk in the newness of life with him: "Through baptism into his death we were buried with him, so that, just as Christ was raised from the dead by the glory of the Father, we too might live a new life." The responsorial psalm (Ps. 23) called to mind that we will never want or have reason to fear with God as our shepherd, who "guides me in right paths." At first sight the gospel seemed a strange choice for a baptism, but it proved to be appropriate given the child's name and her parents' love for the poor. The last judgment scene of Matthew 25 repeats the questions, "Lord, when did we see you hungry and feed you, or thirsty and give you drink? When did we see you a stranger and welcome you, or naked and clothe you? When did we see you ill or in prison, and visit you?" (Matt. 25:37–39, 44), only to hear the same response each time: "Amen, I say to you, whatever you did for one of these least of mine, you did to me" (Matt. 25:40, 45).

Provided with these particular readings in the context of baptism, the homilist was able to point out that little Dorothy Rose was being initiated into a new way of living. Through the example and influence of her parents, godparents, and her local parish community, this girl will grow up seeing the world with different eyes. As with all Christians, she will learn to live a new life, trying to die to her selfishness and self-centeredness so that she will love God and her neighbor. But, of course, the important question remains: who is our neighbor?

Throughout the gospels, Jesus is always expanding the sense of who our neighbor is. In response to the question, "What must I do to inherit eternal life?" Jesus responds with the greatest commandment: "You shall love the Lord, your God, with all your heart, with all your being, with all your strength, and with all your mind, and your neighbor as yourself" (Luke 10:27). This gives rise to the question, "And who is my neighbor?" which Jesus answers with the parable of the good Samaritan (Luke 10:30–37). Here the neighbor is defined, not in terms of common ethnicity, but in terms of the compassionate care for another in need. The good news of salvation that Jesus proclaims in his hometown synagogue in Nazareth is not just for the Jews, but is also for non-Jews like the widow of Zarephath and Naaman the Syrian (Luke 4:16–30). Love and mercy for our neighbor includes even love for our enemies (Luke 6:27–36). Love such as this enables us to be more godlike—"Be merciful, just as also your Father is merciful" (Luke 6:36)—and to imitate Jesus, who forgave his enemies on the cross: "Father, forgive them, they know not what they do" (Luke 23:34).

Love for our neighbor, as we heard in the gospel reading on the occasion of Dorothy Rose's baptism, includes love for the poor, the hungry, the thirsty, the naked, the prisoner, the stranger—for in all of these we find our neighbor—people who are worthy to be treated with dignity and compassion. Indeed, the story of the disciples on the road to Emmaus repeats the lesson of Matthew 25 that care and compassion for the unfortunate and hospitality to the stranger opens the window to experience the presence of the risen Lord in our midst. After all, the disciples came to recognize the presence of the risen Lord in the breaking of the bread only after they welcomed a stranger to stay with them (Luke 24:29–34).

Little Dorothy Rose was given a name that inspires the commitment to the poor that we find in Matthew 25. Dorothy Day (1897–1980) committed her life to defend the poor, the unemployed, and the homeless in New York City. She espoused nonviolence and, with Peter Maurin, founded the Catholic worker movement in 1933. When confronted with the enormous problems of the world—war and peace, prisons, drug addiction, prostitution, and the apathy of the great masses of people—Dorothy Day would be reminded of the little way of St. Thérèse:

Young people say, "What good can one person do? What is the sense of our small effort?" They cannot see that we must lay one brick at a time, take one step at a time; we can be responsible only for the one action of the present moment. But we can beg for an increase of love in our hearts that will vitalize and transform all our individual actions, and know that God will take and multiply them, as Jesus multiplied the loaves and fishes.[2]

The example of Dorothy Day will guide little Dorothy Rose and all disciples of Jesus on the right path (Ps. 23), for it embodies the corporal works of mercy, which consist especially in "feeding the hungry, sheltering the homeless, clothing the naked, visiting the sick and imprisoned, and burying the dead" (no. 2447).[3]

After the liturgy of the word, the parents and godparents, together with all assembled, renounce sin and profess their faith. The parents opted to have Dorothy Rose baptized by immersion. This ritual action of immersing the child into the water of the baptismal font is an apt image for what Paul wrote in his Letter to the Romans: "We were indeed buried with him through baptism into his death, so that . . . we too might live in newness of life" (Rom. 6:4). In fact, immersion was the common practice of baptism in the early church as the clearest sign of what was happening. Baptismal fonts took many shapes, signifying what was happening in a most profound way: a tomb to indicate that the person was dying to his or her old ways, a womb to indicate that the person was being brought to new birth, a step-down font in the shape of a cross to indicate that the person was dying to his or her old self, rising to new life with Christ, or a step-down font in an octagonal shape—the Resurrection of Jesus came on the day after the Jewish Sabbath, i.e., on the "eighth day"[4] of the week—to represent that the old self was drowned so that the person would rise to the new life of the resurrection.

This image of dying to the old self and being reborn into new life with Christ is reinforced through the post-baptismal actions of the anointing with chrism oil, the clothing with the white garment, and the entrusting of the baptismal candle to the parents and godparents. This child is different now; she has been transformed. As she is anointed with the oil of chrism, Dorothy Rose hears: "God the Father of our Lord Jesus Christ has freed you from sin, given you a new birth by water and the Holy Spirit, and welcomed you into his holy people" (no. 98).[5] As she is clothed in her white garment, she is reminded: "You have become a new creation, and have clothed yourself in Christ" (no. 99).[6] And as the light of Christ is entrusted to Dorothy Rose's parents and godparents, they are encouraged to keep the light of Christ burning brightly in this child, so that she will "walk always as a child of the light" (no. 100).[7]

Dorothy Rose's parents have baptized her into the faith of the Christian community and have committed themselves to handing on the faith that they have professed publicly. This faith, however, is not some thing that we possess, but a way that we live. Faith without a corresponding life and practice is not living faith.[8] As she gets older, Dorothy Rose will need to grow in her awareness that a true disciple of Jesus is one "who hears the Word of God and acts on it" (Luke 8:21; 11:28; Matt. 7:21, 24). Acting as Jesus did, with a preferential love for the poor,[9] will most clearly mark her as a follower of his way.

Confirmation

On the eleventh Sunday in ordinary time, twenty young men and women, ages sixteen to seventeen, were confirmed in their parish by the auxiliary bishop of the diocese. Their preparation for the sacrament of confirmation included a public commitment ceremony during a Sunday Eucharist, religious education classes, a retreat experience, and a service project. Over time, they learned that confirmation is a sacrament of Christian initiation, and that by means of this sacrament they would receive "in increasing measure the treasures of divine life and advance toward the perfection of charity."[10] Their preparation also provided an opportunity to grow in relationship with Jesus, discovering his presence in both personal and communal prayer, and in their service to the poor. As the celebration of the sacrament approached, they anticipated that the giving of the Holy Spirit in confirmation would conform them more fully to Christ and strengthen them "so that they may bear witness to Christ for the building up of his Body in faith and love" (no. 2).[11]

The selected readings for the confirmation liturgy announced the gift of the Holy Spirit that would strengthen the young people's relationship to Christ, enabling them as his disciples to be of service to the world. The first reading, from the prophet Isaiah, reminded the assembly that the spirit of the Lord God is given to them "to bring glad tidings to the lowly, to heal the brokenhearted, to proclaim liberty to captives, and release to the prisoners" (Isa. 61:1). The second reading proclaimed that, having received the Holy Spirit, those being confirmed will become witnesses of Jesus "to the ends of the earth" (Acts 1:8). Finally, the gospel reading provided lessons for discipleship and mission: "Whoever wishes to come after me must deny himself, take up his cross, and follow me. For whoever wishes to save his life will lose it, but whoever loses his life for my sake will find it" (Matt. 16:24–25).

The instruction given by the bishop underlined the deeper relationship with Christ that comes from confirmation and the witness that each Christian is called to give in the world: "You have already been baptized into Christ and now will receive the power of his Spirit and the sign of the cross on your forehead. You must be witnesses before all the world to his suffering, death, and resurrection; your way of life should at all times reflect the goodness of Christ" (no. 22).[12] Before the bishop laid hands upon the young people, he asked all gathered to "pray to our Father that he will pour out the Holy Spirit to strengthen his sons and daughters with his gifts and anoint them to be more like Christ the Son of God" (no. 41).[13] The prayers used during the confirmation liturgy echoed these same thoughts. For instance, the prayer over the gifts asks that

God will "send us your Spirit to make us more like Christ in bearing witness to the world" (no. 58).[14] Similarly, the prayer after communion reminds the assembly of its conformity to Christ, having been "anointed with your Spirit and fed with the body and blood of Christ," so that they "by their works of love [will] build up the Church in holiness and joy" (no. 58).[15]

The confirmation liturgy in its prayers, readings, and liturgical actions has a formative influence on the assembly, enabling them to become more deeply immersed into Christ to continue his service in the world. This lofty calling of each Christian to a life of holiness and service in the name of Christ is articulated in the general introduction to Christian initiation, which notes that the three sacraments of initiation—baptism, confirmation, and Eucharist—combine "to bring us, the faithful of Christ, to his full stature and to enable us to carry out the mission of the entire people of God in the Church and in the world" (no. 2).[16] Conformed more deeply to Christ, the newly confirmed are called to imitate Christ as they live in the world, taking up their cross and losing themselves for his sake and the sake of the gospel.

Confirmation complements baptism through the outpouring of the Holy Spirit, enabling Christians to participate in the church's saving mission to the world. The Second Vatican Council's document on the church envisioned that Christians would exercise their priestly, prophetic, and kingly office in the world through their imitation of Christ, particularly through their preferential love for the poor. In their priestly office, all work can be offered as a spiritual sacrifice: prayers and apostolic works, married and family life, their daily work, mental and physical recreation, and even life's troubles if they are patiently borne (no. 34).[17] In their prophetic office, all people are called to carry forth the message of Christ through their words and the witness of their lives in the ordinary situations of life (no. 35). In their kingly office, all those who have been baptized and confirmed are called to make their way into the world with the spirit of Christ so that the world will more effectively attain its purpose in justice, in love, and in peace (no. 36). The document on the church specifically maintains that this will entail such efforts as working for a more equitable distribution of the world's goods and improving secular structures and conditions that are sinful and unjust. It is through these efforts that Christ will progressively illumine the world with his saving light (no. 36). The sacrament of confirmation celebrates the empowerment of the baptized Christian to live in the world in a different way—a way that witnesses Christ's justice, love, and peace—to be salt for the earth and light for the world.

Eucharistic Liturgies

The lectionary readings for the weekdays of the tenth and eleventh weeks of ordinary time were taken from Paul's Second Letter to the Corinthians, various responsorial psalms, and the Gospel according to Matthew. Among the selections from 2 Corinthians, the passage assigned to Tuesday of week eleven would lend itself to preaching about topics pertinent to Catholic social teaching. In 2 Corinthians 8:1–15, Paul is encouraging the Corinthians to complete their efforts of collecting money for the needs of the church in Jerusalem. Mindful that the Corinthians are called to serve the needs of the poor and the vulnerable, Paul sees this gracious act on behalf of others as a test of the genuineness of their love. Indeed, Paul roots the concern and action of the Corinthians in the very example of Christ: "For you know the gracious act of our Lord Jesus Christ, that for your sake he became poor although he was rich, so that by his poverty you might become rich" (2 Cor. 8:9). In addition to the sacrificial example of Christ, Paul cites solidarity with others as a motivation for the Corinthians' generosity: "Your surplus at the present time should supply their needs, so that their surplus may also supply your needs, that there may be equality. As it is written: 'Whoever had much did not have more, and whoever had little did not have less'" (2 Cor. 9:14–15).

We also find values associated with Catholic social teaching in the responsorial psalms for these days. On Thursday of week ten, the psalmody includes Psalm 85, which celebrates the proclamation of God's peace to God's people, a true peace in which "kindness and truth shall meet; justice and peace shall kiss; truth shall spring out of the earth; and justice shall look down from heaven" (vv. 11–12). On Tuesday of week eleven, Psalm 146 praises the God who made heaven and earth and who stands on the side of the oppressed and the vulnerable: "[The Lord] keeps faith forever, secures justice for the oppressed, gives food to the hungry. The Lord sets captives free. The Lord gives sight to the blind. The Lord raises up those that were bowed down. The Lord loves the just. The Lord protects the strangers" (vv. 7–9).

The gospel selections for these two weeks provide a particularly rich resource for preaching about several key principles of Catholic social teaching. The gospel passage for Monday of the tenth week is the reading of the Beatitudes (Matt. 5:1–12), which suggest ways of living—different from any standards or judgments of our world—in which a person will be blessed. Poverty in spirit, mercy, peacemaking, the hunger and thirst for holiness, and persecution for holiness' sake will bring people true fulfillment, for they will have aligned themselves with Christ, sharing in his suffering and new life, as they free themselves from the enslavement to material goods, as they work against hatred and violence, as they care for the vulnerable among us, and as they stand in solidarity with all people who have been marginalized in our society. Rather than being filled up with what our world purports will make us happy—material goods, status, security—the Beatitudes maintain that we will be fulfilled to the degree that we empty ourselves, giving ourselves away for the sake of another, just as Jesus did.

The gospel readings from Thursday of the tenth week and Monday and Tuesday of the eleventh week contain a strong exhortation for Christians to become people of forgiveness, peace, and reconciliation. In Matthew 5:20–26, Jesus reminds his listeners that their righteousness must exceed that of the scribes and Pharisees and that there must be conformity between liturgy and life. He teaches that there must be reconciliation with our brother or sister before an offering can be made on the altar. Monday's reading of the eleventh week (Matt. 5:38–42) urges the listener to not deal with an evildoer through force, but through nonviolent resistance. While it might strike us initially as cowardice or foolishness—to turn the other cheek, to give your cloak as well, to go a second mile—these instructions are meant to confront the oppressor's cruelty, embarrassing the oppressor into seeing his or her own actions as brutality and the victim's resolution as courageous resistance. "The way of the Lord" introduces a different path from either retaliatory violence or passivism that is associated with cowardice.[18] In "the way of the Lord" that is emphasized in the Gospel passage for the next day (Matt. 5:43–48), Jesus urges his followers to "love your enemies, and pray for those who persecute you," and in doing so people will "be perfect, just as your heavenly Father is perfect." Here Jesus appeals to how God loves us—both the good and the bad—and indicates that only by imitating God's ways will we "become children of the heavenly Father." The selections from the Gospel according to Matthew over the course of these days provide an opportunity for the preacher to expand upon the need for love of neighbor and forgiveness in our daily lives, for it is these attitudes and actions that will bring about solidarity in the midst of division, and peace in our hostile world.

In addition to the readings proclaimed, the prayer texts also provide opportunities for the congregation to be mindful of several basic principles that are germane to Catholic social teaching. Images of solidarity, peace, service, love, and unity pervade these liturgical texts, which make frequent reference to Jesus as the example and source for this new way of life. For instance, in the tenth week, the opening prayer asks the God of wisdom and love to "guide our actions in your way of peace," while the alternative opening prayer asks God to "raise us beyond the limits this world imposes, so that we may be free to love as Christ teaches." The prayer over the gifts asks God to "look with love on our service" and to "help us grow in Christian love." In the eleventh week, the opening prayer prays that God will "help us to follow Christ and live according to your will," while the alternative opening prayer rejoices "in the faith that draws us together, aware that selfishness can drive us apart." This prayer continues by asking God to "keep us one in the love that has sealed our lives [and] help us to live as one family." The prayer after communion prays that this Eucharist may accomplish "the unity and peace it signifies."

In addition to the readings and prayers, the ritual action of the liturgy also carries within it the potential to raise awareness of pertinent themes within

Catholic social teaching. The assembled group gathers around the one table and responds with one voice as it signifies its unity as the body of Christ and its solidarity with all God's people and creation. As the Eucharistic prayer is prayed, the community remembers the loving sacrifice of Christ, whose body was broken and whose blood was poured out for the life of the world, especially the poor and the wounded, the oppressed and the neglected. The words of the Eucharist Prayer remind Christians of the responsibility to live a particular way in the world:

> Open our eyes to the needs of all;
> inspire us with words and deeds
> to comfort those who labor
> and are burdened;
> keep our service of others
> faithful to the example and command of Christ.
> Let your Church be a living witness
> to truth and freedom, to justice and peace,
> that all people may be lifted up
> by the hope of a world made new.[19]

Remembering the actions of Jesus, the community pledges itself again to do likewise in memory of him, to be bread for the world, nourishment for the poor and the hungry.

In the Lord's Prayer, people pray for forgiveness and indicate their own willingness to forgive. Through the sign of peace, they demonstrate their willingness to commit themselves to forgiveness, peace, and reconciliation. And as they approach the Lord's Table they are reminded that the communion they receive this day is an anticipation of that day to come when all God's people will be gathered around the one table at the messianic banquet. Here, the poor and the lame, the lost and the wounded, the neglected and the forgotten, the victims of poverty and war, and the objects of hatred will be gathered around God's table. Here, the foolishness of the gospel—strength from weakness, richness from poverty, authority from service, new life from death—will manifest itself clearly as wisdom and truth.

These ritual actions and prayers complement and reinforce the word of God that has been proclaimed. They remind the assembly of the constant need for conversion as it measures itself against a world dominated by individualism, materialism, consumerism, and violence. Further, the ritual actions, liturgical prayers, and the proclamation of God's word challenges the assembly to live in its present actions in a way that anticipates the future coming of the fullness of God's reign as it goes forth "to love and serve the Lord."

Christian discipleship demands conformity to Christ and his gospel values. To act justly, to have compassion for the poor and the needy, and to be a person of forgiveness, peace, and reconciliation in a troubled world can seem to be foolish, naive, and unrealistic. However, the liturgy, in its readings, prayers, and ritual actions, proposes a certain way of living that challenges and clarifies our basic human hermeneutic. Changing our mode of interpreting life, the liturgy challenges us to test the accuracy of its claims by living in a certain way and by discovering the new life that this way of living offers. As a result, the liturgy stands as a locus with the power to shape us as a certain kind of people—people who defend the life and dignity of the human person, seek the common good, serve the poor and the vulnerable among us, hunger and thirst for justice, live in solidarity with the whole human family, work for peace, and become good stewards of God's creation.

Discussion

"Be not afraid; I am with you always"

Fr. Donohue suggests that we think about his chapter by attending Mass and listening for the call to peace, justice, and compassionate care for others and our world. In effect, he asks us to reflect on the liturgy as he has done in the chapter. He offers some guidance: the readings and homily will be the prime source, but attention to concluding prayers will raise our level of awareness to how God calls us to act in the world. With this advice, I tried to listen for themes of justice, peace, and mercy during worship on the fourth Sunday in ordinary time, February 3, 2008. The "ordinary" of ordinary time refers not to something commonplace, but to the numbered (ordinal) weeks, named for their number on the calendar rather than a feast day such as Pentecost or Christ the King. The fourth Sunday in ordinary time is a week between Epiphany and Lent. So far so good: the exercise will work best (Fr. Jim insists) if we do not stack the deck or look for particularly unique liturgy. I did not know what the readings would be for the Mass on the first week in February 2008.

As it turns out, the readings and homily made explicit reference to justice, compassion, and peace. The first reading, Zephaniah 2:3 and 3:12–13, instructed us to seek the Lord and to seek justice and humility. As a prophet speaking in times of trouble and unfaithfulness (the seventh century BC), Zephaniah announces that God will sustain "a remnant . . . a people humble and lowly, who shall take refuge in the name of the Lord." In response to the first reading, the cantor sang Psalm 146, which praises the faithfulness, justice, and mercy of God. The congregation's response to the verses was Matthew 5:3, "Blessed are the poor in spirit; the kingdom of heaven is theirs." The second reading was 1 Corinthians 1:26–31, where Paul (as he often does) preached the foolishness of God in Christ, "who chose the weak of the world to shame the strong, who chose the lowly and despised of the world."

The readings and response were clearly leading up to the gospel (I realized this fact only when it was read). The gospel was the Beatitudes of Matthew 5:1–12: "Blessed are the poor in spirit . . . Blessed are those who mourn . . . Blessed are the meek . . . Blessed are they who hunger and thirst for righteousness . . ." and so on. The homily went straight to the difficulty of living out the Beatitudes even though they promise to be an easy burden and a lifegiving way. The difficulty is that we create obstacles and make the burden heavy. The priest, Fr. Jack, called us to trust in God's grace and to have faith in God's abundant love.

I was pleased. I experimented with the exercise recommended by Fr. Jim; I found plenty to write at the conclusion of his chapter, and I was able to recommend the same exercise to you, the reader. After the homily, however, I forgot what I was doing. It is not that I stopped paying attention; rather, I stopped looking at the Mass as a school assignment. I was taken into the prayers and creed that conclude the liturgy of the word, and I was entirely unself-conscious during the liturgy of the Eucharist. I remember very clearly: after receiving the Eucharist, I was walking back to my seat when I remembered that I was supposed to be listening for phrases and themes that I could write down later. I was a bit annoyed with myself. I kneeled at my pew and figured that I would have to try the whole thing again another Sunday.

As I was kneeling and beginning to pray, however, the communion hymn made its way through me. I say "made its way through me," because I was singing it before I realized that I was singing and before I was aware of the words. The hymn was "Be not Afraid," which takes its verses from various chapters in Isaiah and Matthew 5 (e.g., "Blessed are your poor, for the kingdom shall be theirs. Blest are you that weep and mourn, for one day you shall laugh. And if wicked men insult and hate you all because of me, blessed, blessed are you!"). The chorus is, "Be not afraid. I go before you always. Come follow me, and I will give you rest." I should admit that on that Sunday (and every other Sunday when the hymn was sung), I sang the wrong words. For the purposes of the chapter, I found the lyrics on the internet. Rather than "I go before you always," Christ has been, in my incorrect version, "with you always." I suppose that I have been hearing what I wanted to hear, which is always a temptation during worship.

"Be not afraid." This is the call of God's justice, peace, and mercy. It is the grace of Christ's presence in the Eucharist. If I had been looking for it to include in this chapter, I probably would have missed it. I was looking for words in a philosophical sense. But I was given the word as a call of grace. It came at the moment when I was forgetful of self: I was kneeling to pray and found myself singing with the congregation. I know the words of God's compassion and peace, but I also know fear that holds me back from accepting grace and living it out more fully. Security (financial and otherwise) as well as choice and autonomy (especially choices about how I use my time), are high on my order of values. I often work the gospel around them. I usually think that I take risks of faith recommended by the gospel, but hearing the Beatitudes showed me how far I have to go in trusting in the way of Jesus Christ. "Be not afraid. I go before you (and I am with you) always. Come follow me, and I will give you rest." These words of grace and hope are what I found in the liturgy on the fourth Sunday of ordinary time. These are the words that show the way of God's justice, peace, and mercy.

Now it's your turn. Next time you attend Mass listen for the call to peace, justice, and compassionate care for others and our world, write something down later in the day, and discuss what you heard and found with someone else.

3

Eucharist and Social Justice

RODICA STOICOIU

W here's God? I don't see God!" The child's clear high voice cut through the priest's prayers and reverberated through the Sunday assembly. So did the "tap, tap, tap" of my mother's shoes as she hurried up the center aisle to collect her wayward three-year-old. It was a tolerant community. She was given a knowing look, I was given an indulgent wink, and the liturgy went on. As did my asking that question, no longer as a child but now as a theologian—where is God? Many answers come to mind of course, but there is one that speaks to our question in this chapter and it is found in the Gospel according to Matthew:

> "For I was hungry and you gave me food, I was thirsty and you gave me drink, a stranger and you welcomed me, naked and you clothed me, ill and you cared for me, in prison and you visited me." Then the righteous will answer him and say, "Lord, when did we see you hungry and feed you, or thirsty and give you drink? When did we see you a stranger and welcome you, or naked and clothe you? When did we see you ill or in prison, and visit you?" And the king will say to them in reply, "Amen, I say to you, whatever you did for one of these least of mine, you did for me." (Matt. 25:31–40)

We have heard this story before, perhaps many times, and the meaning is very clear. We are to act like Christ, feeding the hungry and caring for the poor.

What is assumed within the story for Matthew's community, but which is not as clear for us today, is the connection between these behaviors and the celebration of the Eucharist.

This chapter will examine the connection between the Sunday celebration and our actions of justice in the world. The Eucharist is meant to change us, to turn our perspective away from self and toward the other. Hence the Eucharist is a dangerous activity. It is a risky endeavor if we value our self-sufficiency and who we have made ourselves to be. In our celebrations, by contrast, we fully and consciously seek to be transformed by God. We are at risk of loss and change. Yet I know few people who feel that liturgy is a life-threatening event, and even fewer who have felt their own life was in peril by celebrating the liturgy. More often than not we stand condemned by what our liturgies fail to do rather than by what they accomplish (transform us into the ongoing presence of Christ in the world). So what are we to make of the liturgy, which is meant to be the active remembering of a dangerous memory? Especially when so few seem to have had such transformative experiences? What must happen in our celebrations if they are to truly be the experiences of conversion they are meant to be? Especially when the results of such transformative actions lead to mission, to carrying for the poor, to feeding the hungry and to welcoming the stranger?

We will examine the link between the Eucharist and justice in three parts. We will first take a closer look at the Eucharist, what it is, how it forms and transforms us, and how it prepares us to carry out the responsibility which comes from our baptism, to be the ongoing presence of Christ in the world. We will then examine a few areas of the liturgy that are important parts of this transformative experience (symbol, rhythm and silence, and communion). Finally, we will examine how our liturgies shape who we understand ourselves to be. We will look at how the liturgy challenges our identity and shapes us into the body of Christ, and at how our actions in the Eucharist are actions of communal *metanoia*, a communal conversion that leads us to mission in the world and to acts of justice which live out the kingdom of God.

The Eucharist

Eucharist, from the Greek *eucharistia*, means thanksgiving. What we do as we gather on a Sunday morning is to respond to and give thanks for something we have already received. We are responding to a gift. The Eucharist is a gift which we do not control or earn. Indeed, counter to our controlling instincts, the Eucharist is a gift free and clear to which we can do nothing but respond with thanks. Our central posture in this activity, which is the source and summit of our lives as Christians, is one of emptiness and openness, standing in the midst of a community all of whom are equally powerless before this profound gift.

We speak of our response to this gift, of our being transformed as human beings through this celebratory response, but what exactly is it that we are giving thanks and praise for? It is the gift given by Christ of Christ, as in this hymn quoted by Paul.

> Who, though he was in the form of God, did not regard equality with God something to be grasped. Rather he emptied himself, taking the form of a slave, coming in human likeness; and found human in appearance, he humbled himself, becoming obedient to death, even death on a cross. Because of this, God greatly exalted him and bestowed on him the name that is above every name, that at the name of Jesus every knee should bend, of those in heaven and on earth and under the earth, and every tongue confess that Jesus Christ is Lord, to the glory of God the Father. (Phil. 2:6–11)

This gift is the self-emptying (*kenosis*) of Christ, God's son. It is given through the abiding love of the Father, so that we may find ourselves returned to God who is at the heart of our being. David Power, in *Love without Calculation*, shows through a study of this hymn that *kenosis* is the means of our salvation through the transformation of all humankind in justice and mercy.

Power explains, "To fill out the implications of this trans-form-ation, the hymn uses the term *kenosis* to show that he willingly laid aside the form of God, taking on existence in human likeness. To this it adds the act of humiliation whereby he became obedient, even to the point of death on a Cross."[1] Christ enters the human condition, which is marked by biological limitation and death. He becomes a slave (*duolos*).[2] Power notes that in so doing Christ is equated with the powerless, "those who must serve others and have no rights of their own. Their very being is defined by the service they are obliged to render to others."[3] Power continues by noting that the humility shown by Christ, sung in this hymn, is one "of being rendered humble through humiliation."[4] He was put to death by capital punishment. "Not only did Christ take the form of a lowly slave but he appeared as the lowliest and most despised of persons by being put to death on a Cross. It is on this account that God gave him the name and power of Lord, *Kyrios*."[5]

In how he lived, and served, and how he suffered and died, Christ exemplifies how all are called to live "in love and service."[6] The gift we celebrate in the Eucharist, this self-emptying of Christ into which we ourselves are to be transformed, can be summarized thus:

> First, he relinquishes all show of power, glory, splendor, he did not impose himself by any display of his role as God's envoy. Second, he took on a common humanity, the human form which all possessed under the reign of sin and death, so as to be like unto those he was to liberate. Third, within this estate he appeared

as socially inferior, as one to be ranked among the servant classes. Fourth, he
was humiliated before the eyes of all by being subjected to the most despised of
deaths, by being shown in the lowliest conceivable condition. Therein lies the
full import of the *kenosis* of Christ. It was by such passage that he was given
lordship, so that with God he exercised the power of releasing humankind from
servitude and from death itself.[7]

What Christ did in servitude, we are called also to do through humiliation.
Through our baptism we are called to give ourselves away to those who are
slaves, in order to stand against slavery of all kinds and to serve with humility
those who are humiliated. Our Eucharistic celebrations are our means for our
transformation, our response to the *kenosis* of Christ. When we are baptized
we take on the call (or in most cases our parents and godparents take on the
responsibility for us) to be the presence of Christ in the world. We no longer
live for ourselves, rather we set aside the limits of biological isolation and
death, and live in a new way, having a new way of being human. This way is
one which is communal and radically relational (as we have seen in chapter 1
on biblical justice). We are baptized in the name of the triune God. Even as
we die to self and rise to new life in Christ through the waters of baptism,
we rise as a new creation in the image of a relational God, a God in whose
very heart is a relation of Father, Son, and Spirit. We are most fully and truly
human when we are in relationship. In Christ, our relationships are not limited
by social class, status, or economic level.

In our Eucharistic celebrations we are reminded of this new way of being
human which began in our baptism and which continues as we reach out in
relationship first within the liturgy, and afterward outside the door of the
church. The Eucharistic gathering is first a community in which we experience this new ontological reality that continues to challenge us by word and
gesture, transforming us into an authentic expression of Christ's (kenotic)
way of being human. Eucharist, therefore, is first of all an action, not an
object. It is an action expressing the kenotic gift of Christ with the intention
of continuing our transformation. Thus transformed we can carry out the
mission of Christ in the world, bringing forth the kingdom of God through
service to the poor, to those who are slaves, those who daily face humiliation
and death in a thousand different ways. In the Eucharist we give thanks for
the gift of Christ, we are altered and move out into the world to continue this
self-emptying in justice to those in need.

Symbol, Rhythm and Silence, and Communion

Our next task is to look at some areas of our celebrations and to ask how
these aspects of the liturgy aid in the overall event of the Eucharist and hence
in the transformation of the assembly.

Symbol

The language of the liturgy is a language of action, silence, and word. It is the language of gesture, taste, touch, movement, and stillness. In other words, it is the language of symbol and ritual, a language our culture has to a great extent lost. We are suspicious of this language. Take symbol, for example. We confuse it with sign, which is univalent, shallow, and often juxtaposed with what is truly real. Think of a stop sign. How many meanings does it have? Just one. Now think of the symbol of the cross. Symbols are multivalent. They draw us into a rich tapestry of meaning, connection, and transformation that opens us to the Other in sacramental encounter.[8] One cannot define a symbol; it cannot be reduced to an explanation. One cannot narrow the multiple layers of meaning in a symbol and still retain the symbol intact.[9] Symbols help us communicate with God and one another a reality that, at its core, is a mystery.

Rhythm and Silence

By its very nature, the liturgy is countercultural; this is embodied in the liturgy's silence. Silences in our society are voids to be filled. We are familiar with such terms as "awkward pauses" and "deathly silence." Rarely is silence accepted as something to aid us, as something to be looked forward to and settle into. But this is exactly what liturgical silence helps us understand. Silence in the liturgy is one means of entering into the mystery at the heart of our prayer. Silence can help us more deeply approach that mystery. And the liturgy is full of such silences. "Let us pray"—this phrase is to be followed by silence in which the assembly actually prays. It is then followed by the collect or prayer gathering that assembled prayer in offering to God. Silence is part of the very fabric of the liturgy as both invitation and expectation. It is invitation into the mystery, and it is expectation of that which is to come. But no matter which dynamic is at play, these silences are communal and active, not private or isolated. They are not introspective but radically public. These are silences which are "expressions of the assembly's corporate attentiveness to the word of God proclaimed in the scriptures, and of its receptivity to the Spirit present in the celebration of Christ's mysteries in memory and in hope. . . . Silence is understood as that dimension which enables the person and the community to be brought more fully into the mystery of Christ's presence celebrated in liturgy."[10]

The rhythm and dynamic of the liturgy is also countercultural. It sets a pace of call and response, praise and thanks which aids in the transformation of the community. We embody, in this community and in these relationships, the deeper reality of our baptism—we are the body of Christ. In order to form and transform human persons in this dynamic of ritual action and word, liturgical performance is also repeatable and predictable. We do not reinvent the wheel with each liturgy. Rather, we carry out the same ritual words and actions week after week, with the same call and response; and yet each time we are ever more made new, ever more changed. We enter into this public prayer with an ease and confidence that comes from familiarity.

Communion

We are shaped into the body of Christ to be the body of Christ. We are called by our baptism to a radically new way of life, to rise from the waters of baptism as new creations, expressing our lives in Christ through our actions as church, a communion of persons—as *koinonia*. It is in our celebration of the Eucharist, in the gathering of the body around the table of the Lord, that this ecclesial reality is most fully expressed. Augustine himself noted "[t]herefore if you yourselves are the body of Christ and his members, then your own mystery lies on the altar. . . . Be what you see, and receive what you are."[11]

Through our baptism we are called into a new way of being, transformed by Christ. Paul argued, "[t]here is no longer Jew nor Greek, there is no longer slave or free, there is no longer male and female; for all of you are one in Christ" (Gal. 3:28); and again, "I have been crucified with Christ; and it is no longer I who live, but it is Christ who lives in me" (Gal. 2:19–20). Through our baptism we are radically reoriented to God, into a relationship that finds its ultimate expression in the gathering of the community around the eucharistic table, a relationship that is begun in the water but only fully disclosed in the eating and the drinking of the body and blood of Christ as a communion of persons.

Thus communion is the activity which draws the church together as the body of Christ and reveals the nature of the church both as an eschatological reality, living expectantly for the fulfillment of God's kingdom, and as a body that bears responsibility in the world. A key point here is the identification of Eucharist as an activity, and communion as the high point of all our eucharistic actions. We give the fullest expression of our identity in our communion, the common union of persons with Christ through the working of the Holy Spirit sent out for the healing of the world. We are *koinonia*, a relational body formed in the image of the triune God responding to the kenotic gift of the Christ.

Liturgy as Formation

Taking this point one step further, it is important to note the ramifications that all these liturgical actions have upon our formation, especially the emphasis upon communion as the central point of eucharistic identity. When silences are hurried or lacking entirely, when the rhythm of the liturgy is disrupted either by being rushed, skipped, or reinvented each week, and when we fail to envision through our own communion the communion with Christ in the world, then we are attempting to resist our transformation through God's self-giving. In the context of our resistance, our liturgical actions can hardly hope to form us into the body of Christ that the liturgy, properly carried out, is meant to accomplish.

When we refuse to celebrate the liturgy in the radical identity forming manner of Christ's self-emptying, we fail to open ourselves to embodying the relationships envisioned by our baptism. When we open ourselves to these relationships, they will be transformative. With the eucharistic communion of God in Christ comes a call, and the responsibility of the church is both to strengthen itself as a communion and also to reach outside itself in its mission. In expressing our identity as one body through eucharistic communion we are, in turn, committed to manifest that reality outside the church, to act as a sign of God's love and to call the world into this relationship. The Eucharist is the most public, radically social act we do as church. In it we are joined to the saving action of Christ and his cross!

Are our eucharistic liturgies authentic expressions of our faith? We must ask some difficult questions. Of whom are our communities composed? What boundaries have we set for ourselves, perhaps out of fear of having our comfort disrupted, so as not to confront the risks of our faith and the discomfort of God's call to us in the scriptures? There is no indication in liturgy or scripture that the relationships we are called to enter through our baptism are meant to be comfortable ones. As followers of Jesus, we do not have the option of picking and choosing those with whom we relate as the body of Christ. Rather it is through our eating and our drinking of the body and blood of Christ that we are called to manifest a new way of being in relationship, one which does not shy away from humiliation, social inferiority, poverty, slavery, or shame. We are called to reach out in openness to the world around us. "I don't see God! Where's God?" Practically speaking, God is found where our ritual actions are strongest, where our silences speak loudest, where we embody the self-emptying of Christ, when we empty ourselves to each other and give ourselves away to serve the world, even if this self-giving challenges our preconceived notions and comfort levels.[12]

Discussion

A Reflection on Eating

As a way to reflect on her chapter, Rodica Stoicoiu suggests that we consider how we eat and the characteristics of our meals. She asks us to begin with the bread and cup of the Lord's Supper—our sharing the body of Christ and the blood of new covenant. Recall the connections that she makes in the chapter between the Eucharist as an event of God's self-giving and our formation as a healing, reconciling, and loving community in the world. Pope Benedict XVI develops this theme in his encyclical, *Deus Caritas Est* (*God is Love*). He links the Eucharist with the command to love our neighbors.

Faith, worship and *ethos* are interwoven as a single reality which takes shape in our encounter with God's *agape*. Here the usual contraposition between worship and ethics simply falls apart. "Worship" itself, Eucharistic communion, includes the reality both of being loved and of loving others in turn. A Eucharist which does not pass over into the concrete practice of love is intrinsically fragmented. Conversely . . . the "commandment" of love is only possible because it is more than a requirement. Love can be "commanded" because it has first been given.[13]

John Paul II, in his *Ecclesia de Eucharisti* (2003), underlines this problem of fragmented love and the fragmented meal by citing St. John Chrysostom, the fourth century archbishop of Constantinople.

In a homily on the Gospel according to Matthew, Chrysostom connects the Eucharist with the parable of the judgment of nations (Matt. 25:31–46).

Do you wish to honor the body of Christ? Do not ignore him when he is naked. Do not pay him homage in the temple clad in silk, only then to neglect him outside where he is cold and ill-clad. He who said: "This is my body" is the same who said: "You saw me hungry and you gave me no food," and "Whatever you did to the least of my brothers you did also to me." . . . What good is it if the Eucharistic table is overloaded with golden chalices when your brother is dying of hunger? Start by satisfying his hunger and then with what is left you may adorn the altar as well.[14]

John Paul II holds that eucharistic love and Christian hope must shine forth in a world "where the weakest, the most powerless and the poorest appear to have so little hope . . . [T]he Lord wished to remain with us in the Eucharist, making his presence in meal and sacrifice the promise of a humanity renewed by his love."[15]

Benedict XVI and John Paul II offer us the starting point in the Eucharist—from which Dr. Stoicoiu asks us to begin our reflections. We now can consider how we eat, and we will take this step by turning to a book by Robert J. Karris, OFM, *Eating Your Way Through Luke's Gospel*. The book asks us to investigate the nature of the meal from the basis of the Gospel according to Luke. (1) "In Luke's Gospel Jesus is either going to a meal, at a meal, or coming from a meal." (2) "In Luke's Gospel Jesus got himself killed because of the way he ate."[16] As a natural good, food is sustenance for life, and the meal is the basic social form through which we are nourished. Eating in the gospel is both an ordinary social activity and a surprising and joyful practice of the kingdom of God.

On the first point (#1 above), Fr. Karris catalogues references (either figurative or literal) to food, eating, or table fellowship in every chapter of Luke. Jesus frequently eats with the likes of tax collectors and sinners, and the reign of God is represented by a great feast (Luke 14:15–24). But food and the meal are also intertwined with the gospel in less obvious places. For example, in Luke

5:1–11 Peter's first encounter and call from Jesus come through the medium of fish: first empty nets, then an abundance of fish when Jesus appears, and finally the call to be a fisher of the gospel. At the end, Jesus predicts Peter's denials during the Last Supper (Luke 22), and as the risen Lord he offers reconciling peace to Peter and the other disciples before they share a meal of baked fish (Luke 24:36–43).

On the second point (eating as the way to the cross), we need only recall the opposition that Jesus creates when he eats with sinners and announces the coming banquet of God's reign. Agriculture—rights to the land, farming, the taxation of production and trade, and so on—is a realm of political and economic tension and oppression in Israel under Roman rule.[17] The meal (and household hospitality) is a site for the expression of religious boundaries and political power. Jesus's way to the cross is set in motion when he gathers Israel for the great feast of God's reign. The meal is a sign and enactment of the kingdom. Before his death, during the Passover meal, he instructs the disciples about the bread and cup: "This is my body, which will be given for you; do this in memory of me" (Luke 22:19).

Karris, in *Eating Your Way Through Luke's Gospel*, considers the instruction, "do this in memory of me," not only in terms of eucharistic worship, but also in the broader sense of a eucharistic framework for our ordinary meals. The meal is opportunity for conversation and hospitality. Jesus is distinguished for encouraging conversation with uninvited guests and for accepting hospitality from the wrong kinds of people (Luke 7:36–50). The meal is opportunity for reconciliation and conversion (Luke 19:1–10), and we, in our meals today, have opportunity of living out parables of the kingdom.

Too often, however, our meals are hardly meals at all and our food (our fast or processed food) is hardly real food. We have lives filled with work and various activities. We are almost always on the move from here to there, and we have changed how we eat to accommodate our schedules. What would happen if we accommodated our schedules to how we should eat and welcome guests—strangers perhaps—to a meal? What would happen if we took the time to cook, eat, and enjoy conversation with our guests? It is striking how much our lives would change if hospitality were an everyday (or even weekly) affair. And in taking time for our meals, we might also discover that we have made room in our lives, we have made a place, to live out the gospel more fully. Sadly, for most of us the change would be too drastic. The whole of our day-to-day lives would have to change. As noted in the discussion section of chapter 2, the words of the risen Christ to the disciples apply to us, "do not be afraid." We should trust that hospitality will free us from the squirrel cage of "work and spend" and free us for the joy of faith.

However, if regular hospitality is too distant a goal, here's a small step. Eat less meat. Fr. Karris makes a correlation between Jesus's mealtime hospitality and the simple petition of the Lord's Prayer, "Give us each day our daily bread" (Luke 11:3).[18] Karris emphasizes the plural—give "us" and "our" daily bread. Jesus instructs us to depend upon God from day to day, and he calls us to reconciliation and hospitality. He eats his daily bread with both Pharisees and sinners. The daily bread of the Lord's Prayer points not only to our dependence upon God, but also to our dependence upon one another. The bread in my house is not an isolated product but represents a web of interdependence and, often, injustices and imbalances in the politics and economy of food. Beef, for example, appears in our grocery stores neatly displayed and wrapped, but its production plays a role in our current environmental crises and imbalances in world hunger and nutrition.[19]

We in the United States have an excessive and unhealthy appetite for meat.[20] According to the USDA, the average total meat consumption (red meat, chicken, and fish) per person in the United States, in 2005, was 200 pounds per person or over a half a pound each day.[21] The adverse effects on our health are well documented.[22] Michael Pollan, author of *In Defense of Food: An Eater's Manifesto*, shows that our carnivorous habits are far more the result of economic and cultural pressures than nutrition and taste. His advice is: eat food, not too much, mostly plants ("A little meat won't kill you, though it's better approached as a side dish than as a main").[23] The health effects are clear, but other consequences might be more surprising. I am citing these effects of meat consumption from John Sniegocki's "Implementing Catholic Social Teaching."[24]

- A recent United Nations Report, for example, concluded that livestock production is responsible for more greenhouse gases than all forms of transportation combined! The raising of animals for meat is also a major contributor to problems such as deforestation, desertification, groundwater depletion, and water pollution.[25]

- With regard to the contribution of meat-based diets to world hunger, it takes on average about twelve pounds of protein from grains and beans to produce one pound of protein from feedlot beef. The remaining 90+% of the protein (along with similar proportions of many other nutrients) is lost to human consumption. The conversion ratios for other animals vary, but all are inefficient. Many third-world nations devote much of their land to growing animal feed crops to satisfy the demand for meat by the world's wealthy consumers while local people go hungry. While reducing meat consumption will not by itself bring about an end to world hunger (various unjust political-economic structures also need to be changed), it is nonetheless one essential component of the response that is needed.[26]

In short, our diets are not free from the interdependence and interconnections with others. As Fr. Karris suggests, Jesus's instruction, "Do this in memory of me," calls us to live out eucharistic grace in our everyday meals.

4

Pope Leo XIII and a Century of Catholic Social Teaching

JOHN F. DONOVAN

Great teachings of the church invite us in and create a history of commentary. They command our attention. This is surely true of the foundational document of modern Catholic social teaching, Pope Leo XIII's *Rerum Novarum*. The custom in naming church documents is to use the first few words of the Latin translation. "Rerum Novarum" points to "new things" or revolutionary changes in the modern world. The subtitle of the document is "On the Condition of Labor," and the first sentence is: "It is not surprising that the spirit of revolutionary change, which had long been predominant in the nations of the world, should have passed beyond politics and made its influence felt in the cognate field of practical economy."[1] Although revolutionary changes were not surprising, it was unclear to many Catholics how the church should respond to the new things brought into the world by modern economic relations. In their workaday laboring lives, industrial workers were in the grip of economic forces that appeared hostile to the religious tradition affirmed in their Sunday worship. The dilemma they faced was the following: Could they affirm the reality of the modern economic order in a way that was congruent with their Catholic faith? Or were they forced to choose between them?

Published in 1891, *Rerum Novarum* initiated and facilitated a tradition of Catholic thought on modern economic practices aimed at solving this dilemma. Forty years after the document's publication, Pope Pius XI revisited these issues in *Quadragesimo Anno (After Forty Years)*, and again on the eightieth anniversary, Paul VI issued *Octogesima Adveniens*. Pope John Paul II commemorated both the ninetieth anniversary with *Laborum Exercens (On Human Work)* and the hundredth year with his *Centesimus Annus*.

This chapter will discuss Pope Leo's *Rerum Novarum* from the perspective of its engagement with the philosophical suppositions of the Enlightenment (the 18th century flowering of the modern era), which were for the most part deeply hostile to Catholicism. Given this hostility, a simple authoritarian appeal to church teachings would have fallen on deaf ears. Authority—with its apparent support of premodern social conditions and institutions—was itself under attack. In this intellectual climate, *Rerum Novarum*'s effectiveness turned on the strength of its arguments, and its arguments themselves needed to be cast in categories that the modern world could understand and accept. In order to understand how *Rerum Novarum* was able to initiate this kind of dialogue, we must first understand the intellectual community to which the encyclical was addressed.

Modernity's Conception of Social Order: the Myth of the Machine

Alexander Pope captured the spirit of modernity in these famous lines: "Nature and Nature's Law lay hid in night—God said 'Let Newton be'—and all was light." Modernity's self-characterization is that it is a time of enlightenment. This implies that the past with its traditions was a time of darkness. The evidence for such a characterization of modernity as "enlightened" was the overwhelming success of the emerging sciences, especially physics. As the quotation from Pope shows, there was the well-justified belief that the triumph of modernity is best exemplified in Newtonian mechanics, and the not so well-justified belief that, if a Newtonian explanation could be brought to bear on any area of culture, the truth would emerge. The world appeared to early modern science to be a marvelously constructed machine to which intelligence could discover the keys. Given this belief, it is important to understand what a Newtonian explanation looks like, for it is this kind of explanation that *Rerum Novarum* must acknowledge as a starting point of dialogue yet interpret in a way that is congruent with Catholic orthodoxy.

The Enlightenment's "Atomic" Individuality

A Newtonian explanation begins with an interpretation of the nature of its subject matter. Applied to physics, the really "real" is interpreted as a series of atomic particles in motion, each discrete or separate from the others. Motion appears to be imparted from the outside and thus is described as "force." The task of science is to formulate the laws that describe and explain the forces that cause atoms to interact. There are laws of various generality that explain specific levels of atomic interaction. Thus Galileo describes free fall, Kepler the pathways of the planets, Boyle the circulation of blood. The final task in this kind of explanation is to formulate a general principle that explains and locks together the various specific laws, some of which are mentioned here. This is Newton's principle of universal gravitation. The physical universe appears to be a wonderfully integrated machine with each part fitting smoothly into the whole. Questions about how things work dominate. The questions about "why" tend to disappear. In the famous explanatory commentary to his major work, the *Principia*, Newton asserts: "I make no hypotheses." That is, he poses no explanation for why the world is as it is. Rather, he rests satisfied with an explanation of how it works.

Given the great success of this kind of explanation when applied to the physical universe, it is only natural to wonder if similar progress could be made if this pattern of explanation were applied to the social, psychological, and economic realms. When applied to the social order, the atoms to be studied are individual human beings. As in the case with physical atoms, discrete individuality is the starting point. No response to questions such as, "where do such individuals come from?" or "aren't families prior to individuals?" is considered. What is the nature of this atomic political individualism? To be a person is to be free in the sense of self-ownership. To be a person is also to have the right to own the goods needed for personal survival.

The rest of the explanation follows the pattern outlined above. One looks for explanations of why such self-sufficient individual atoms gravitate together to form various kinds of communities. The final level of explanation is the principle integrating the lower-level explanations. It is the principle of the social contract formulated variously by Hobbes, Locke, Rousseau, and Kant. In social contract theory, associations are always secondary and derivative. Their function is to serve the needs and desires of individuals. Viewed from this vantage point, notions of the human person as essentially part of groups and as incomplete without communities appeared to be unjust limitations on human freedom. Rejecting the medieval notion of the self as essentially embedded in social relationships, social contract theory stressed the atomic individual's right to privacy, a notion closely related to freedom as independence. Outside influences are seen as forces to be minimized.

The Atomic Individual's Right to Privacy and its Impact on Religion

As noted above, the social and political setting in which modern philosophy developed was one of unrest and revolution. Thus Leo XIII's title, "New

Things" or "Revolutionary Change," recognizes this upheaval as the general framework into which modernity's self-understanding is cast. The unrest took many forms. Prominent among them was philosophy's insistence on a private notion of self-identity. This for the most part entailed a rejection of its own past, especially for its notion of a communal sense of the self. Thus we see the "father of modern philosophy," René Descartes (1596–1650), who cut his philosophical teeth as a quartermaster in the Thirty Years War, arguing that anything outside of individual consciousness is something other than the self. He saw the self as disconnecting from outside "forces" to achieve a sense of private self-certainty. We see John Locke (1632–1704), famous for the social contract political theory that we discussed above, and equally famous for his strong defense of the individual's right to privacy as the twin pillars of England's Glorious Revolution of 1688, championing a notion of selfhood based on individual memory. They—and many of their contemporaries who defended the right to privacy—deplored the role that religion appeared to be playing in augmenting and fueling civic unrest and discord. The great enemy of enlightenment—in their view—was *enthusiasm*, which they defined as the *public* expression of religious fervor. Their solution was to remove religion from the public order and make it a *private personal* matter.[2]

.Given the historical context in which the privatization of religion and the atomization of the human being became important intellectual projects, such claims appear to provide a rationally plausible solution to a pressing social problem. That is to say, the treatment of religion as private and personal was fueled by a public social need, the need for civil peace and order. There is no denying that this need was real. Its impact, of course, was to deny religion a public voice. Moreover, when that voice was heard it appeared as an apology for the pre-modern social order where the "parts" are fully integrated in the social whole, thus confirming modernity's belief that religion—and especially Catholic religion—was essentially an enemy of and incompatible with the emerging culture of individual freedoms rooted in rights claims. In other words, the privatizing of religion was a necessary but not sufficient condition for a coherent presentation of the new philosophical anthropology and new conception of the human being undergirding modernity. How could the Catholic Church enter into dialogue with the proponents of Enlightenment individualism?

Rerum Novarum: Bridge between Catholicism and Modernity

What will guide us as we look back on *Rerum Novarum*'s engagement with the proponents of the privatized self and its rights claims? We will organize Pope Leo's engagement with the Enlightenment by reflecting on John Paul II's call for a rereading of *Rerum Novarum*.[3] In John Paul's view, such rereading has three dimensions:

- *looking back* to recover the significance of *Rerum Novarum* as a text addressed to an audience that was to a great extent hostile to religion. Given our historical distance from the text, a natural misreading would be to judge it solely from the perspective of our present social concerns and—using those criteria—to judge it as an anachronistic failure;

- *looking around* to understand the different challenges and problems that we confront in the present. Great texts respond to the questions put to them. What does *Rerum Novarum* mean to us, given our contemporary vantage point that allows us to see social issues and problems not visible in the nineteenth century?

- *looking ahead* to exercise the church's prophetic mission as we enter a new millennium. What challenges and opportunities should the church expect in view of the key questions that distinguish our horizons from those presumed by *Rerum Novarum*?

One might think of both popes—Leo XIII and John Paul II—as recognizing that important truths are incarnational. That is, truths of human life reveal themselves in time and are deeply historical. For *Rerum Novarum* and subsequent documents (like John Paul II's *Centesimus Annus*) to speak to us as Christian believers, we must have the humility and patience to hear and respond to what they are able to tell us about issues of the present from the vantage points of their own horizons. We should read them in a visionary way as pointing the way to a future that is congruent with the truths of faith. Both men stand in the shoes of the first pope, Peter the fisherman. Both possess a nautical wisdom: when rowing a boat one goes forward by sighting what is behind.[4] Real progress is not the Enlightenment's tendency to respond to perceived error by clearing the deck and beginning all over again. Rather, what is needed is a sympathetic reading of past texts that orient us, from the perspective of distance, to what lies ahead.

In looking backward to *Rerum Novarum*, we can see that its real impact should be viewed as a bridge that allowed Catholicism to cross over from its role as the dominant institution in premodern times to an engagement with modernity.[5] That is, the encyclical is a bridge that spans a deep trench. On one side of the trench is the church's embeddedness in premodern social and political forms in contrast to the modern rise of nationalism, *laissez faire* ("hands off" or strict free market) economics, and the socialist ideology of Marxism. On the other side of the trench is the secular claim that religion is an alienated self-consciousness, an ideological opium that masks the pain of an unjust world. The greatness of *Rerum Novarum* is that it bridges this divide in a way that insured that authentic Catholicism could be preserved and brought into dialogue with modernity. In order for us to appreciate this, we must avoid an unhistorical issue-based reading of the text. We should not focus on what one views as outdated in the encyclical, such as the place of women in society or its agriculturally based understanding of the economy. Rather, we need to see the manner of argumentation and its historical significance: in the antiauthoritarian time in which it was written, *Rerum Novarum*'s impact had to stand on the strength of its arguments. How strong is it philosophically? Having laid out the presuppositions of modernity—the Newtonian atomic self with is notion of the right to privacy and the privatization of religion—we must assess the text's power to enter into conversation with the prevailing viewpoints that composed the great intellectual battlefield of modernity.

Pope Leo's Adoption and Deepening of Rights Language

Modernity's atomic and privatized self expressed its claims in terms of the possession of inalienable and indefeasible rights. A right is inalienable in the sense that it cannot be given away or sold. It is indefeasible in the sense that it cannot be taken away. It is important that we have some notion of what exactly a right is, for it is in Pope Leo's decision to use such language that the church's overture to modernity consists. It is instructive to note that, although Catholic social teaching, both in *Rerum Novarum* and in subsequent documents, relies heavily on rights language, there are only five references in the index to *Catholic Social Thought: The Documentary Heritage*. Only one of the references is to *Rerum Novarum*. Given the centrality of the concept, it is best to start with Locke's classic definition. Rights are expressions of a person's "perfect freedom to order actions, and dispose of their possessions and persons as they think fit, within the bounds of the law of nature, without asking leave, or depending upon the will of any other man."[6] Let us unpack this proposition.

1. It is an assertion of the social atom's independence: rights claims do not require the permission of any other individual or collective.
2. It is a claim to the legitimacy to initiate action: rights claims go beyond thinking to doing.
3. It is an identification of a domain of agency: within that domain in which one may freely act are one's person and one's property. Rights language forbids intrusions into this domain by unnatural forces such as interference by other individuals, social organizations, the state, and the church.
4. It is the recognition of a sphere of the duties. One atomic self has duties to another and thus expresses the only natural limitation on one's otherwise perfect freedom.

To be a person is to be a possessor of such rights. Foremost among these rights is the right to private property.[7] Locke used the term "property" in two senses. (1) It meant the human self: one owned oneself and one's body. (2) It referred to ownership of those things needed for personal survival and well-being that are procured by the individual through her own labor.

Rerum Novarum on Human Nature—Pope Leo's Deepening of Rights Language

Having seen the classic expression of modernity's new rights-based anthropology, our task now is to see how *Rerum Novarum* accepted rights language, and especially the right of private property as foundational, while deepening its philosophical foundations by an appeal to a Christian understanding of the human person.

The encyclical begins with what appears to be a total acceptance of modernity's viewpoint as we have studied it above. Appealing not to church authority but to the power of reason, Leo judges that the arguments for private property "are so strong and convincing that it seems surprising that certain obsolete opinions should now be revived in opposition to what is here laid down." What are the arguments?

1. Given our rational foresight, humans can possess not only the fruits of the earth but also the earth itself . . . to make provisions for our needs.
2. The earth and its use is given to the human race in general since we cannot distinguish the fundamental needs of one person as having rational priority over another.
3. To say that the earth is given for the use and enjoyment of the universal human race is not to deny that there can be private property. But it does imply moral and social limits to the use of property.
4. Private ownership, according to the law of human nature, is required for the preservation of life and for our well-being. What we need is produced in great abundance by the earth, but not until we bring it into cultivation and with great care and skill.
5. When we properly cultivate the earth, we make a part of the earth and its fruits our own (private property), and in the process, a person "leaves, as it were, the impress of his own personality."
6. Before the application of our labor, nature was barren, a wasteland.
7. The common reasoning of human beings and cultures has put form to the principle of private ownership.

8. The right to private property is not grounded in the state. Man is older than the state and he holds the right of providing for the life of his body prior to the state.

Rerum Novarum's Deepening of this Rights-based Argument: "A Family Right"

In *Rerum Novarum*, the deepening of this rights-based argument begins immediately after the rights of labor and property are outlined. While accepting the individual's right to property, Pope Leo places the understanding of the proprietor in a much stronger light by locating it "in relation to man's social and dogmatic obligations" (no. 12).[8]

> That right to property . . . which has been proved to belong naturally to individual persons, must in like wise belong to a man in his capacity of head of a family . . . that right is all the stronger in proportion as the human person receives a wider extension in the family group. (no. 13)

The pope deepens the notion of self to include the concrete roles that an agent plays. The formula "head of household" can lead us into a discussion of gender issues, but I argue that its historical significance lies in a redefining of the notion of personhood based on the Christian notion of community; here in terms of the basic society of family. It has always been the church's practice in evangelizing the world to start with cultural givens that can be read analogically as stepping stones into the historical cultures to which the gospel is addressed at a given time. It would not occur to Enlightenment writers such as Locke to raise gender issues in regard to the Pope's redefinition of the person as possessing rights. What would be new to Locke is the Pope's reassertion of a communal notion of the person in a way that is congruent with the emerging culture of rights (of which Locke is an important architect). Rights, then—and especially the right to private property—are set in the context of reciprocal duties which depend on a non-atomistic account of social relations.

A Deepened Notion of Self as Owner Applied to the Right to a Just Wage

Having established the right to be heard by rehearsing and deepening the notion of the modern self as owner, Pope Leo XIII applies the concept critically to classic economic theory. In view of the argument for a communal view of personhood, what can be said of modern economic notions, such as "the iron law of wages" and the "invisible hand"? *Rerum Novarum* begins by rehearsing classical economic theory. Leo XIII begins with a statement of individual freedom that rests uneasy with the determinist nature and mechanistic theories of classical economics.

> Wages, as we are told, are regulated by free consent, and therefore the employer, when he pays what was agreed upon, has done his part and seemingly is not called upon to do anything beyond. The only way, it is said, in which injustice might occur would be if the master refused to pay the whole of the wages, or if the workman should not complete the work undertaken. . . . (no. 43)

We have here a statement (which Leo will rebut) of the contractualism for which Locke argued so forcefully. But Pope Leo argues: "To this kind of argument a fair-minded man will not easily or entirely assent" (no. 44). The Lockean argument is abstract in a bad sense: "It is not complete, for there are important considerations which it leaves out of account altogether." One thing the pope finds missing is a clear statement of the nature and purpose of work. Rather than seeing work as a simple agreement between two parties, he defines it in terms of its goal: to work is to exert one's self for the sake of procuring what is necessary for life, for self-preservation. Far more than simply free exchange between contracting parties, work has the characteristic of being necessary to the human being as a human person. Moreover, since it is directly connected with self-preservation, work has the characteristic of a moral duty. Viewed as supporting the person and the family, the laborer is not free to accept just any wage, and the employer is morally prohibited from pressuring the acceptance of low wages based on the worker's need. "If through necessity or fear of a worse evil the workman accept harder conditions because an employer or contractor will afford him no better, he is made the victim of force and injustice" (no. 45).

Conclusion

Given such judgments, Pope Leo XIII is rejecting the notions of society and economic theory that present relationships under the metaphor of natural necessity and the atomistic self. He deepens the notion of the self to include concrete moral relationships (within family and between employer and employee). He frames the question of labor and wages with the notion of labor's goal: to serve the life and well-being of the worker. In this way, supporting relationships (of family and employment) bring out the moral dimensions of economic exchange that lay underdeveloped or even absent in classical Enlightenment theory. It is upon such kinds of moral enrichments that Catholic social teachings will come to rest in the century following *Rerum Novarum*. Leo XIII's encyclical is the basic text in the twofold meaning of the term. It is basic in the sense of being just the beginning, as well as in the sense of being the foundation upon which things rest.

Discussion

Private Property and Common Work

John Donovan's presentation of Leo XIII's *Rerum Novarum* points to different conceptions of the human being which correspond to different conceptions of social and economic relationships. On one hand, the new things of the modern economy (and Locke's notion of ownership) presuppose a conception of the human being as an isolated atom. On the other hand, Catholic social thought sees the individual always (from the very beginning of creation) within reciprocal, social, and personal relationships. In other words, our personal and social identities are intrinsic to our roles and place in relationship to others.[9] Dr. Donovan indicates that our roles and duties (in family, for example) are both a justification for private property and the way we draw moral limits on the use of private property.

In response to Donovan's chapter, we will discuss relationships between employers and employees in terms of what is called "the universal destiny of property." Universal destiny can be illustrated with the example of food. My wife and I have a refrigerator full of food that is our private property. As Pope Leo indicates, we use this property to sustain ourselves and our children. However, our ownership is not absolute. If we were to throw all the food away for no good reason, we would be committing a moral wrong. Perhaps we should call the wrong a sin of selfishness and ingratitude, or maybe greed and the sin of pride (our arrogant claim of absolute ownership). Why a moral wrong? The "universal destiny" of food is to satisfy hunger and to nourish human beings. This destiny is the primary and universal purpose of food, and we properly use our food when we apply this universal purpose within our particular relationships and duties of family. When our ownership of food exceeds our use, the food still retains its human purpose, and our duties to those who hunger are sustained (even though those who hunger are no longer our children). To sustain the purpose of food, it ought to be given to a food bank or, in some other way given to those who are hungry and need nourishment. (Maybe we should host a great banquet and invite the poor from the highways and byways.) In any case, food is put to its universal destiny whether we use our food for our children or for others who are hungry. Waste violates food's inherent and universal purpose.

If this is the meaning of universal destiny, the question for discussion is how this conception of purpose might fit with the ownership of businesses and the means of production and employment. Let's begin with Pope Leo's agrarian framework, which forms the bridge between his conception of property and the relationships between capital/employer and labor/employee.

1. Ownership comes through the cultivation of the earth. On this point, review Dr. Donovan's eight points above in the section titled, "*Rerum Novarum* on Human Nature."
2. A wealthy landowner has farmland that he is not able to cultivate on his own, so that he needs the labor of others if he is going to put his land to its proper use and destiny. Compare the food example. My wife and I had food that we could not put to use, and the landowner has agricultural lands to be used for human sustenance.
3. Landless laborers need land to cultivate if they are to acquire the fruits of the earth and fulfill their destiny as human beings. Again, consult John Donovan's eight points.
4. The landowner and the laborer have a relationship along with reciprocal rights and duties that is based primarily, not on the demands of the market or on an economic contract, but on what it means to be a human being. The supply and demand of labor can determine wages to a degree, but the base line of wage is determined by the basic needs of the worker.

This same framework of reciprocal duties and rights is used, by Leo XIII and the tradition that follows, to understand the relationship between factory owner and industrial worker or a corporation in a service industry and its employees.

Please bear with a short detour, so that I can indicate the wider significance of this framework of ownership. In *Centesimus Annus*, John Paul II uses this conception of ownership to discuss the relationship between wealthy and poor nations. In reference to Leo XIII, he notes that in the late twentieth century economy (in the global economy), "there exists another form of ownership which is becoming no less important than land: *the possession of know-how, technology and skill*. The wealth of the industrialized nations is based much more on this kind of ownership than on natural resources" (no. 32). John Paul holds that this shift of resources, from the land to the skilled person, makes Pope Leo's framework all the more important. Good work in a technological and service economy increasingly depends upon cooperation and interdependence: the person is a resource, so that relations between persons are all the more vital to dignified work. The danger is that the poor, especially in the poor parts of the world and in underdeveloped economies, will be merely used for their labor or simply ignored. "The fact is that many people, perhaps the majority today, do not have the means which would enable them to take their place in an effective and humanly dignified way within a productive system in which work is truly central" (no. 33). John Paul II applies Leo XIII's framework of ownership and the universal destiny of goods to those in the first world who have ownership of the new economy in relationship to the poor in the world who do not have access to the system. The economic system of technology and know-how is, in a sense, the "land" that has the purpose of providing the poor the opportunity for dignified work. Global markets, however, are not giving the poor a dignified place in the global economy. This claim is also important to John Paul II's call to give poor countries relief from foreign debt (*Centesimus Annus*, no. 35). Massive foreign debt (which is no fault of the poor citizens of a poor country) excludes the population from the fruits of good work (such as basic nutrition, health care, and education).

Now back to the main point: we return to Leo XIII's conception of the relationship between employer and employees. Pope Leo's agrarian frame establishes mutual dependence between owner and worker and reciprocal duties. Given this mutuality, Catholic social teaching has been critical of both market-dominated capitalism and state-dominated socialism. From Pope Leo to Benedict XVI, Catholic thought has challenged both capitalism and socialism by means of its integrated view of human work and the duties that are intrinsic to the relationship between employer and employee. Leo XIII presents their reciprocal rights and duties in this way. The worker ought "fully and faithfully to perform the work which has been freely and equitably agreed upon," and the owner/employer ought to "respect in every man his dignity as a person . . . [T]o misuse men as though they were things in the pursuit of gain, or to value them solely for their physical powers—that is truly shameful and inhuman" (no. 20).

Later in *Rerum Novarum*, Pope Leo will attend in length to the rights of the laborer. Indeed, he writes the encyclical because the dignity of the worker is threatened by new things of the industrial economy. Leo XIII outlines the rights of workers to attend to spiritual and intellectual fulfillment through work which does not create servitude and through adequate time off for religious observance and leisure pursuits. The worker has the right to work in such a way that will sustain physical health and a good life. For this reason, employers should limit the hours of work and the kinds of labor that a person is required to do. Finally, the worker is due a wage that is determined (in part) by what is needed to sustain a family, to allow the modest acquisition of property, to plan for the future, and to have opportunity to give to the poor and contribute to the common good.

One hundred years after *Rerum Novarum*, John Paul II offers a similar account of the purpose of a business.

> The Church acknowledges the legitimate *role of profit* as an indication that a business is functioning well. When a firm makes a profit, this means that productive factors have been properly employed and corresponding human needs have been duly satisfied. But profitability is not the only indicator of a firm's condition. It is possible for the financial accounts to be in order, and yet for the people—who make up the firm's most valuable asset—to be humiliated and their dignity offended. Besides being morally inadmissible, this will eventually have negative repercussions on the firm's economic efficiency. In fact, the pur-

pose of a business firm is not simply to make a profit, but is to be found in its very existence as a *community of persons* who in various ways are endeavoring to satisfy their basic needs, and who form a particular group at the service of the whole of society. Profit is a regulator of the life of a business, but it is not the only one; *other human and moral factors* must also be considered which, in the long term, are at least equally important for the life of a business. (*Centesimus Annus*, no. 35)

What Can We Do?

For a number of years, I have required students to respond to John Paul II's conception of a business as a community of persons. I have found that many are cynical. They assume that the Catholic tradition's view of ownership is not realistic. They assume that John Paul II's appeal to human and moral factors, as well as his concern for the common good, is usually a hindrance to profit and economic survival. I know several successful business people who think otherwise. For a few years, I have been part of a group of business people (some small business owners and others executives or managers). I have been impressed with their profound commitment to their employees as persons. I will give one example, and hopefully it will help us think about the question, "what can we do?" from the sides of both employer and employee.

C. Merediethe Adams Jr. (who goes by Bo) owns the Adams Insurance Agency, which has a Nationwide Insurance office in Frederick, Maryland, an independent office in Bethesda, and eight employees. I should add that he is a graduate of Mount St. Mary's in nearby Emmitsburg. You might want to take a look at the agency's website: www.adamsinsuranceagency.net/. You will find the company's mission.

> Adams Insurance Agency is dedicated to providing our clients with professional insurance and financial expertise and advice, tailored to meet your individual and business needs. We care about our clients, offering quality and value coupled with a personal, hands-on approach to help you *protect what you don't expect*. Our goal is to develop a good understanding of your needs, so that our insurance professionals can make the appropriate risk management recommendations.
>
> At Adams Insurance, we are committed to teamwork, innovation, education, and most of all communication. We promise to treat each and every client with honesty, fairness, trust, and integrity.

I asked Mr. Adams a series of questions, first about the mission and the company's service to society, and then about his relationship to his employees and their good.

When asked about the good of society as a whole, Bo pointed directly to the mission of the insurance agency. People need protection for their businesses, personal security, and for their families. He and his employees want to provide the best protection (not too much and not too little), based on an individual's needs and for the best possible price. I mentioned to him (it just seemed to pop into my head), that security and protection against unemployment, sickness, and the disabilities of aging are first on the list in Pope John XXIII's list of human rights in *Pacem in Terris* (Peace on Earth, 1963).[10]

"Precisely," Bo responded, "insurance is not simply a commodity." I was confused: isn't that exactly what insurance is, a marketable product? Bo admitted that many agencies and corporations have reduced insurance to a commodity, but that the insurance business is primarily a relationship. He explained that people do not have many advisors in their lives (a problem, perhaps, of our individualist age). His agency provides an advisory relationship by listening to the needs of its clients in terms of their lives as a whole—including a person's goals in life (like educating children). This advisory role can create strong personal bonds, which must be respected and not reduced to a product. Bo noted that people will stop by his office to run a problem or financial opportunity by him, even when it is not directly related to their accounts with the agency. Sometimes he worries that this openness and availability puts too much of a strain on the business; nonetheless, he considers this broad advisory relationship an essential part of doing good business (good in both the financial and human/relational senses). It is necessary because his clients are not anonymous consumers; he and his coworkers want a full picture of their concerns and needs.[11]

Next we discussed Bo's relationship to his employees. He explained that he thinks about his relationship with employees in terms of shared ownership. I noted to him how interesting shared ownership is in relationship to Catholic social teaching. Pope Leo XIII holds that work and wages should enable ownership, so that persons can provide for their families, plan for a secure future, and contribute to common life. This task of enabling ownership seems to weigh heavily upon Bo. His worries about the health of his business are also worries about protecting the jobs of his employees. He wants them to be secure and successful. Further, as we will see in the discussion section at the end of chapter 8, Pius XI (in 1931) frames the relationship of employer and employee in terms of shared ownership of the work. This sense of ownership—ownership of the mission—is where Bo began his discussion of employer-employee relations.

He sees himself as both a mentor to and a coworker with his employees. He is a collaborative leader who shares the company's success with employees and asks them to share the responsibility of the work. We talked about both of these—the benefits of success and the responsibility of the work—as forms of ownership.

- Part of ownership of the mission is taking on responsibility for setting goals and providing ideas (models) for how to achieve these goals. Employees are asked to take an active role in the direction of the company.

- Another aspect of ownership is sharing in the success of the company. Employees receive 100% of commissions on accounts that they secure as well as annual raises based on the growth of the agency.

In owning the mission, Bo finds that he has a teaching role. He mentors employees in understanding and carrying out the mission of the company: both the role of helping people gain security and the role as advisor (with its openness and availability to the whole person). He explained to me a downside to this approach. Some employees do not want the responsibility. They want insurance to be simply a commodity, and they want to work just for a paycheck. These employees eventually find work elsewhere. Other employees flourish, however. During our conversation, it was clear to me that Bo is concerned, not simply with the business, but sees ownership of the mission and responsibility for the work as important to the personal growth of his employees. He has high expectations about what kind of people his employees are becoming through their work. He backs these explanations up with opportunities for sharing in the financial success of the company.

I will end with a personal experience. If you were to have a discussion with Bo, you too would hear and see his deep concern for his employees. I also experienced his concern for his clients: we have life insurance with the Adams Insurance Agency. One thing that strikes me about financial advising (not just with Bo) is how intimate it is. When we lay out the facts about what we do with our money, we show what we think is important in life. We might say we value one thing, like education or time with our families, but the numbers and how we use money might say otherwise. My wife and I found Bo to have skill and insight in understanding the numbers and to have courage to ask the tough questions. Our two-hour discussion with him was not just about a policy. It was about my wife, me, and our children. It was about our worries and hopes, about what we can and cannot live without. One thing that struck us is that he gave advice opposite to what we have received from brokers and mortgage companies. We have found the general attitude to be, "borrow and spend to your limits." Bo's advice was to live modestly, be clear about what is important, and spend as much time as you can with your family. That is financial advice that serves the common good.

PART TWO

Love

5

Saint Augustine of Hippo

Love, Community, and Politics

WILLIAM COLLINGE

Saint Augustine (354–430) holds a central position in Western political thought. He has been claimed as an ancestor of both medieval Christendom and the modern secular state, and both claims can draw support from his writings. Augustine's dominant position in Western thought—by no means confined to the political—arises from the quantity and quality of his works, partly because the collapse of Roman cultural institutions in the centuries immediately following his death precluded anyone from rising to the status of a rival.

Augustine's Life

Augustine was born in the small town of Thagaste (now Souk Ahras, Algeria) in the Roman province of Numidia in North Africa. His father, Patricius, was a pagan; his mother, St. Monica (or Monnica), was a Christian. Augustine was not baptized as a child but was given a vaguely Christian upbringing, as well as the best classical education his family could afford. His *Confessions*, written between 397 and 401, describe his spiritual wanderings, culminating in his baptism by St. Ambrose in Milan at Easter in 387.

He returned to Africa, where in 391 he was forcibly ordained to the priest-hood (a solution to the priest shortage that is now out of favor) at Hippo (modern Annaba, Algeria). In 395 he became bishop at Hippo, a position which he held for the rest of his life. He wrote close to one hundred books, more than two hundred letters (which were semipublic documents), and more than four hundred sermons. Previously unknown letters and sermons still turn up from time to time. His most influential works are the *Confessions* and *The City of God*, both of which are discussed below.

Augustine on Love

A key term in Augustine's writing, one which connects his thought on moral matters, the state, the church, and even the nature of God, is love. Actually it is three terms in Latin—*amor*, *caritas*, and *dilectio*—but they are more or less interchangeable. Love is an inclination, tendency, or movement of the will. In turn, the will (Latin *voluntas*, a term that Augustine brought to prominence in Western philosophy) is simply the power of the soul to move toward a certain object (if you are mathematically minded, you could think of the soul as a vector).

For Augustine, love is good or bad depending on its object. Augustine is firm, however, in his insistence that no thing is bad in itself—all that God created is good. The will becomes evil not in itself and not through loving evil things but through a wrong ordering of its loves. If I love bodily pleasures more than spiritual goods, if I love material wealth more than my fellow human beings, if I love myself more than God, then my will is evil and I am sinning.[1]

In *On Christian Instruction* (*De doctrina christiana*), begun about 396, Augustine introduces two helpful distinctions. The first is between enjoyment (*frui*) and use (*uti*). To enjoy something is to love it for its own sake. To use it is to love it for the sake of something else. Strictly speaking, only God, who alone gives us happiness, is to be enjoyed; all other creatures are to be used. It may sound strange, even offensive, to speak of using ourselves and others. In contemporary English, "using" people suggests taking advantage of them for our own selfish purposes. Augustine's point, however, is that love of self and neighbor is to be subordinated to love of God. If our love is to be "rightly ordered," Augustine says, "every human being should be loved for the sake of God, and God should be loved for his own sake."[2] At times, in fact, Augustine speaks of "enjoying a human being in God," which means loving the other person in such a way that both of us are drawn toward God, the only one who is to be loved for his own sake.[3]

The second important distinction in *On Christian Instruction* is between *caritas* and *cupiditas*. There is no good idiomatic English translation of these terms—the translation quoted below very nearly leaves them in Latin—but "self-giving love" and "possessive love" come close to conveying the meaning. Note how both are expressed in terms of enjoyment.

> I call "charity" the motion of the soul toward the enjoyment of God for his own sake, and the enjoyment of one's self and of one's neighbor for the sake of God; but "cupidity" is a motion of the soul toward the enjoyment of one's self, one's neighbor, or any corporeal thing for the sake of something other than God.[4]

This distinction becomes Augustine's basic principle for biblical interpretation, which is the main subject of *De doctrina christiana*: "Scripture teaches nothing but charity, nor condemns anything except cupidity, and in this way shapes the minds of human beings."[5] Or, as Jesus says in Matthew's gospel, "The whole law and the prophets depend on the two commandments, to love God with all your heart, soul, and mind, and to love your neighbor as yourself" (Matt. 22:37–40).[6]

Friendship

All human communities, Augustine thinks, are based on shared love. He speaks of the community of fans of an actor; we might also think of the fans of an athletic team.[7] As individuals may be judged in accordance with what they love, so too may communities. In particular, this is true of the intimate form of community called "friendship" (*amicitia*), which Augustine especially cherished. He was rarely without the company of friends, and in the *Confessions* he gives many examples of the role of friends in his life, for good or ill.

Book 2 of the *Confessions*[8] features an episode in which the sixteen-year-old Augustine and a gang of friends vandalize a pear tree belonging to a neighbor. Why, critics sometimes ask, does Augustine spend so much time on so trivial an event? There are two reasons. One is that it is a pure case, an example of an evil deed done for its own sake (the boys didn't want the pears). The other is that it shows the negative moral effects of friendship, when directed toward the wrong ends. "Alone I would not have committed that crime, in which my pleasure lay not in what I was stealing but in the act of theft. . . . Friendship can be a dangerous enemy."[9] Augustine is not making excuses here; his point is that friends can goad one another to commit acts that they would otherwise refrain from as morally wrong. Any reader who was ever a teenage boy can probably find parallels in his own experience. Moreover, this story—involving a tree, its fruit, and partners in crime—is intended to echo a more famous story of sin: that of the original sin, told in chapter 3 of Genesis, which portrays how the whole human race became a community of sin.

Book 4 contains some of the most eloquent language about friendship in all of ancient literature. Augustine narrates the death of a close friend and his own grief at the loss: "My home town became a torture to me; my father's house a strange world of unhappiness; all that I had shared with him was without him transformed into a cruel torment."[10] He takes consolation, however, in the company of his remaining friends:

> to make conversation, to share a joke, to perform mutual acts of kindness, to read together well-written books, to share in trifling and in serious matters, to disagree though without animosity—just as a person debates with himself—and in the very rarity of disagreement to find the salt of normal harmony, to teach each other something or to learn from one another, to long with impatience for those absent to welcome them with gladness on their arrival. These and other signs . . . [act] as fuel to set our minds on fire and out of many to forge unity.[11]

Despite all these good things, Augustine concludes that his friendship with the young man who died and the others who survived was not true friendship. For one thing, "I had poured out my soul on to the sand by loving a person sure to die as if he would never die."[12] In addition, Augustine and this group of friends were joined by their adherence to a religion that, from the point of view of Augustine writing the *Confessions*, was "a vast myth and a long lie."[13] This was Manichaeism, a dualistic religion that saw the world and the human soul as a battleground between good and evil divine, coeternal principles.[14] In two ways, Augustine's love was wrongly ordered: he was loving a mortal person as if he were eternal, as only God is, and he was loving a false God, a false image of God as not truly all-powerful. So the friendship "was less than a true friendship";[15] the friends did not (to use the language of *On Christian Instruction*) "enjoy one another in God."

"True friendship," Augustine immediately goes on to say, "is not possible unless you [God] bond together those who cleave to one another by the love which 'is poured into our hearts by the Holy Spirit who is given to us.'"[16] This passage cites St. Paul's Letter to the Romans 5:5, one of the two scripture texts on which Augustine relies most heavily in his theology of the church; the other, which also echoes what Augustine says of friendship, is Acts of the Apostles 4:32: "The community of believers was of one heart and one mind."[17] The church is the community that is bonded together by true love of God, which comes through the gift of the Holy Spirit. So true friendship is to be found in the church. As Augustine describes, in books 6 through 9 of the *Confessions*, how he draws closer to the church, he gives many examples of the role of friendship in this process. In book 6 we read the story of Augustine's best friend, Alypius. Book 8 speaks of a number of Christian friends and acquaintances who are instrumental in Augustine's conversion—including Alypius, who is with him at the decisive moment and is himself converted at that time. Book 9, the last autobiographical book, tells of the community of friends with whom Augustine is living between his conversion and his baptism, and finally of a brief period of ecstatic contemplation of God shared by Augustine and his mother—the *Confessions'* most striking instance of humans "enjoying one another in God." A literary indication, first noted by Frederick Crosson, of Augustine's movement from false to true friendship is that in the first half of the autobiography (book 1 to the middle of book 5), he names almost none of his contemporaries—not his dead friend, his mistress of fifteen years, or even his parents and his son—whereas the second half, especially books 8 and 9, is full of personal names. "The second half," says Crosson, "is not only an ascent toward God; it is a progressive return to community."[18]

The Church

When Augustine became bishop at Hippo, he was brought into a long-standing conflict between the Catholics and a rival Christian church that its opponents called the Donatists, after Donatus, one of its early leaders.[19] The Donatists claimed that the Catholics were fatally compromised by the fact that, in the last persecutions of the Christians, late in the third century, some Catholic clergy had handed over sacred vessels and books to be destroyed by the Romans. In Augustine's vicinity, Donatists probably were the majority of Christians, but for Augustine what mattered was that they were not in union with the church of Rome (headed by its bishop, the pope) and the other great churches of the empire. Central to Augustine's response to the Donatists was the argument that by breaking with the larger church they had broken the bond of love that unites it.

This argument is developed especially in a series of ten homilies Augustine preached in 407 on the First Letter of St. John. "We shall not be in darkness," he says, "if we love the brethren; and the proof of love for the brotherhood lies in not rending our unity, in maintaining charity."[20] Sometimes Augustine speaks of the love that binds the church as the Holy Spirit himself, while at other times it seems to be the effect in us of the presence of the Holy Spirit. As in the following passage, Augustine does not clearly distinguish the two: "On what is anyone to ground assurance that he has received the Holy Spirit? Let him enquire of his own heart: if he loves his brother, the Spirit of God abides in him. . . . There can be no love without the Spirit of God."[21]

The Donatists emphasized the purity of the church. One of their favorite scripture passages was Ephesians 5:25–27, which speaks of the church as "without spot or wrinkle." They themselves, they said, had kept the church pure of the terrible sacrilege of handing over the sacred books and vessels. Augustine, however, did not think that the church in this life could ever be pure. Rather, he argued that the true community of those bound together by the love given by the Holy Spirit is not always visible. The visible or empirical church—those who are on the membership rolls, those who attend Sunday liturgy, even priests and bishops—is a mixed church, including some who are united by the Spirit and some who are not. The latter are like weeds among the wheat, goats among the sheep, to be separated from the rest at the end of time.[22]

There is another complication here. Go back to Romans 5:5: "The love of God is poured into our hearts by the Holy Spirit who *is given to us*"—and note the italicized words. The Holy Spirit is God's gift; whether or not we receive him is up to God, not up to us. As Augustine's theology of divine grace develops, it hardens into a theory of predestination. Predestination does not simply mean that God knows our choices in advance of our making them (called foreknowledge); it means that God has chosen in advance who will be saved and who will not. Those are saved to whom God chooses to give the gift of the Holy Spirit, which is the grace of salvation; all others are damned because of original sin. Augustine does not deny human free will; rather, he says, it takes grace to make it functional. In the *Confessions* he speaks of sin as a sort of addiction: "By servitude to passion, habit is formed, and habit to which there is no resistance becomes necessity."[23] He uses the metaphor of chains here, and you can make sense out of it when you think of people who want to be free from an addiction—say, to cigarettes or alcohol—but are unable to free themselves from the compulsion to smoke or drink. In a sense, original sin causes a collective enchainment of the human race to sinful habits, from which only grace can break people free.

We do not need to go into all the difficulties of Augustine's theory of predestination and whether or not it preserves human free will.[24] Augustine continued throughout his life to urge people to do good and avoid sin, as if the choice were theirs, and he emphasized that in this life no one knows whether he or she belongs to the saved or the damned. But as we approach his great work, *The City of God*, we need to be aware of the theory of predestination lying in the background.

The Two Cities

The City of God, on which Augustine worked from 413 to 427, began as an answer to pagan charges that the Christians were responsible for the sack of Rome in 410 by the Visigoths under Alaric, in that they had brought down the wrath of the gods against the city. It expands into a massive treatise (more than a thousand pages in English translation) relating Christianity to classical culture and arguing for the superiority of Christian to pagan theology. Not many contemporary readers—if you don't count graduate students—succeed in making their way through the whole book, as it wanders through details taken from mythology, philosophy, the Bible, experience, and lore,[25] seemingly for readers who had all the time in the world (which the wealthy, educated pagans to whom Augustine was writing more or less did). Yet it has few rivals in its influence on Western political thought.

The City of God compares two cities (*civitates*, political communities) which, like all communities, are joined by the object of their love: "The two cities were created by two kinds of love: the earthly city was created by self-love reaching the point of contempt for God, the Heavenly City by the love of God carried as far as contempt of self."[26] Ultimately, these two cities are the two communities created through predestination: "By two cities I mean two societies of human beings, one of which is predestined to reign with God for all eternity, the other doomed to undergo eternal punishment with the Devil."[27]

Some passages in *The City of God* lend support to the idea that the city of God, the heavenly city, is to be identified with the church, while the earthly city is to be identified with the Roman empire or the political order. But it is only at the end of time that the heavenly city is to be separated from the earthly one. Here the church is a mixed church, as Augustine argued against the Donatists. And in this life the members of the heavenly city have a real concern for the political order.

All political society aims ultimately at peace, which Augustine defines as "the tranquillity of order—and order is the arrangement of things equal and unequal in a pattern which assigns to each its proper position."[28] The earthly city, Augustine says, "aims at an earthly peace," while the heavenly city aims at a heavenly, eternal peace. But in this life, in which they must make use of temporal things, the two cities have a common interest in the earthly peace. "The earthly city, whose life is not based on faith, aims at an earthly peace, and it limits the harmonious agreement of citizens concerning the giving and obeying of orders to the establishment of a kind of compromise between human wills about the things relevant to mortal life." The heavenly city seeks a heavenly, eternal peace, but its members, in this life, "must needs make use of this peace also, until this mortal condition, for which this kind of peace is essential, passes away."[29]

Thus, the members of the heavenly city do "not hesitate to obey the laws of the earthly city by which those things which are designed for the support of this mortal life are regulated; and the purpose of this obedience is that, since this mortal condition is shared by both cities, a harmony may be preserved between them in things that are relevant to this condition."[30] Because of their common interest in the earthly peace—even though it is not the final purpose in their lives—Christians can and should take part in the institutions of civil society. Because they love their neighbors they will live with them, as much as possible, in the earthly peace, "that ordered harmony; and the basis of this order is the observance of two rules: first, to do no harm to anyone, and, secondly, to help everyone whenever possible."[31]

From the superiority of the heavenly city and heavenly peace over the earthly city and earthly peace, many medieval thinkers drew the conclusion that the church should govern the state, that is, that kings and emperors should be subordinate to bishops and popes. But Augustine never draws that conclusion himself. For him, a mixed church lives among a mixed political society, comprising members of both cities, who will be separated only at the end of time. True members of the heavenly city will obey the laws of whatever political system in which they find themselves (not just the Roman empire), "so far as may be permitted without detriment to true religion and piety."[32]

In turn, the obligation of Christians to cooperate with others for the sake of earthly peace, and therefore ordinarily to obey the laws of the state, is the aspect of Augustine's thought that can be said to provide a basis for the modern secular state. Augustine would have objected to modern totalitarian states' pretensions to provide ultimate human fulfillment and to modern democratic states' pretensions to be religiously and morally neutral, but he does provide a Christian legitimation of a state that is distinct from, and to some degree independent of, the church.[33] In such a state, Christians can cooperate with others to preserve the earthly peace, to help each other and protect each other from harm. In any political order, however, they will be "a society of aliens,"[34] who have not yet arrived at the heavenly peace toward which they are journeying.

Discussion

Gaudium et Spes: Pastoral Constitution on the Church in the Modern World

William Collinge's treatment of Augustine and love gives us opportunity to investigate the place of love in a key document in contemporary social thought. The *Pastoral Constitution on the Church in the Modern World* (1965) is a lengthy document produced by the Second Vatican Council (Vatican II), which convened between 1962 and 1965.[35] This ecumenical council (a council of bishops of the whole church) spent a great deal of time giving account of the church's place and role in modern society and politics. This concern is seen in *The Church in the Modern World* and in documents dealing with such matters as religious liberty and the relationship of the Catholic church to non-Christian religions. The Latin title of *The Church in the Modern World*, *Gaudium et Spes*, identifies the first three words and the basic theme of the document: "The joys and hopes, the griefs and anxieties of the men of this age, especially those who are poor or in any way afflicted, these too are the joys and hopes, the griefs and anxieties of the followers of Christ" (no. 1). After the chapter on Augustine, we can see that at the heart of this solidarity—the sharing of joys and grief with the people of our age—is the friendship and love of God.

The chapter of *Gaudium et Spes* that we will consider is titled "The Community of Mankind." It follows a chapter on the dignity of persons, as we are made in the image of God. In the chapter on human dignity, the image of God—that is, the distinctive nature of the human being as created by God—is organized by three themes. We are created as (1) knowing subjects (self-conscious and intelligent), (2) free persons (moving ourselves through the will), and (3) social beings (fulfilled in common life). We have basic capacities to know the truth, to act and to choose freely, and to be in truthful and free relationship to others. Likewise, we are fulfilled through our knowing (the truth), choosing (the good), and participating in (seeking the good in and for) the lives of others. The chapter titled "The Community of Mankind" develops this third theme. In doing so, the *Pastoral Constitution on the Church in the Modern World* does not draw directly from Augustine. The majority of its citations are from scripture and the encyclicals of Pope John XXIII.[36] However, Collinge notes that Augustine's influence in the West is profound. An interesting exercise for the reader is to compare what follows to Collinge's chapter on Augustine in order to find parallels between Augustine's account of love, friendship, and social life and the use of scripture in *Gaudium et Spes*.

The chapter, in *Gaudium et Spes*, on "The Community of Mankind" begins and ends with a discussion of Christian revelation. The final paragraphs of the chapter note again that human beings are made in the image of God, not as isolated individuals, but as social beings—represented, first, in the calling out of Israel to be a chosen people, a holy people of God and later "developed and consummated in the work of Jesus Christ" (no. 32). Jesus Christ is the fulfillment of solidarity and love.

> For the very Word made flesh willed to share in the human fellowship. He was present at the wedding of Cana [John 2:1–11], visited the house of Zacchaeus [Luke 19:1–10], ate with publicans and sinners [Mark 2:13–17]. He revealed the love of the Father and the sublime vocation of man in terms of the most common social realities and by making use of the speech and the imagery of plain everyday life. . . .
>
> As the firstborn of many brothers and through the gift of his Spirit, he founded after his death and resurrection a new brotherly community composed of all those who receive him in faith and love. This he did through his Body which is the Church. There everyone, as members one of the other, would render mutual service according to the different gifts bestowed on each. . . . (no. 32)

The revelation of God's love in Jesus Christ, the document proposes, should "lead us to a deeper understanding of the laws of social life which the Creator has written into man's spiritual and moral nature" (no. 23).

In order to let *Gaudium et Spes* speak for itself, I will cite long paragraphs which highlight our social nature and the social nature of love.

God, who has fatherly concern for everyone, has willed that all men should constitute one family and treat one another in a spirit of brotherhood. For having been created in the image of God, who "from one man has created the whole human race and made them live all over the face of the earth" (Acts 17:26), all men are called to one and the same goal, namely God Himself.

For this reason, love for God and neighbor is the first and greatest commandment. Sacred Scripture, however, teaches us that the love of God cannot be separated from love of neighbor: "If there is any other commandment, it is summed up in this saying: Thou shalt love thy neighbor as thyself. . . . Love therefore is the fulfillment of the Law" (Rom. 13:9–10; cf. 1 John 4:20). To men growing daily more dependent on one another, and to a world becoming more unified every day, this truth proves to be of paramount importance.

Indeed, the Lord Jesus, when He prayed to the Father, "that all may be one . . . as we are one" (John 17:21–22) opened up vistas closed to human reason, for He implied a certain likeness between the union of the divine Persons, and the unity of God's sons in truth and charity. This likeness reveals that man, who is the only creature on earth which God willed for itself, cannot fully find himself except through a sincere gift of himself [Luke 17:33]. (no. 24)

Along with this call for unity and self-giving, *Gaudium et Spes* calls us to protect human dignity and "consider . . . every neighbor without exception as another self, taking into account first of all his life and the means necessary to living it with dignity [James 2:15–16], so as not to imitate the rich man who had no concern for the poor man Lazarus [Luke 16:18–31]" (no. 27). Further, we ought to love our enemies: "Respect and love ought to be extended also to those who think or act differently than we do in social, political, and religious matters, too" (no. 28).

Central to human solidarity is the common good, which is defined by the good that fulfills the human being and draws us more closely in common life.

Every day human interdependence grows more tightly drawn and spreads by degrees over the whole world. As a result the common good, that is, the sum of those conditions of social life which allow social groups and their individual members relatively thorough and ready access to their own fulfillment, today takes on an increasingly universal complexion and consequently involves rights and duties with respect to the whole human race. Every social group must take account of the needs and legitimate aspirations of other groups, and even of the general welfare of the entire human family.

At the same time, however, there is a growing awareness of the exalted dignity proper to the human person, since he stands above all things, and his rights and duties are universal and inviolable. Therefore, there must be made available to all men everything necessary for leading a life truly human, such as food, clothing, and shelter; the right to choose a state of life freely and to found a family, the right to education, to employment, to a good reputation, to respect, to appropriate information, to activity in accord with the upright norm of one's own conscience, to protection of privacy and rightful freedom even in matters religious.

Hence, the social order and its development must invariably work to the benefit of the human person if the disposition of affairs is to be subordinate to the personal realm and not contrariwise, as the Lord indicated when He said that the Sabbath was made for man, and not man for the Sabbath [Mark 2:27].

This social order requires constant improvement. It must be founded on truth, built on justice and animated by love; in freedom it should grow every day toward a more humane balance. An improvement in attitudes and abundant changes in society will have to take place if these objectives are to be gained.

God's Spirit, Who with a marvelous providence directs the unfolding of time and renews the face of the earth, is not absent from this development. The ferment of the Gospel too has aroused and continues to arouse in man's heart the irresistible requirements of his dignity. (no. 26)

What Can We Do?

This chapter of *Gaudium et Spes* on "The Community of Mankind" builds to the same point with which Collinge concludes his essay on Augustine. Collinge presents Augustine's view that "Christians can cooperate with others to preserve the earthly peace, to help each other and protect each other from harm." Likewise, *Gaudium et Spes* urges us to journey with Christ and to reject the dominance of "individualistic morality" in our world. We are asked to "contribute to the common good, according to [our] own abilities and the needs of others," to "consider it [our] sacred obligation to count social necessities among the primary duties of modern man" (no. 30), to encourage one another to "play one's role in common endeavors" and "to take part in the activities of the various groups which make up the social body" (no. 31). In short, we ought to cooperate as good neighbors and citizens with an eye both to earthly peace (to the shared goods of common life) and to our eternal peace in union with our neighbors in the love of God.

One example of cooperation of the common good is provided by David Cloutier (the author of chap. 7). He is a member—and therefore part owner—of the Common Market, a food cooperative in Frederick, Maryland (commonmarket.com). Similar cooperatives can be found in cities across the United States. David notes that the Common Market (although a non-religious organization) corresponds to the fundamentals of Catholic social teaching.[37] Its conception of ownership and employer-employee relationships fits with the discussion of Leo XIII's *Rerum Novarum* in chapter 4. It asks its employees and members/shareholders to take ownership of its mission and commitment to the common good, as well as offering profit sharing and an environment for good work.[38] Like any business, the Common Market looks to make a profit, but unlike many businesses its profits are directed to the common good—distributing profits back into the community. The Common Market's commitment to the common good is expressed by its efforts to provide excellent goods at a low price (often by selling in bulk and marketing non-packaged foods), to sustain a free market for local farmers, to support organic farming and its environmental stewardship, and to educate the community on healthy foods, fair and local trade, environmental issues, and sustainable living.

But how is grocery shopping a matter of love? As the extended quotes from *Gaudium et Spes* indicate, the love intended by God is not simply a fuzzy feeling or a private romantic emotion. Rather, love is meant to be the order found in all our social relationships, with every neighbor. Love means that our social relationships express a participation in the fundamental unity of humankind which God creates and which God hopes for at the end of time. This sort of love and hope, in which we can participate now, depends on the sort of knowledge that is built up by organizations like food cooperatives, where people pay a great deal of attention to where food comes from and how those who produce it—as well as the land itself—are treated. Such knowledge allows us to exercise our free will in choosing to love in all we do. Thus, the cooperative is an instantiation of love insofar as it manifests the basic human capacities of knowledge, free choice, and participation in a loving social order that *Gaudium et Spes* identifies as the fundamental capacities that make us fully human.

As we will see in chapter 8, the Common Market is a subsidiary (intermediate and local) institution that is fundamental to Catholic social thought. David Cloutier's commitment to the food cooperative is having its effect on us—his coworkers and friends. We are inspired to join in the work.

6

A Contemporary Augustinian
Approach to Love and Politics

Pope Benedict XVI's Deus Caritas Est

WILLIAM COLLINGE

Joseph Ratzinger, who became Pope Benedict XVI in 2005, had previously been a distinguished academic theologian. He began his career in 1951 with a lengthy doctoral dissertation on Augustine's theology of the church,[1] and throughout his career Augustine has been one of the strongest influences on his theology. As pope he has, as of 2008, issued two encyclicals, of which the first, titled *Deus Caritas Est* (*God is Love*), is the focus of this chapter.[2] The document comprises two parts. The first addresses love in general, while the second considers the church's organized activities of charity. The document cites Augustine directly five times, more than any other non-biblical author, and its content has significant links with Augustine's theology.

In part 1, Benedict speaks of the unity of love, somewhat as Augustine does in *On Christian Instruction*, though without reference to Augustine. He argues[3] that there is no fundamental opposition between *eros* (the love of desire, especially sexual desire) and *agape* (selfless concern for the other), but rather that "'love' is a single reality, but with different dimensions" (no. 8).

The biblical view of love, he says, culminates in Jesus Christ, in whom God gives himself to us—in the Incarnation, the cross, and the Eucharist.

The conclusion of part 1 and the beginning of part 2 resemble Augustine's Homilies on the First Letter of John.[4] Benedict draws on 1 John, from which the encyclical takes its title,[5] in reflecting on the bond between love of God and love of neighbor. Because God has loved us, we are enabled to love God in return and to love our neighbor:

> The saints . . . constantly renewed their capacity for love of neighbor from their encounter with the Eucharistic Lord, and conversely this encounter acquired its realism and depth in their service to others. Love of God and love of neighbor are thus inseparable; they form a single commandment. But both live from the love of God who has loved us first. (no. 18)

Benedict opens part 2 with a quotation from Augustine's book, *On the Trinity*: "If you see charity, you see the Trinity."[6] He proceeds to relate love to the Holy Spirit in Augustinian terms:

> The Spirit . . . is that interior power which harmonizes [believers'] hearts with Christ's heart and moves them to love their brethren as Christ loved them. . . . The Spirit is also the energy which transforms the heart of the ecclesial community, so that it becomes a witness before the world to the love of the Father, who wishes to make humanity a single family in his Son. (no. 19)

"The entire activity of the Church," Benedict goes on to say, "is an expression" of that love (no. 19).

From that starting point, Benedict examines the church's organized charitable activity, beginning in the New Testament. Examples today in the United States of what Benedict has in mind are Catholic Charities and Catholic Relief Services. These organizations are officially sponsored by the Catholic church, and their work is done in the name of the church. Benedict is not speaking of charitable organizations (for example, Girls and Boys Town) that are founded by Catholics motivated by their faith but are not directly controlled by church authorities.

Benedict regards charitable activity as "one of [the Church's] essential activities, along with the administration of the sacraments and the proclamation of the word" (no. 22). Earlier he speaks of these activities as constitutive of the church, which means that they are one of the things that make it what it is; without these activities, it is not the church.

In section 26, he responds to a common objection to the church's charitable activity: that what the poor need is justice, not charity; that charity, without pursuit of justice, merely props up the existing, unjust social order. Charity, one might say, alleviates the symptoms of poverty, while doing nothing to fix its causes. Thus the church must commit itself to action for justice. This argument can draw support from the 1971 Synod of Bishops' statement: "Action on behalf of justice and participation in the transformation of the world fully appear to us as a *constitutive* dimension of the preaching of the Gospel, or, in other words, of the Church's mission for the redemption of the human race and its liberation from every oppressive situation."[7]

For Benedict, though, the pursuit of justice is not constitutive of the church, as charity is; in fact, it is not the church's direct duty to pursue justice.[8] Rather, Benedict says, citing *The City of God*, "The just ordering of society and the State is a central responsibility of politics," and, "A just society must be the achievement of politics, not of the Church" (no. 28). Again, "The formation of just structures is not directly the duty of the Church, but belongs to the world of politics, the sphere of the autonomous use of reason" (no. 29).

Benedict has several concerns in mind when he makes these statements. One is that he wants to make it clear that church and state are distinct, and that the church should not have power over the state. Another, and more immediate, concern is that the church should not identify itself with any particular political program, as he appears to believe liberation theology did.[9] A third concern is to preserve the religious identity of Catholic social service organizations, especially when they collaborate with governments. Contemporary antidiscrimination laws, for example, sometimes prevent such organizations from giving preference to Catholics in hiring employees. The risk is that the organizations can deteriorate into generic social service organizations that give no particular witness to Christian love.

None of this means that the pursuit of justice is unimportant. Benedict is not saying that members of the church should not pursue justice in society, nor that the church as a whole is unconcerned with social justice. Rather, "The direct duty to work for a just ordering of society . . . is proper to the lay faithful" (no. 29).[10] Laity must be motivated by Christian charity in their political activity, but they must be willing to collaborate in politics with those who do not share their faith. Laity engage in politics as members of the Church but not in the name of the Church.[11] It is worth noting that, while Benedict twice attacks the view (which he labels Marxist) that action for justice should replace charitable activity (nos. 26, 31), he never holds that action for justice is unnecessary in addition to charitable activity. In fact, to act for justice is the laity's obligation.

What is the church's official role in politics? Benedict says it has an indirect duty in the formation of just structures, not a duty to bring them about, but a duty to "contribute to the purification of reason and to the reawakening of those moral forces without which just structures are neither established nor prove effective in the long run" (no. 29). It is in pursuit of this duty that the church issues encyclicals and other documents of Catholic social teaching.

The Church's indirect duty includes encouraging its members to act for justice, but the expressions "the purification of reason" and "the reawakening of moral forces" imply more than that. As Augustine argued, reason must be purified because it is vulnerable to corruption through sin. If our love is disordered, it tends to disorder our understanding. Thus, the common sense of a society can accommodate itself to grave injustices, such as slavery or racial segregation. Sometimes this involves simply taking injustice for granted, as part of the natural order of things; sometimes it involves generating rationalizations that give an apparent but spurious justification to the interests of those who benefit from the injustice. The church, through its preaching and teaching and the example of its charitable activities, must seek to help people see things as they really are and to motivate them to act accordingly.

Augustine's *The City of God* sheds light on the points that Benedict is making here. Because the church (insofar as it represents the heavenly city) aims at the heavenly peace, its proper purpose is not "the just ordering of society and the state." But its members, while here on earth, must cooperate with others in promoting the earthly peace, taking part in "the harmonious agreement of citizens concerning the giving and obeying of orders to the establishment of a kind of compromise between human wills about the things relevant to mortal life."[12]

With help from Augustine, we may distinguish two senses of justice. In one sense, "justice is the virtue which assigns to everyone his due," including God. Because ancient Rome never gave due worship to God, it never had true justice, and therefore it was never a true *res publica* or commonwealth.[13] The Romans were never truly a people, in the sense of "a multitude 'united in association by a common sense of right and a community of interest,'"[14] because a common sense of right implies, in Augustine's view, a commitment to true justice. This sense of justice resembles the biblical sense of the term, or at least part of it. Biblical justice incorporates God's saving disposition toward his people and, in turn, the people's right relationship with God and with one another, including especially the right treatment of the poor and oppressed. It is not very different from love or *caritas*. This *is* the church's duty to promote.

A second sense of "justice" is related to a second sense of "people." In this sense, "a people is the association of a multitude of rational beings united by a common agreement on the objects of their love,"[15] and the Romans were a people. "The better the objects of this agreement, the better the people,"[16] Augustine says. In turn, the better the people, the greater the prospect that the citizens of the heavenly city may cooperate with them in pursuit of the earthly peace. This peace entails a form of justice, which involves the right ordering of earthly goods, the assignment to each of his due. This justice (Augustine does not use the word "justice" but speaks of "order"), in the pursuit of which the citizens of the heavenly and earthly cities collaborate, is close to the sense in which Benedict speaks of justice in *Deus Caritas Est*, as "a just social order in which all receive their share of the world's goods" (no. 26).

There are, nevertheless, two respects in which the church has a direct duty to promote earthly justice. These are developed in the 1971 Synod document, *Justice in the World*. Pope Benedict neither denies nor mentions these in *Deus Caritas Est*. In one respect, the church must maintain justice in its internal working. "While the Church is bound to give witness to justice," the Synod says, "she recognizes that everyone who ventures to speak to people about justice must first be just in their eyes."[17] Thus, the effectiveness of its witness—one of its direct duties—depends on such things as its respect for the rights of its members, fair wages for its employees, due process in judicial procedures, and participation of its members in decision making.[18] But second, the church also must act justly in society. This includes its corporate involvement with government—it must withhold taxes, get its vehicles licensed, and otherwise observe the civil law—and, even more important, the position it holds in society:

> In the case of needy peoples it must be asked whether belonging to the Church places people on a rich island within an ambient of poverty. In societies enjoying a higher level of consumer spending, it must be asked whether our lifestyle exemplifies that sparingness with regard to consumption which we preach to others as necessary in order that so many millions of hungry people throughout the world may be fed.[19]

As important as these duties are, however, they are not constitutive of the church, in the sense of making it be what it is. They are duties that obligate every human person and organization. Admittedly they are amplified in the case of the church, in that failure to fulfill them undermines its ability to carry out its proper mission in a way that would not undermine the ability of, say, Wal-Mart to carry out its mission. But they are not constitutive of the church in the sense that embodying God's gift of charity, both within itself and to those outside, is constitutive. For the Church, as Pope Benedict says, they are not "a part of her nature, an indispensable expression of her very being" (no. 25).

Discussion

Forming Consciences for Faithful Citizenship

Every four years since the 1970s the United States Conference of Catholic Bishops (the USCCB) has issued statements on the responsibilities of Catholics in social and political life.[20] The statements correspond to the year of campaigning prior to the presidential election, but the importance of the call to social responsibility is certainly not limited to the moment when a voter pulls a lever or taps an "X" onto a computer screen. The bishops take the presidential election as an occasion to remind Catholics of their role in social and political life. In

2007, the USCCB issued *Forming Consciences for Faithful Citizenship*.[21] If we follow the distinctions developed in William Collinge's chapter on Benedict's *Deus Caritas Est*, we see that the main concern of *Forming Consciences* is not Catholic institutions *per se* (like Catholic Relief Services), but the call of the laity to sustain their faith while they work together in politics with those who do not share their faith.

On this point, the U.S. bishops note (like Dr. Collinge in his discussion of *Deus Caritas Est*) that the Christian faith is not a political program, but that same faith is the Christian's indispensable contribution to common life. The bishops explain that the Christian moral framework "does not easily fit ideologies of 'right' or 'left,' 'liberal' or 'conservative,' or the platform of any political party" (*Forming Consciences for Faithful Citizenship*, no. 55). On occasion, Catholics might find the decision to vote very difficult as none of the candidates represent good options (no. 36). Like Collinge, *Forming Consciences* cites *Deus Caritas Est*, no. 29.[22]

> The direct duty to work for a just ordering of society . . . is proper to the lay faithful. As citizens of the State, they are called to take part in public life in a personal capacity. So they cannot relinquish their participation "in the many different economic, social, legislative, administrative and cultural areas, which are intended to promote organically and institutionally the common good." The mission of the lay faithful is therefore to configure social life correctly, respecting its legitimate autonomy and cooperating with other citizens according to their respective competences and fulfilling their own responsibility. Even if the specific expressions of ecclesial charity can never be confused with the activity of the State, it still remains true that charity must animate the entire lives of the lay faithful and therefore also their political activity, lived as "social charity."[23]

Appealing to the example of the Good Samaritan (Luke 10:29–37), Pope Benedict XVI holds that this social charity is simply "a way of making present here and now the love which man always needs" (no. 29).

The Bishops' *Forming Consciences* presents seven themes of Catholic social teaching as the framework for the activities of Catholic laypeople in the public square. The following points are cited from a condensed version of *Forming Consciences*, issued by the USCCB:[24]

> 1. Human life is sacred. Direct attacks on innocent human beings are never morally acceptable. Within our society, life is under direct attack from abortion, euthanasia, human cloning, and destruction of human embryos for research. These intrinsic evils must always be opposed. This teaching also compels us as Catholics to oppose genocide, torture, unjust war, and the use of the death penalty, as well as to pursue peace and help overcome poverty, racism, and other conditions that demean human life.

2. The family, based on marriage between a man and a woman, is the fundamental unit of society. This sanctuary for the creation and nurturing of children must not be redefined, undermined, or neglected. Supporting families should be a priority for economic and social policies. How our society is organized—in economics and politics, in law and public policy—affects the well-being of individuals and of society. Every person and association has a right and a duty to participate in shaping society to promote the well-being of individuals and the common good.

3. Every human being has a right to life, the fundamental right that makes all other rights possible. Each of us has a right to religious freedom, which enables us to live and act in accord with our God-given dignity, as well as a right to access to those things required for human decency— food and shelter, education and employment, health care and housing. Corresponding to these rights are duties and responsibilities—to one another, to our families, and to the larger society.

4. While the common good embraces all, those who are in greatest need deserve preferential concern. A moral test for society is how we treat the weakest among us—the unborn, those dealing with disabilities or terminal illness, the poor and marginalized.

5. The economy must serve people, not the other way around. Economic justice calls for decent work at fair, living wages, opportunities for legal status for immigrant workers, and the opportunity for all people to work together for the common good through their work, ownership, enterprise, investment, participation in unions, and other forms of economic activity.

6. We are one human family, whatever our national, racial, ethnic, economic, and ideological differences. Our Catholic commitment to solidarity requires that we pursue justice, eliminate racism, end human trafficking, protect human rights, seek peace, and avoid the use of force except as a necessary last resort.

7. Care for the earth is a duty of our Catholic faith. We all are called to be careful stewards of God's creation and to ensure a safe and hospitable environment for vulnerable human beings now and in the future.

What Can We Do?

As a different way of thinking about social and political life, Christian charity and faithful citizenship do not represent isolated Good Samaritan moments or occasional questions about voting every two or four years. Catholic participation in social life is a way of life that draws from our faith in Jesus Christ: to be formed by the presence of God in worship, to be shaped by the story of scripture, and to join together in imaginative ways to allow God's love to animate our roles in social life. What we can do (hopefully aided by the chapters of this book) is to take the themes of faithful citizenship out of the voting booth and into the institutions and activities of everyday life. William Collinge offers a good example for us, particularly on theme six (from the list above). He has invested himself—his energy, time, and talents—in peacemaking and community building in his own town of Gettysburg, Pennsylvania.

Dr. Collinge tells an interesting story of his involvement in civic affairs in Gettysburg. The end of the story (at least as this point in his life) is that he is the organizer of an annual multicultural festival—the Adams County Heritage Festival. The Heritage Festival in Gettysburg (the Adams County seat) is not simply an event. As anyone who lives in a small town and rural county knows, an annual festival, if it is indeed a community celebration, occupies a sizeable portion of the community for several months of the year and is the medium for sustaining important lines of communication and habits of cooperation. In other words, the Heritage Festival is a social institution. It contributes to political life in the most basic sense of community and social interaction and organization for the common good.

Bill (Dr. Collinge) tells the story in this way:

"It began with an effort to be, not a good Catholic, but a good Catholic theologian. When the U.S. bishops came out with their pastoral letter *The Challenge of Peace* in 1983, I was chair of the theology department, and it seemed as if we needed a response at Mount St. Mary's. I joined with a small group of faculty, who proposed (1) a discussion group on *The Challenge of Peace* (held in 1984), (2) an interdisciplinary course in war and peace (taught between 1985 and 1991), (3) the formation of a chapter of Pax Christi USA (which flourished for a few years in the late 1980s), and (4) the creation of a minor in peace studies (finally approved in 2007).

"In consequence of this, I was asked (along with a colleague) to represent Mount St. Mary's on a multi-institutional committee to plan an academic conference in 1988 on the occasion of the 125th anniversary of the Battle of Gettysburg. The community's celebration of the anniversary featured the relighting of the peace light on the Gettysburg battlefield and a series of events, of which the academic conference was one, with the general theme of 'The Search for Peace in a World United' (derived from the motto of the peace light).[25]

"In consequence of those events, I was invited the following year (1989) to join the board of the Interfaith Center for Peace and Justice in Gettysburg, the organization that first proposed the theme for the community celebration. By 1993, I had floated up to the position of vice president, an office whose sole specific duty was to chair board meetings in the absence of the president. Or so I thought. Then in 1993, the organization ran out of money and let go its two paid staff members, and its president moved out of town, and I found myself in charge.

"It was either shut down operations or keep them going with volunteers, and we have done the latter since then. Lots of people share responsibility for that, but I have handled organizational details and record keeping, edited the quarterly newsletter (for more than fifty issues now), and supervised the organization of our annual multicultural festival, the Adams County Heritage Festival.

"If you're not from Gettysburg, what you have heard of it is about the battle, and our most prominent annual events all have something to do with the Civil War heritage. At a meeting in 1991 at which I was not present, a group of residents of Adams County proposed to have a festival that featured the local ethnic heritages—especially the African-American, Hispanic, and Asian—that were being overlooked in the other festivals. This became a project of the Interfaith Center, and, after joining the committee in 1993, I became its chair, which basically means the festival manager, in 1996.

"Each year on a Sunday in September, the festival is held in the Gettysburg town park, a central location near African-American and Hispanic neighborhoods. It features musical and dramatic entertainment, ethnic foods, arts and crafts, children's activities, and exhibits by local non-profit organizations. Attendance is over a thousand (the population of Gettysburg is about seven thousand), admission is free (we are supported mainly by grants), and the weather is usually good.

"Managing a festival is a job that is hard to hand off to someone else. Once you start doing it, it is difficult to stop until you have your heart attack. So now I am probably the only theologian in Pennsylvania who also holds a state promoter's license. I have had to learn things about state and town regulations, insurance, wiring, sound system specifications, and all sorts of other things that do not usually come with the job of theologian.

"What have we accomplished? The Heritage Festival is well-entrenched in local civic life. It is an event that people look forward to. Perhaps many people are there mainly for the music and the food, but when they come they share an afternoon of community with their neighbors of all ethnicities. We have gathered five days after September 11, 2001, and two weeks after a Ku Klux Klan rally on the battlefield in 2006. In today's climate of fear and hostility directed toward immigrants, I hope that the festival is an occasion for people whose ancestors willingly or by coercion became immigrants to recognize their common ground with those who are immigrants today, as they enjoy their heritages in food, music, and the arts together.

"The Adams County Heritage Festival is not a Catholic festival or even a religious one (although there is an opening prayer), but it is a local instance of the solidarity that the Catholic (meaning universal) church champions worldwide."[26]

The heart of Bill's story, as I see it, is the living out of his call by filling needs when his neighbors do the calling. In other words, he begins with his call as a

Catholic theologian and lives it out by being attentive to the needs of his community. For example, he becomes the president of the board of the Interfaith Center for Peace and Justice not because he campaigns for it, but because he is faithful to the need (when everyone else steps back, he stays and leads). His story is unique in the sense that he responds within his particular role as a Catholic theologian to the needs of a particular place (Adams County). None of us will follow his steps in Gettysburg, but we can do something similar where we live and with what we have to offer. Like him, we can be open and attentive to how our gifts and talents meet the needs of our communities.

Bill begins with his role as a theologian, but it is easy enough to imagine becoming involved in an analogous way if one were an accountant, carpenter, or office manager. In fact, as I see it, Bill's role as organizer of the Heritage Festival highlights gifts in him that are not characteristic of many theologians (like me). He has skills needed for scheduling, organizing, record keeping, and publishing a quarterly newsletter (for over twelve years). His civic activity fills out his potential for contributing to common life. The lesson for us is Bill's responsiveness and willingness to give his time and energy to the good of his community—to be attentive to his call in a particular place. Twenty-five years ago he took a few steps in being conscientious about what the U.S. bishops call the theme of solidarity (number six above), and from there he found that opportunities for service presented themselves to him. The same will happen to us if we are attentive to the themes of Catholic social thought and dare to take a few steps to contribute to the common good.

7

Modern Politics
and Catholic Social Teaching

David Cloutier

"The attainment of the common good is the sole reason for the existence of civil authorities." Pope John XXIII, *Pacem in Terris*, no. 54

"Cooperate and no one gets hurt." T-shirt for the Linden Hills Food Co-op, Minneapolis, Minnesota

On the steps of many courthouses, there stands a statue of Justice. This statue is a great starting point for beginning to understand what justice means in our political system, and how it compares to the justice described by modern Catholic social teaching. Justice holds scales in her hand, but perhaps the most important feature of the statue is that she is wearing a blindfold. Justice cannot see; she is blind. Why? The assumption built into the statue is illustrated by the motto carved into stone above the entrance to the United States Supreme Court building: "Equal justice under law." The blindfold is meant to insure equality, that justice treats every person equally and impartially. She does not look at their beauty or their social status or their money—she does not look at who they are. Rather, she treats everyone equally. Hence, the blindfold shows us how central equality is to our modern conception of justice.

However, this image does not tell the whole story. Imagine if we took mothers to a playground and insisted that they all wear blindfolds, so that they would treat every child in exactly the same way. Or imagine if we all walked around campus blindfolded, so that we treated our friends no differently than anyone else we happened to run into. Absurd, right? So if we naturally believe that parents should give special attention to their own children and friends give preferred treatment to friends, why then do we expect government to wear a blindfold in order to insure justice?

The difference between the two is a distinction between the public sphere and the private sphere, and it is central to modern politics. Some matters are public, and involve the government, and in these matters justice requires equal treatment, and therefore must wear a blindfold. However, in our private lives, the blindfold can come off, and we can treat others differently, according to their status in relation to ourselves. Political philosophers call this (obviously) the public-private distinction. The public sphere is the sphere of government, but we are not owned or controlled by the state—rather, we are more like customers of the state, which provides impartial services that facilitate our private lives. Most important, the state enforces and protects what we call our individual rights, so that everyone plays by the same set of rules, regardless of their status.

This model of politics is known as the social contract model, since each individual is assumed to sacrifice some small part of his or her freedom in order to receive the protection and services of the state. More broadly, the system is known as liberalism.[1] This does not mean liberal as in Democratic (in the sense of the American political party structure). Rather, it derives from the word "liberty," and it indicates that the purpose of the state is to provide freedom (liberty) to everyone in order that each of us can pursue our own lives.

It might be even better to call this system of politics individualism, because the state exists to serve the individual, rather than the other way around. We can see this picture in two ways. One, the theories upon which this system of government is based start with a certain picture of human beings before government—in what they call "the state of nature." It is assumed that humans are individuals by nature, but that they discover certain hardships in nature, and so they form a social contract, banding together as a society for mutual protection and defense.[2]

However, individualism as a political system is seen most clearly by contrasting it with a different (and, in terms of history, a more typical) system of government, one in which a society is a common project to which everyone contributes. Instead of the state serving individual projects, individuals live their lives in service to the larger project of the society.[3] In individualism, there really isn't any common project for the society. We talk much about freedom and democracy, but these do not name common projects, but rather the parameters necessary to pursue our own individual projects. By contrast, some versions of collectivism (as it is sometimes called) assume that each person has a part to contribute to the overall project of the state. This may be the glory of Rome, or the sustenance of the tribe, or the worldwide spread of communism. But in all these cases there is no public/private distinction. There is no limited social contract. There is no blindfold, because the purpose of the state is not simply to help people do their own things, but rather to do something together.

Indeed, we can see a little version of collectivism in the non-blindfolded relationships we described above. In a family, everyone contributes to the good of the whole, especially parents to children, or else the whole thing breaks down. In friendships, bonds are forged through undertaking common projects, where friends work together toward a similar vision. If someone only has friends in order to facilitate his or her own individual happiness, we call the person selfish. If someone has children for their own amusement, we may say something even worse. The same attitude might be seen in collectivist political systems: the goal is not to use the society and the government for your own individual happiness, but to contribute your own life to the good of the society.

The Common Good

The history of modern political thought and practice is a battle, often *literally*, between these two pictures. It is assumed that politics can be either a matter of the state serving each individual or a matter of individuals serving the state. Catholic social teaching is often described as a third way—a picture of politics that is neither individualist nor collectivist.[4] How so? We can begin to develop the distinctive Catholic vision by thinking about groups and social spaces—communities—where the public/private distinction gets blurred. We can think about teams or musical ensembles. We can think about small towns, where the owner of the hardware store is also your neighbor and your friend, as well as a member of the city council. We can think about small colleges, where your classmates, your class officers, and your best friends may all be the same people. What these communities have in common is the absence of a clearly defined public space, a space where the blindfold is on. Because there is no such space, there is also not a stark opposition between looking out for yourself and looking out for the collective. For example, on a team your individual good and the good of the team are not really separable—or, if you do try to separate them, the team will break down. In a small town, doing a favor for the hardware store owner may not simply be looking out for another, since it may be reciprocated and make your life easier the next time your refrigerator breaks down.

The phrase that Catholic social teaching uses to express this relationship is "the common good." A common good suggests that you and others are not simply isolated individuals pursuing isolated goods, but also that you and your neighbor are not simply cogs in a larger social collective. Rather, there is a shared good that belongs to everyone. In the rest of this essay, we will develop this notion of the common good, but first we need to notice why this idea is absent from the modern political picture explained above.

At the root of the two modern pictures above is a conception of the individual and society *in competition*. Either society serves the individual or the individual serves the society. We may try to maintain some sort of balance, but it is a tension-filled, competitive balance, between competing forces. In an individualist society like our own, the result is that everyone is always trying to get ahead, and people use social and political institutions to further their own interests. Political scientists call this "interest-group politics," and we can see an example in the prominence of competing political lobbyists, each attempting to manipulate the political process to further its own group's interest. At best, such politics yields compromises, which are a balancing force, but the balance is always unstable and eventually breaks, since the interest groups do not go away once there is some sort of compromise. The collectivist picture overcomes such an endless competition, but only by subordinating all individual interests to the interests of the state.

The fundamental error of modern politics, Catholic social thought says, is its picture of human beings as individuals or interest groups in endless competition.[5] Rather, human beings form a single unity. The Vatican II Constitution on the Church in the Modern World states it this way: "God, who has fatherly concern for everyone, has willed that all men should constitute one family and treat one another in a spirit of brotherhood."[6] The use of family language should already alert us to the problems with both the individualist and collectivist pictures, since a family is neither of these. In a family, the individual and the whole cannot be separated. Thus, "man's social nature makes it evident that the progress of the human person and the advance of society itself hinge on each other. For the beginning, the subject and the goal of all social institutions is and must be the human person, which for its part and by its very nature stands completely in need of social life."[7] This statement is very careful to avoid the errors of either individualism or collectivism. On the one hand, social institutions must serve persons, and not enslave them to a king or a supreme leader; on the other hand, persons are social by nature and are completely in need of social life. Ideally, the team helps every member play at his or her best, but that individual best is completely dependent on the coordinated play of the team.

Two comments will help flesh this idea out further. First, the whole idea of a team, family, or any sort of genuine community depends on individuals recognizing that the primary task is not competition, but rather cooperation, with others. This chapter began with a quote from a T-shirt: "Cooperate and no one gets hurt." That's the sort of thing we expect a bank robber or a kidnapper to say. The T-shirt is humorous because, by placing the phrase in a different context (a food cooperative), it suggests that if we aim our actions at cooperation with one another, everyone will win and no one will lose. No one will get hurt, if we recognize, as members of a food co-op, that the customers, employees, and the farmers are not in competition with one another. Rather, we seek to cooperate and share.

The second comment, however, helps us see why this is a challenging way to look at politics. Pope John Paul II writes that "there is a growing inability to situate particular interests within the framework of a coherent vision of the common good. The latter is not simply the sum total of particular interests; rather, it involves an assessment and integration of those interests on the basis of a balanced hierarchy of values."[8] In other words, what makes it possible for us to see the common good on a team or a food co-op is that there is a coherent vision of what is good—for example, the team follows the rules of a sport, everyone has their own positions, and everyone knows what the goal of the game is. In a food co-op, everyone shares a common vision of the importance of healthful food, fair compensation, preservation of land, and shared responsibility, as opposed to a regular grocery store. There the ultimate goal of the customer is the lowest price or the greatest selection, and the ultimate goal of the store is maximizing profit. In turn, the farmer usually simply wants to keep farming, so he or she exploits the land just to stay economically afloat. In the latter scenario, there is no way to see the common good because there is no coherent shared vision, only each part with its own vision. Properly speaking, there is no common good in such a system. Thus there cannot be cooperation, strictly speaking, only negotiation and compromise.

But if we can start to see the common good of a sports team or a particular business, what is the common good of a political society? How can there be cooperation? Pope Pius XI writes: "First and foremost, the State and every good citizen ought to look to and strive toward this end: that the conflict between the hostile classes be abolished and harmonious cooperation of the Industries and Professions be encouraged and promoted."[9] Pius goes on to repeatedly stress the fundamental responsibility of all to "cooperate amicably" not merely in their own individual pursuits, but for the "common good."[10] Everyone cannot be out for themselves.

John Paul II develops this need for cooperation further in his concept of solidarity:

It is above all a question of interdependence . . . accepted as a moral category. When interdependence becomes recognized in this way, the correlative response as a moral and social attitude, as a 'virtue', is solidarity. This then is not a feeling of vague compassion or shallow distress at the misfortunes of so many people, both near and far. On the contrary, it is a firm and persevering determination to commit oneself to the common good; that is to say, to the good of all and of each individual because we are all really responsible for all.[11]

Thus, if we recognize real interdependence, we will then feel solidarity—something like what we may feel for our family, for example—and recognize that when someone else is suffering misfortune, we cannot say, "well, that's their problem, not mine." We are all in it together.

Growing up in the 1980s, I participated in a nationwide event called Hands Across America, where, long before the Internet and cell phones, there was a massive effort to coordinate a chain of people holding hands that stretched from coast to coast. The line passed a couple miles south of my house in Chicago, and so we went out and joined in, as the radio played the theme song for the event. The lyrics went:

> We must learn to love each other/See that man over there, he's my brother/And when he laughs, I laugh/And when he cries, I cry/And when he needs me, I'll be right there by his side. . . .[12]

The lyrics, cheesy 80s as they may be, express very powerfully exactly what John Paul II is teaching. It suggests that we share in the joys and sorrows of others, but even more importantly, we don't just feel for others, we actually *act* for them when they are in need. The symbolic gesture of holding hands coast-to-coast was a way of concretely expressing this interdependence, this solidarity.

Subsidiarity

Most people will respond in one of two ways to this vision: it is either inspiring or overwhelming. In fact, you may respond with both feelings. On the one hand, if we are truly one family in God's eyes, then we should live out this common responsibility to one another. But how can we be responsible for "all," as John Paul II puts it? It seems exhausting and impossible.

There might be one way to do it: have the government impose this common responsibility on everyone by law. But by now you should recognize what this is: this is collectivism, not cooperation. The church's social teaching is highly critical of individualist societies like ours, but it is also (and perhaps even more so) critical of collectivist societies. Why? We might imagine the difference between a team that plays well together because it wants to and a team that plays well together because it is commanded by a strong-willed dictator coach. Ultimately, the good coach is the former coach, since he or she guides everyone to share responsibility, rather than forcing it through obeying orders. Most importantly, the individual players develop much better under the former coach.

What we can see on the level of a sports team can be captured on a political level by introducing the second key concept (the first being the common good) of Catholic social teaching: subsidiarity. John Paul II explains the necessity of subsidiarity this way: "The social nature of man is not completely fulfilled in the state, but is realized in various intermediary groups, beginning with the family and including economic, social, political, and cultural groups which stem from human nature itself and have their own autonomy, always with a view to the common good."[13] The principle of subsidiarity teaches that a nation is not so much one big team, but rather a large number of smaller teams, in which the state can foster cooperation. Without subsidiarity, the very examples we have been using—of sports teams and local food co-ops—break down. For example, in the former Soviet Union sports and athletics were not good in themselves, but instruments to demonstrate the superiority of the Soviet society to all others in international competition. Farmers were organized into collectives, on state-confiscated land, and directed by central orders. In both cases, the system did great harm, because while individual competition was eliminated, cooperation was imposed from the top down, and each area was not given what John Paul II terms its "own autonomy." Subsidiarity suggests that the goal is not one big sports team for the country or one big food system, but lots and lots of teams and local cooperatives, fostered by the state. These are what are called "intermediary groups" or "intermediate associations."

These intermediate groups are the key to not being overwhelmed. The weakness of a gesture like Hands Across America is the idea that I (as an individual) have responsibility for 250 million other individuals. This is impossible. But perhaps, if my local neighborhood, local business, local school, local city or state were organized properly, I could share responsibility for specific groups of others—and by doing so, on a larger scale, I would help and support others in other places. At specific and catastrophic times of need (the most recent being Hurricane Katrina in New Orleans), there might be a larger responsibility. But at least one of the reasons Katrina was so devastating was that years of neglect of the common good plagued poor southern cities and poor neighborhoods in New Orleans. In other words, we may seem generous in times of catastrophe, but the real challenge of Catholic social teaching is making such generosity and cooperation the norm of social system, perhaps preventing such disasters in the first place.[14]

Unfortunately, both individualism and collectivism tend to decimate intermediate organizations. As noted above, collectivism views any autonomous group as a potential threat to the overall power of the state. But in individualist societies, John Paul II writes, "the individual today is often suffocated between two poles represented by the state and the marketplace. At times it seems as though he exists only as a producer and consumer of goods or as an object of state administration."[15] Because of the competition and independence prized in individualist societies, intermediate groups are discouraged or eliminated in favor of individual preference. As one well-known defender of local communities has written, "Neither our economy, nor our government, nor our educational system runs on the assumption that community has a value—a value, that is, that *counts* in any practical or powerful way."[16] While everyone uses the word "community," when actual choices are made, the choices depend on what really counts, individual rights, economic profit, or national power.

Common Life

Having developed the two key concepts of modern Catholic social teaching which challenge ordinary modern political systems—the common good and subsidiarity—we now turn to specifics: What does this mean concretely? In particular, what does common good encompass when we are talking about politics and governments? Vatican II states that the common good, which is the purpose of any political community, "embraces the sum of those conditions of social life by which individuals, families, and groups can achieve their own fulfillment in a relatively thorough and ready way."[17] Thus, "the common good is a good that is common to the whole social community and to the individuals that are parts of the whole."[18] The "and" in this statement is crucial—it is a good that is both for others and for the self.

Virgil Michel (1890–1939), best known for his ideas on liturgical reform and social justice, goes on to further clarify two distinct aspects of the common good, which are helpful in giving concrete content to the notion. First, the common good involves "the common conditions of social life that are necessary before individuals can attain to the good life."[19] Typically, this includes the enforcement of laws, the protection of rights and property, and the provisioning of universally necessary services. We are all aware, at least from a distance, of what happens in a society when basic law enforcement and services are no longer available for all. Everyone, every group and individual, needs these in order to flourish. But note as well that this is not simply a matter of self-interest: the assumption here is that these conditions and necessities are needed by all, not just by some.

If only some need them, then they are not necessary to the good life. Moreover, these conditions ought to be ordered to the good of all, and not just to some. For example, a stable currency and monetary system is a responsibility of the government. But such a system can be ordered to the flourishing of all, or it can be ordered to the flourishing of a particular class, company, type of business, and so on. Thus, we see that this description of the common good emphasizes distribution over individual maximization.[20] What is important is that these conditions are common and shared by all, that no one is excluded from having them. For example, if educational opportunity is necessary for all, whatever their life, then government-sponsored education ought first to insure that everyone has access to *good* education before giving a *better* education to some instead of others. As John Paul II points out, the social order will be "stable" when it "does not place in opposition personal interest and the interests of society as a whole, but rather seeks ways to bring them into fruitful harmony."[21] The choices and policies of governments can either favor some at the expense of others or can harmonize everyone's interests—cooperate, and no one gets hurt.

Michel then points out that the responsibility of the government for the common good also includes "the attainment of this good life by all members of the community, by everyone at least to a minimum degree."[22] Ultimately, the attainment of the good is not a task of the state, but of individuals and groups. However, because of human solidarity the failure of some to attain the good life hurts us all. Hence, beyond creating the conditions, the community "must come to the rescue—not merely for the sake of those unfortunate individuals, but for the sake of all the other individuals whose permanent attainment of the good life must eventually suffer from the non-attainment of the common good by all."[23]

This tends to be the point of greatest controversy. In an individualist society like our own, we may seek fairness in the conditions of life—equality of opportunity—but then if someone fails to flourish, we believe it is no longer our responsibility. It is their failure, not ours. However, Catholic social teaching founded on solidarity suggests that, while the society cannot actually attain the good life for anyone (they have to take the responsibility on themselves), it should offer any and every kind of help for those who have failed or are failing in some way. The common good is ultimately a matter of all participating in it. In a family, if there is one "problem child," the family will (hopefully!) offer further help to that child, rather than exclude him or her from the family. The same will be true for a classroom, a sports team, a neighborhood, and of society itself.

Concretely, what does this mean? Here we need to take on what might be called the "level-playing-field" myth. Nearly everyone in American society, at least in their words, supports a level playing field for all as a part of justice in society. However, the myth is that there exists, at any given time, a level playing field. In fact, the playing field is always already skewed. Insofar as it is, Catholic social teaching can speak of "structures of sin," which "are rooted in personal sin and thus always linked to the concrete acts of individuals who introduce these structures, consolidate them, and make them difficult to remove. And thus they grow stronger, spread, and become the source of other sins and so influence people's behavior."[24]

A convenient example from our own history might be racism. While racism in American society ultimately is rooted in the specific sin of slaveholding, it introduces a structure which is difficult to remove and thus perpetuates racism, even after individual people stop holding slaves. Thus, the society has a responsibility to act against such a structure, taking steps to help those who are victims of racism, even if no one today holds slaves. This example obviously requires a careful analysis of how structures of racism actually work; however, the underlying question is a matter of helping those who, because of structures, are hindered from achieving their good "in a relatively thorough and ready way," in the words of Vatican II.

Again, it is important to stress that everything here hangs on the anthropological picture: if human beings are simply separate individuals, with no common good, then the suffering of someone else has nothing to do with my life, but if we are in fact all one family under God, then (like in a family) someone else suffering does affect my own life, and thus helping them attain their good is not contrary to my own good, but a part of it. Thus, the government's role is not simply to balance competing forces, nor simply to create equal conditions, but rather to promote actual harmony and cooperation, as we have described before.

But as these problems are addressed, it is also crucial to keep in mind the principle of subsidiarity. That common education is the responsibility of the society to the common good may not be disputed, but the design and attainment of a common educational system is not always clear. The principle of subsidiarity reminds us that more local communities ought to be allowed to do what they can do, so long as other principles of the common good are not violated.

Inequality, Alienation, and Human Ecology

Having considered in more depth the question of what the common good is, and some of the actions governments should take to achieve it, we can turn finally to the question of what makes this task so difficult. Why do we tend to favor competition over cooperation? We can discuss four problems that are prominent not only in Catholic social teaching, but (to some extent) also in secular critiques of modern political thought.

The first is inequality. The eighteenth-century philosopher Jean-Jacques Rousseau insisted that humans, while not selfish by nature, learn selfishness because of their introduction into a society that constantly seeks to make hierarchical distinctions between people. The source of inequality is any and every form of social competition, whether in terms of money, power, looks, fashion, cultural tastes, and so on.[25] While Catholicism does not endorse Rousseau's solution of some form of absolute equality, it does recognize that existing inequalities make it difficult to achieve the common good, since typically those of higher status seek to perpetuate their power by maintaining their control of a given system. That is to say, we establish our own identity by, in one way or another, seeing ourselves as better than others. We may think immediately of money here, but such inequality happens in many ways. For example, in our individualist society friendships tend to be based on personal preference, and so people with affable personalities and attractive appearances tend to do better in seeking the good life than those who do not have such looks and personality. In all sorts of ways we perpetuate this inequality, because our own status depends on it. Hence, seeking the common good requires those who are rich (in money, power, charm, etc.) to use such status for the benefit of the whole, rather than to increase their riches even further.

The second problem is alienation. "Alienation" is a term most prominent in Karl Marx for describing what happens in capitalist society because a person does not work for themselves, but rather for someone else, thus alienating one's own labor.[26] However, John Paul II, no friend of Marxism, reappropriates the term in criticizing individualist societies:

> [Alienation] happens in consumerism, when people are ensnared in a web of false and superficial gratifications rather than being helped to experience their personhood in an authentic and concrete way. Alienation is found also in work, when it is organized so as to ensure maximum returns and profits with no concern whether the worker, through his own labor, grows or diminishes as a person, either through increased sharing in a genuinely supportive community or through increased isolation in a maze of relationships marked by destructive competitiveness and estrangement, in which he is considered only a means and not an end.[27]

The Pope sums up his analysis by saying, "A society is alienated if its forms of social organization, production and consumption make it more difficult to offer this gift of self and to establish this solidarity between people."[28] John Paul II is here pointing out that our lives as workers and consumers make us into particular sorts of persons: either those who give gifts and share, or those who think in terms of getting for the self. We become alienated from ourselves if we live within systems where everything is about self-interest, rather than in systems in which everything is about solidarity.

Third, this teaching is difficult to realize because of the loss of what John Paul II calls the human ecology of communities.[29] As we have already mentioned, Catholic social teaching assumes that pursuit of the common good requires local structures—intermediate associations—in which the common good is readily apparent. It is, we might say, the natural habitat of the human person, and so just as animals die when deprived of their ecological system, so too the human person shrivels up when he or she lacks community. What this means may take many forms—unlike animals, for example, we are able to survive and thrive in various climates and terrains—but any setting requires the sort of personal bonds and support and sharing characteristic of intermediate associations.

Finally, John Paul II is explicit in naming two particular sins which afflict us and create disharmony: "on the one hand, the all-consuming desire for profit, and on the other, the thirst for power, with the intention of imposing one's will upon others."[30] These are the real forms of idolatry—the false gods—which afflict today's world. The desire for profit may come in many forms—the consumer trying to always get the best deal, the investor ignoring how companies operate and looking only at their profit, the manager who cuts jobs and deals with workers solely in terms of the company's financial statements. Similarly, the desire for power may come in the form of explicit political power-seeking to forward one's own interests, or it may come through idolizing technology (e.g., stem cell research), in which technological power is sought for its own sake, without attention to the common good.

Conclusion

Any form of ethics seeks to determine the good purpose of any given action or structure. In the case of politics, Catholic social teaching unequivocally maintains that the purpose of the state is to promote the common good, both for individuals and in terms of conditions appropriate for all. This common good is promoted by means which enhance and support subsidiary associations in which teamwork, cooperation, and sharing form participants in the virtue of solidarity. Such teaching offers fundamental challenges to all forms of modern politics, both individualist and collectivist, insofar as they lose sight of the social nature of human beings and their personal interdependence. In this chapter, we have outlined the conceptual framework of the teaching, and offered some ways in which it might be fleshed out, while also noting some major challenges that afflict us in contemporary American society.

The Catholic social vision is challenging, but it is ultimately an invitation to life, to genuine human happiness. As Leo XIII exclaims, "Where this teaching flourishes, will not all strife quickly end?"[31] But it is not the sort of teaching that can be implemented by a single individual or office. It is fundamentally a bottom-up, not a top-down challenge, one in which individuals and local groups seek out and implement practices of cooperation that very gradually build the new society in the shell of the old, competitive one. Such work, as Wendell Berry notes, is small work, but it is also immensely satisfying.[32] We might consider first and foremost how our local governments and the governing bodies of our workplaces can be oriented toward a common good, so that they are more like a team and less like a competition of isolated individuals. We can begin to find ourselves rooted in some particular human ecology, rather than always seeking to use our environments to foster individual goals. And we can start to see other humans, both close by and far away, as persons to whom we are joined through God, members of one another with whom we share both joy and suffering.

Discussion

Politics and Health

A number of issues could be used to exemplify David Cloutier's comparison between Catholic social teaching and the dominant options in modern politics. As we are putting together this volume, presidential primary season is just getting underway for the 2008 presidential election, and Democratic and Republican candidates are offering their policy proposals. Health-care reform is a major issue, and its problems form such a mess that we imagine the topic will be relevant even if this book is in print beyond this presidential election. In a short discussion, we cannot expect to wade through the complex web of problems, but it will be helpful to focus on topics treated in the chapter— the common good, solidarity, subsidiarity, individualism, collectivism, and consumerism.

The problem that prompts calls for reform is the high cost of health care. Cost is not necessarily the basic problem, but it is the prominent symptom. It is clear that as medical technology has advanced, costs have risen. We are paying more, but those who have insurance are getting far more than decades ago. Compared to other countries, it is common practice in the United States to provide and undergo a broad range of tests and procedures, some or most of which turn out to be unnecessary. However, "studies by reputable economists have concluded that spending on such advanced treatments as cardiac drugs, devices and surgery; neonatal care for low-birth-weight infants; and mental health drugs have more than paid for themselves by extending lives and improving their quality."[33] Here the problem might be not high costs per se, but the fact that high costs increase the divide between those who can afford insurance and those who cannot. If the health-care consumer wants more and better care, let her get it and pay for it. The problem is that many are shut out of the market entirely.

As with any issue of consumption, the health-care market offers little or no means to think about what we are getting and who is getting it in terms of the common good. We have a fragmented system. What we have today in the United States is a private-sector health-care and insurance system that is paid for by a government-mandated but private-sector and employment-based system. Obviously, when the employer-based system developed in the 1930s and 1940s, it was not a burden. But by the 1960s, costs of health care started to rise. Today, it has become prohibitive for many employers.[34] Federal and state governments, in an uneven and often provisional manner, have implemented programs (such as Medicare and Medicaid) to fill some gaps for some of the uninsured. But the cost of these programs is becoming prohibitive as well. Here is a statistical picture (for 2006), according to the U.S. Census Bureau. Almost 16 percent, or 47 million people in the U.S., are uninsured. Just about 60 percent of the population is covered through an employer, and 27 percent are covered by a government program. The percentage of children (under 18) without insurance is 11.7 percent.[35]

Consider now "A Framework for Comprehensive Health Care Reform," issued in 1993 by the U.S. Conference of Catholic Bishops.[36] It attempts not to provide a policy, but instead an outline of human goods: the respect of life from conception to natural death, solidarity and concern for the poor, comprehensive benefits and access to health care, pluralism, cost containment, and equitable financing. A few of these terms need further explanation. "Natural death" is a term rich with background in Catholic thought. The Catholic moral tradition is against various forms of euthanasia, but it does not require that patients be submitted to extraordinary and disproportionate treatment. Persons near death should be allowed to die rather than have their lives sustained entirely by artificial means. Solidarity refers, in the citation from John Paul II, to active concern for the poor and the common good, but here it also takes health care partly outside the market and sets it in social relationships and our care for one another. Health care, like education, is a necessary good for all persons, and hence a part of the common good, as defined earlier. Finally, pluralism points to the concept of subsidiarity, that health-care reform should encourage a wide array of intermediate groups and institutions, public and private, profit and nonprofit, all contributing to the common good.

Along with the concept of subsidiarity, the bishops do not propose a collectivist/state-controlled system or an individualist policy entirely provided by the private sector. We can think about the basic options in this way. On the individualist side, there are arguments that the market will find a way to make the proper adjustments.[37] We need only to provide tax breaks and get government out of the way. This theory avoids the question of why governments (state and federal in the U.S. and governments across the world) have become involved in health care in the first place—namely, the recognition that health care is something needed by all persons in order to flourish. As early as the 1950s, the private system began to break down in providing adequately for the common good. On the other side, there are calls for some version of a national health-care system. On the positive side, we would be providing universal coverage. On the negative side, most analysts doubt whether costs could be contained, and if they were contained there are doubts that a gargantuan government bureaucracy would be able to contain costs fairly and appropriately so that individuals would receive the care that they need. Further, with universal coverage the amount of consumers will rise, and even if limits are set, the use of expensive medical technology and treatments will only increase.

What should we do? Candidates and elected officials will be offering proposals for many years to come.

What Can You and I Do in the Meantime?

From the point of view of Catholic social teaching, a solution will require cooperation, responsibility, and change from all of us. We need to begin to see health care as a personal and social good within a network of social duties and social relations, and not merely as a market commodity. In order to simplify matters for further discussion, I will depart from policy recommendations and think in terms of solidarity and subsidiarity. Here are some suggestions of what we can do.

- Cooperation rather than consumerism. We could become less like consumers and more locally cooperative in how we think about health care, much like local food cooperatives. We could approach local clinics and physicians groups in order to think about ways that health care could become less narrowly professionalized and more part of community life. We might contribute our resources, both financial and practical, so that physicians and nurses could set aside time and energy for community education, extended consultations with patient's families, and care for the uninsured. By and large, doctors and nurses would welcome the opportunity. They would probably experience a renewal of their calling to medicine.

- Assist medical professionals. Medical professionals, especially physicians, accrue a great deal of debt in paying for their education. Debt affects not only where doctors practice (there is a shortage of physicians in rural areas), but also what they practice. We in civic and church groups could make an effort to help fund education for nurses and doctors so that they might be freer to identify their particular vocations and be constrained less by the market.

- The medicalization of modern life. We need to think about how our lives have become "medicalized." On one level, some natural processes like aging skin and hair loss have become medical conditions, though most of us remain skeptical. But what about hyperactivity in children or a declining sex drive among the elderly? Are these medical conditions? Are they diseases which need treatment? If so, or at least in some cases, is medical treatment the best option? On another level, we hold out hope that medicine will cure any illness or disease. We go to the physician's office for a cure to the common cold. One study reports that "each year [the common cold] makes for 25 million unnecessary visits to doctors' offices—and some 1.6 million trips to emergency rooms."[38] My mother would give me her mother's concoction of whiskey, honey, and tea, and then send me to bed. Is that bad?

• Midwifery and hospice. A great deal of medical expense (most would say a disproportionate amount) is attributable to care at the very beginning and at the end of life. It varies, of course, but a good amount of time during the last two years of life is spent undergoing curative treatment; yet, "across the U.S., the data shows that more services, treatments, hospital stays, and doctor visits don't generally translate into improved quality of care."[39]

At the beginning of life, we might think about a combination of care from a midwife and physician. Midwifery is a time-honored and community-based network of care during pregnancy and childbirth. Hospice care is the same for the last years and months of life. With the help of hospice care organizations, people are able to receive palliative care as they die at home or in a hospice care facility.

Like the first suggestion (cooperation rather than consumerism), "de-medicalizing" childbirth and dying will not succeed if we enter the process only when we need the service. Bearing and raising children, as well as caring for the dying, ought to be ordinary matters of life that are shared by networks of kin and community. These networks are still present, but often their place has been reduced to the baby shower and the funeral. We only need to expand the networks of independence that already exist, and take time to enliven these subsidiary institutions and practices.

PART THREE

Justice

8

Natural Law

St. Thomas Aquinas and the Role of Reason in Social Order

JOSHUA P. HOCHSCHILD

In Sophocles' *Antigone*, there is a character whose passionate will defies reason. The tyrant king Creon declares and then even more foolishly enforces a law against the burial of fallen soldiers. His general stubbornness, and his insistence on his right as political ruler to make laws as he sees fit, lead ultimately to his ruin.

But a tragic story involves ill fortune befalling a great figure and the tragic character in Sophocles' play is Antigone, not Creon. Antigone clearly sees that Creon's law is unreasonable. She too is full of passion, especially because the law would prevent her from honoring her brother's corpse. But Antigone's passion, far from obscuring or usurping reason, instead fortifies it: she heroically resists the bad law to do what is right. She is so sure in her perception that, against the authority of human law, she invokes a higher law, an eternal and divinely authored law to which she owes primary obedience. Thus, when Creon seeks to confirm that she "dared to break [his] laws," Antigone replies

not just with a confession, but with a confident testimony that her allegiance
lies elsewhere:

> Yes. Zeus did not announce those laws to me.
> And Justice living with the gods below
> sent no such laws for men. I did not think
> anything which you proclaimed strong enough
> to let a mortal override the gods
> and their unwritten and unchanging laws.
> They're not just for today or yesterday,
> but exist forever, and no one knows
> where they first appeared.[1]

In a noble act—an act of what we might today call civil disobedience—Antigone follows the unwritten higher law and fulfills her duty to honor her brother.
She does so with a peaceful steadiness and determination, knowing that she
will suffer punishment, but willing to endure it for the sake of true justice.[2]

Thomas Aquinas, Doctor of Faith and Reason

This chapter aims to introduce the contributions of a medieval theologian,
Thomas Aquinas, to the tradition of Catholic social teaching. It begins with
reference to Antigone, however, because Sophocles' story helps to highlight
three aspects of Aquinas's contribution to Catholic thought that this chapter
will address. Two of these will be taken up in subsequent sections: under the
heading of natural law, the notion of a higher or eternal law that governs
human actions; and under the heading of subsidiarity, a manifestation of that
higher law that concerns the relationship between different kinds of human
authority. Another feature, however, must be addressed first: the role of reason
in Catholic teaching. Classical Greece stands as a symbol for philosophical
insight untouched by Jewish and Christian revelation, and Aquinas is honored
by the church not just for exploring dogmatic teachings of revealed theology,
but for helping the church negotiate its relationship with philosophy.

St. Thomas Aquinas lived for almost fifty years right in the middle of the
thirteenth century, from 1225 to 1274. Against the will of his aristocratic
family, he joined a religious order, the Order of Preachers, or Dominicans.
His intellectual talent was quickly evident in school, and he spent the rest
of his life in scholarly communities, mostly at the University of Paris and in
Naples in his native Italy. In his short lifetime he produced an extraordinary
amount of writing—legend describes his dictating several works at a time to
teams of scribes—in genres and subjects ranging from philosophical treatises,
general and specialized theological works, philosophical commentaries, biblical commentaries, prayers, hymns, sermons, and letters. He was canonized

in 1323—although he received an unofficial canonization a few years earlier when Dante placed him in the circle of theologians in the *Paradiso*.

Undoubtedly Aquinas is properly classified as a theologian, and he would not have called himself a philosopher. Yet the church has commended him as a philosopher, appealing to him when calling for the reform of philosophy.[3] To understand this we must recognize that one of Aquinas's accomplishments as a theologian was to help develop the church's relationship to philosophical reason, or intellectual investigation considered apart from Christian revelation. While his official profession was theology, his vocation was surely as philosopher in the classical sense: a lover of wisdom, genuinely open to the truth, willing to find it wherever it may be, and dedicating his life to it. One scholar says that "St. Thomas is, properly speaking, a metaphysical poet, taking the word in its broadest sense to signify one who interprets the universe: a prophet of being—of God, humanity, nature."[4] Another likens the mind of Aquinas "to a lake-basin that absorbs the waters streaming in from every quarter, lets sink whatever of rubbish they bring along, so that the surface forms a clear and tranquil mirror in which the blue vault of heaven is solemnly reflected."[5] The thrust of such images is that Aquinas's brilliance does not lie in esoteric genius, but in a capacious intellect able to make sense of everything. Thomism is, in Chesterton's words, "the philosophy of common sense."[6]

Today, the name of Aquinas is often a code word for tradition and orthodoxy, but in his own day he was regarded as an independent-minded pioneer, demonstrating a sometimes controversial openness to other traditions and new intellectual influences—especially from Arab, Jewish, and pagan authors. He was especially concerned to help theological education assimilate the rediscovered philosophical works of Aristotle. We can appreciate the difficulty of Aquinas's project when we realize the diversity of criticism to which it has been subject. Many secular intellectual historians have found Aquinas too dogmatic, a fideist, subordinating philosophical reason to the constraints of religious authority. On the other hand, some Protestants have accused him of rationalism, granting too much autonomy to philosophy apart from faith.

The truth is in the middle. Aquinas did affirm the ability of human reason to discover much truth—including truth about God and the human soul. He thus has more confidence in the power of reason than many modern philosophers and scientists. On the other hand, reason is still limited in its power, and cannot attain to the highest truths, the mysteries of Christian faith, without supernatural help. Note that "the faith," meaning the *content* of divine revelation (the sum of Christian doctrine) is grasped by "faith" considered as an *act or habit of the human mind* in trusting that revelation, and made possible by supernatural grace. In both senses, faith in this context implies truth, which is why Aquinas thinks that faith is compatible with reason—not because reason is concerned with the material world and faith with the spiritual, nor because reason is concerned with facts in contrast with faith as a matter of opinion or personal preference. Faith is compatible with reason because both give insight into the nature of reality, including reality beyond the physical world.

Some of what reason can grasp by its own power are theoretical truths—truths about the way things are. But others are practical truths—concerning what ought to be done. In the context of this volume, the significance of this should be obvious: Catholic ideas about just social order are not only or even primarily religious doctrines of faith, but are part of rational human inquiry into the nature of the world. Most of Catholic social teaching does not consist of mysterious precepts accepted and submitted to by faith, but of universal truths illuminated and grasped by the natural power of the human mind.

Natural Law

In the Catholic intellectual tradition, the notion of universal moral truths discernable by reason has been most commonly addressed under the rubric of natural law. The concept of universal moral truths is historically quite common, but it took some time for Western thinkers to become comfortable with the designation "natural law." [7] For the ancient Greeks, nature (*physis*) was the realm of forces beyond human control; law (*nomos*) was something instituted by human will, as a corrective or constraint on human action. Nature is common to all, but law varies among nations and peoples; thus, many Greek sophists exploited the different meanings of the terms to contrast the necessary (and universal) with the contingent (and variable). The theoretical and linguistic innovations that allow one to speak of a "law of nature"—which must initially have sounded like something of a paradox—are usually attributed to the Stoics, who thought of nature itself as having a divine *logos* order, or reason. Even before that, however, Aristotle was willing to speak in a way of a "law according to nature." With explicit reference to the passage from Sophocles' *Antigone*, quoted at the beginning of this essay, Aristotle says that general or common laws are those based upon nature, as opposed to those established by people. [8]

Aristotle is considered the grandfather of natural law theory in another sense too: he clearly connects justice with the notion of law (*Nicomachean Ethics*, Bk. V, chs. 2–5), and, if it wasn't already evident that justice is not just a matter of convention, he distinguishes between a justice that depends on human law and "natural justice" (*Nicomachean Ethics*, Bk. V, ch. 10). But Aristotle never elaborated what we might call a theory of natural law, and in the Catholic tradition it is Aquinas who is credited with developing Aristotelian insights into what could be regarded as a natural law theory. [9]

The universe is governed by a God who knows what is best and orders all things accordingly. [10] (Even this, for Aquinas, was not a specifically Christian notion—it was a historical fact that other philosophers, such as Plato,

Aristotle, and Stoic authors, found good reason to believe in a benevolent divine providence.) The universal or "natural" moral law governing human life, then, is just the particular way in which free and rational human beings share in this divine governance. Hence Aquinas defines natural law as the rational creature's participation in the eternal law.[11] This apparently simple definition allows Aquinas to show that natural law fulfills the requirements of genuine law: (1) it is an intelligible command, "a dictate of reason," which (2) comes from a legitimate authority (God), who (3) makes the command for the good of those he governs.[12] It should be noted that on this conception law is not understood as an expression of power or force, meant to coerce or punish; it is an expression of intelligence, meant to lead things toward their fulfillment.[13]

It should be clear also that natural law is not called "natural" because it is somehow independent of or apart from God: the natural law is the very dictate of the divine mind.[14] But then why is it called natural? The answer to this addresses the fourth requirement of genuine law: (4) that it be promulgated. How does God promulgate the natural law? By making us the kinds of creatures we are, and giving us reason to discern what is good for us. Natural law is "natural" then, in two senses: it is rooted in human nature—its moral precepts conform with and help to fulfill the kinds of being we are—and it is discernable by natural reason—the human intellect, by its own power and apart from direct revelation, can discover at least its most essential truths.[15]

A common objection to the notion of natural law argues that we find more disagreement about morality than we would expect if universal moral principles were discernable by all. This objection needs to be answered on two levels. First there is in fact a surprising degree of agreement, across times and cultures, about the basic outlines of good human action.[16] Second, to posit a universal moral law is not to suggest that everyone automatically has equal insight into it; rather, moral insight has to be learned, through habituation and training. Some—like a spoiled child, may lack the training; others may be slower to learn, like a tone-deaf person trying to appreciate an elevated musical style. Natural law theory, indeed any theory of universal morality, can and should include an account of why, and in what ways, those who are not habituated to conform to the natural law are weakened in their ability to perceive it.[17]

A somewhat more academic objection to natural law theory holds that claims about what is good, or about what one ought to do, cannot be based on observations about what things are. This objection has its roots in David Hume's empiricism and twentieth-century positivism, and outside of a philosophy class it falls rather flat. In everyday life, knowing the nature of a plant helps me know whether it ought to have sunlight or shade, or whether it is good for it to have a little water or a lot. Knowing what kind of tool or machine one picks up helps one to determine what it is supposed to do, and to evaluate whether it is any good at doing it. Likewise, knowing what a human being is means knowing what is natural for a human being—not in a statistical sense of what is normal, but in the deeper sense of what conforms to human nature—and from this we can infer those conditions under which a human being can flourish. For instance, given that human beings are embodied and rational, and knowing the rates of physical and intellectual development of human beings, I can know that children need a lot of attention and love in their first several years, and that parents ought to care for their children. The general principle here is sometimes referred to as *teleological metaphysics*, the notion that things have intrinsic purposes (from Greek *telos*, "purpose" or "end") determined by their natures. The technical terminology need not obscure a widely recognized and natural observation: to know what is good for something, one must know what it is for, and to know what it is for, one must know what it is.[18]

To see how naturally this insight accompanies moral reflection, recall that famous American invocation of natural law by civil rights activist Martin Luther King Jr. Like Antigone, King saw that the notion of natural law was essential if we are to measure the justice or injustice of human laws—which seems like a necessity in a just society. King had been chided for breaking the law. In his "Letter from a Birmingham Jail" (April 16, 1963), he responds:

> One may well ask: "How can you advocate breaking some laws and obeying others?" The answer lies in the fact that there are two types of laws: just and unjust. I would be the first to advocate obeying just laws. One has not only a legal but a moral responsibility to obey just laws. Conversely, one has a moral responsibility to disobey unjust laws. I would agree with St. Augustine that "an unjust law is no law at all."[19]

Here is a classic statement of natural law as an expression of natural justice independent of human convention. But King saw further that an appeal to natural justice above human law required an appeal to the conditions of human flourishing:

> How does one determine whether a law is just or unjust? A just law is a man made code that squares with the moral law or the law of God. An unjust law is a code that is out of harmony with the moral law. To put it in the terms of St. Thomas Aquinas: An unjust law is a human law that is not rooted in eternal law and natural law. Any law that uplifts human personality is just. Any law that degrades human personality is unjust.[20]

A just law "uplifts human personality." In other words, it allows the human person to flourish. An unjust law is unjust precisely insofar as it limits or prevents the flourishing of the human person. If there are some actions—such as murder, adultery, or theft—that by their very nature frustrate human flourishing, then these things should not be done. But the emphasis here is not just prohibiting what is bad, but pointing one in the direction of what is good. Natural law is a gift from God intended to nurture and guide us toward genuine fulfillment. Thus, John Paul II's *Veritatis Splendor* (*The Splendor of Truth*) links the Catholic natural law tradition to the notion of promoting human freedom, the freedom of living a life according to the truth (particularly nos. 35–53). While the fullness of truth is revealed only in Christ, Christ is the answer to a question already asked, and the completion of an answer already partially discerned, by the natural longings of the human heart and the natural insight of the human mind.[21]

Subsidiarity

The natural law governs the actions of human beings considered not just as individuals, but as members of communities and polities, families and associations. One particular manifestation of the natural law that has become increasingly talked about in modern society is the principle of subsidiarity. Although articulated as a principle only within the last century or so, it embodies fundamental insights about social order that have always been a part of natural law thinking.

A key text in the emerging consciousness of the principle is the social encyclical *Rerum Novarum* (*On the Condition of Labor*, 1891). In response to political and economic changes that affected European workers, the document insists that individuals and families must retain their own freedom of action, and that their various functions should not be "absorbed by the State" (no. 52). *Quadragesimo Anno*, Pope Pius XI's anniversary encyclical forty years later, more directly invokes a "weighty principle" that "every social activity ought of its very nature to furnish help to the members of the body social, and never to destroy and absorb them." Pius XI seems to be formulating the principle in this highly influential passage:

> Just as it is gravely wrong to take from individuals what they can accomplish by their own initiative and industry and give it to the community, so also it is an injustice and at the same time a grave evil and disturbance of right order to assign to a greater and higher association what lesser and subordinate organizations can do.[22]

Sixty years later, in 1981, John Paul II explicitly formulated the principle of subsidiarity in *Centesimus Annus*—a passage that was then quoted in the *Catechism of the Catholic Church*:

> A community of a higher order should not interfere in the internal life of a community of a lower order, depriving the latter of its functions, but rather should

support it in case of need and help to coordinate its activity with the activities of the rest of society, always with a view to the common good.[23]

If we take only these passages as our guide, we can see that the principle of subsidiarity regulates the relationships between different parts of a social order, especially between different levels of association. Larger or higher levels of association are required to offer help or assistance (Latin *subsidium*) to the activities of lower, smaller, or more local levels of association, and are neither to interfere with nor absorb their activities.[24]

Although articulated only in light of modern economic and cultural developments, as a principle of social order the basic insight here is classical, and would have been implicit in all premodern social activity and tacitly recognized in premodern political theory. It only came to be explicitly invoked with the rise of forces that could systematically violate it. Before the rise of the nation state, familial, feudal, guild, and other organic and local relationships would have ensured that the principle of subsidiarity was more or less naturally observed. Both the modern nation state and the modern economy, however, have the ability to systematically curtail, absorb, or undermine the functions of more organic local communities.

In this sense, the principle of subsidiarity emerges with, but is also an alternative to, modern doctrines of socialism and political liberalism. Marx rightly saw that capitalism was eroding an old social order that had protected workers within networks of associations and obligations; classical liberals recognized that it would be dangerous to entrust the modern state with too much power. Catholic social teaching goes beyond these insights by insisting that human beings belong to natural communities that precede the nation state, and by insisting that the good of these communities, and the good of larger political entities, is inseparable from the good of the individuals who constitute them.[25]

In America the traditions of federalism and classical liberalism have given the principle of subsidiarity an obvious place as a rationale for limited government: state authority should not usurp the functions of lower social orders.[26] But the principle of subsidiarity does much more than provide another argument against the grasping nation state. For one thing, its scope is wider. Even if papal documents most often find occasion to invoke the principle when discussing the state, the principle is concerned not narrowly with specifically public, state power, but with general relationships between parts and wholes in any community. It can apply not only to different levels of government, but also within families and private associations, within corporate administration, within ecclesial polities, or within different parts of the economic order.

Moreover, as a principle of natural law, subsidiarity carries with it a conception of human society that is not implied in classical liberalism. The principle of subsidiarity presupposes that individuals and communities have proper activities, social functions with intrinsic integrity and value. Rather than treating social order as purely conventional or artificial, the product of the choices of sovereign individuals, the principle assumes that certain forms and activities of social order are natural. Marriage, for instance, is not just whatever two consenting adults want it to be. It has an intrinsic nature and authority to which individuals may be subject; as a certain kind of association, it has particular functions and therefore responsibilities—such as the honoring of parents, the fidelity of the spouses, and, in the normal course of events, the rearing of children. It is for this reason that Aristotle's *Politics* does not begin with a consideration of different forms of government, but with a discussion of the nature of the most basic unit of political order, the family. Only after inquiring into the nature of a healthy household can one know what kinds of laws would appropriately lead individuals and families to their fulfillment.

Put another way, the principle of subsidiarity is not so much a principle about rights—the license to act without interference from above—as it is about duties or vocational responsibilities. Papal documents use the term *munus*, often translated as "task," "role," or "function," but the real sense of the term is *mission* or *vocation*, a *gift of service*. Thus it may be advisable to avoid altogether using the language of rights or even proper functions in characterizing the principle of subsidiarity; one scholar of Catholic social teaching describes it instead as a principle regulating *the plurality of gifts within a community.*[27]

Aquinas referred not to the principle of subsidiarity as such, but to the fundamental insight about the relation between the parts and wholes of social bodies. This insight is implicit throughout his political and moral thought. The principle of subsidiarity, if it is even to make sense, clearly depends on the rest of natural law theory. For while subsidiarity tells us that various social functions or gifts must be respected and fostered, it does not tell us what those functions or gifts are. Only rarely, in fact, does human law determine the function or gift of an individual or community. Rather, an important function of human law is to recognize those functions or gifts determined by natural law. If this is the case, the first responsibility of government is not to establish the just distribution of material resources through force or coercion, but to recognize and foster the natural ordering of social gifts. In a just society, there is a distribution of responsibility for all members to seek the common good; both ruler and ruled are expected to act appropriately, through perception of how the natural law bears on their particular circumstances.

Here we might recall Antigone once more. We have seen that her reasoning is easily interpreted as an appeal to the higher (divine) over the lower (the human). But Antigone is also appealing to the primacy of the lower (the more fundamental obligations of family) over the higher (the more distant association of the state, which should serve, rather than usurp, the good of families). She recognizes that the state is supposed to support its members, and that it ought not to undermine her responsibility to her fallen brother. She sees that the law of Creon is unjust because it upsets the order of gifts and vocations within his community. Her choice to defy Creon's law is not a personal preference for some distant abstraction, but a rational human insight into how the good should be pursued here and now. She is not rationalizing a private judgment with a dangerous religious ideology, but using her reason to see how best to realize the concrete good for herself, her family, and her community.

Conclusion: Rethinking Social Justice

The common theme of this chapter on Aquinas's contribution to Catholic social teaching has been the role of reason in determining the just social order. In conclusion, let us make explicit what consequences this theme has for what the tradition of Catholic social teaching can mean by "social justice."

The term, it should be noted, should seem somewhat redundant, for justice already implies a social context.[28] The term also has an ambiguity that could suggest that it pertains simply to the fair allocation of goods in a society. Social justice has thus been confused with what the Aristotelian tradition calls *distributive justice*, which involves the equitable distribution of common social resources. Distributive justice is primarily a concern of the ruling authority who has care of the community (and so, in a democratic community, it is only a concern of individual members insofar as they are responsible for the governing authority). Rather than taking place among and between members of a community, distributive justice pertains to how the community as a whole treats its component parts.

By contrast, *legal justice* pertains to how parts of a community contribute to the common good of the community. This is legal insofar as it bears on how well the individuals fulfill the demands of the law ordering the community. Strictly speaking, the law in question need not only be human law, but can include natural law. The considerations of this chapter help us to see that if social justice is to make sense in the tradition of Catholic social teaching, it must concern how individuals and more basic communities order themselves to the common good of the larger community. Social justice should thus be understood not as distributive justice but as legal justice, where the relevant law is not the law of the state but the moral law by which all things are ordered to God.

In this light, we can see that it would be a mistake to conceive of social justice as a template that can be imposed on society by political force. Rather, it must be realized in society by the rational, moral participation of its members. As one scholar has put it,

> Social justice is not a magic formula out there somewhere, waiting to be applied automatically to concrete situations. As a virtue it has a *medium rationis*, which

means that its mode of action must be constantly determined by one's reason. Consequently, all appeals to the concept of social justice must be supported by cogent rational arguments that show why the common good requires such and such an act in these specific circumstances.[29]

So social justice in this sense is not a policy initiative that can be implemented in a community, but the virtuous activity of the members of a community; it thus requires the rational participation of the members, together seeking to order their actions for the common good.[30] As the principle virtue of a virtuous community—the virtue by which the members of a community are conformed to the law of the community—Aquinas can propose legal justice (social justice) as the natural correlate of the theological virtue of charity:

> As charity may be called a general virtue in so far as it directs the acts of all the virtues to the Divine good, so too is legal justice [a general virtue], in so far as it directs the acts of all the virtues to the common good.[31]

Discussion:

Subsidiarity, Labor Associations, and Family

To put Dr. Hochschild's chapter in summary form, we can look to Pope Leo XIII's *Rerum Novarum* (1891). Pope Leo's encyclical, *On the Condition of Labor*, connects human work, property, family, and the framework of subsidiarity through natural law arguments. These arguments and connections are sustained all the way through modern Catholic social teaching. In Catholic thought, family and associations based on work (e.g., labor unions) are considered basic to the social order.

Consider two excerpts from *Rerum Novarum*.[32] The first (from nos. 8–9) understands work as a natural human activity and a law of our nature that implies a subsidiary claim to property existing prior to various social or economic policies. On the one hand, socialism was making a claim to the fruits of a person's labor; on the other hand, nineteenth-century capitalism, ironically, resulted in the same problem—low factory wages did not sustain the natural condition of human life. We are sustained by and contribute to the common good through our work.

> Moreover, the earth, even though apportioned among private owners, ceases not thereby to minister to the needs of all, inasmuch as there is not one who does not sustain life from what the land produces. Those who do not possess the soil contribute their labor; hence, it may truly be said that all human subsistence is derived either from labor on one's own land, or from some toil, some calling,

which is paid for either in the produce of the land itself, or in that which is exchanged for what the land brings forth.

Here, again, we have further proof that private ownership is in accordance with the law of nature. Truly, that which is required for the preservation of life, and for life's well-being, is produced in great abundance from the soil, but not until man has brought it into cultivation and expended upon it his solicitude and skill. Now, when man thus turns the activity of his mind and the strength of his body toward procuring the fruits of nature, by such act he makes his own that portion of nature's field which he cultivates—that portion on which he leaves, as it were, the impress of his personality; and it cannot but be just that he should possess that portion as his very own, and have a right to hold it without any one being justified in violating that right.

After these arguments on the natural law of human work, Leo XIII turns to the primary place of family which must be served by other levels of society (nos. 12–13).

The rights here spoken of, belonging to each individual man, are seen in much stronger light when considered in relation to man's social and domestic obligations. . . . No human law can abolish the natural and original right of marriage, nor in any way limit the chief and principal purpose of marriage ordained by God's authority from the beginning: "Increase and multiply." Hence we have the family, the "society" of a man's house—a society very small, one must admit, but none the less a true society, and one older than any State. Consequently, it has rights and duties peculiar to itself which are quite independent of the State.

That right to property, therefore, which has been proved to belong naturally to individual persons, must in like wise belong to a man in his capacity of head of a family; nay, that right is all the stronger in proportion as the human person receives a wider extension in the family group . . . The domestic household is antecedent, as well in idea as in fact, to the gathering of men into a community, the family must necessarily have rights and duties which are prior to those of the community, and founded more immediately in nature. If the citizens, if the families on entering into association and fellowship, were to experience hindrance in a commonwealth instead of help, and were to find their rights attacked instead of being upheld, society would rightly be an object of detestation rather than of desire.

Consider, especially, the last two sentences: the rights and duties of the call to family are prior to any conception of the state, and the proper role of the state is to give help and assistance to the vocation and call to service of family.

In the following section, "What can we do?" we will treat the institution of family in more detail. At this juncture, we will turn to labor associations as subsidiary institutions. The long excerpts from *Rerum Novarum* serve not only to show natural law arguments pertaining to family, but also to indicate that work is a law of our nature as well. Indeed, along with family, subsidiary associations based on common work are fundamental to Catholic social teaching. The tradition of Catholic thought, from Pope Leo XIII to Benedict XVI, does not provide a macroeconomic theory but a set of claims about the subjective and objective—the personal, material, and social—meaning of human work.

First, Pope Pius XI introduces the term "subsidiarity," in *Quadragesimo Anno*, as he turns to a social and economic problem: the fragmentation of society into classes based on conflicts within the labor market (nos. 80–87). Capitalism privileges capital and capitalists, and wage laborers suffer under the rule of the labor market. Socialism makes this class conflict the very meaning and course of history. In this context, Pius XI indicates that workers that unite in voluntary associations establish subsidiary institutions to protect workers from the rule of the market, on the one hand, and the rule of the socialist state, on the other. Further, he thinks of labor associations as groups which resist class divisions and contribute to the common good.

John Paul II summarizes this contribution of common life in his *Laborum Exercens* (*On Human Work*, no. 20). First, people join together on the basis of their craft, which is to say on the basis of the internal goods of their work (and not simply on the basis of external goods like wages). Second, the labor association contributes to the common good by protecting the worker (for instance, through union-organized unemployment insurance and the promotion of healthy working conditions). Third, such unions join with owners and employers to promote good work for the good of society, and in this sense labor associations are political. They should not play politics, but be political in the sense that they are concerned with good work and the common good. Finally, the union ought to be concerned not only with the conditions of work, but also with the personal growth and education of the worker.

Now we turn back to Pius XI. In *Quadragesimo Anno*, he proposes that associations based on the natural good of work are a means to resist class conflict and the self-interest that is often attributed, rightly or wrongly, to both capital and labor.

> [The cure to class conflict] will not come until . . . well-ordered members of the social body—Industries and Professions—are constituted in which men may have their place, not according to the position each has in the labor market but according to the respective social functions which each performs. For under nature's guidance it comes to pass that just as those who are joined together by nearness of habitation establish towns, so those who follow the same industry or profession—whether in the economic or other field—form guilds or associations, so that many are wont to consider these self-governing organizations, if not essential, at least natural to civil society.[33]

Your response to this conception of labor associations might be cynicism: workers like anyone else in the economy should just look out for themselves.

It would be interesting to ask instead if we can find examples (such as Bo Adams at the end of chapter 4) where people are joined together by their work to form subsidiary institutions and to contribute to the common good. This idea, in fact, is how John Paul II defines the good of a corporation (in *Centesimus Annus*, no. 35): it combines two natural goods—good work and forming an association for the common good.

What Can We Do?

Our consideration of what we can do could continue with our discussion of work, but we ask the reader to refer back to the discussion sections following chapter 4. Instead, Josh Hochschild and I thought it better to turn again to the theme of family. As we have seen with Leo XIII, family is a basic social institution, antecedent to the state and to economic systems. In his *Letter to Families* (1994), John Paul II likens the family to a culture—a "culture of love" where we human beings become persons (no. 13).[34] Given this role in human life, family is, obviously, a social institution that has a vocation to the common good. However, it is not uncommon in our society to think about family simply as a private arrangement (and marriage simply as a contract). In this regard, there is a degree of correspondence to labor unions. In the marketplace, families, like unions, are sometimes reduced to organizations that merely pursue shared self-interests. Home life is reduced to being a site of consumption—it procures goods and services provided by the state and market and, in doing so, the family's role as a distinct social body and the function of the household as a place of distinctive social interaction are undermined.

Josh suggests that we focus on ways that the family is co-opted by the market and on ways in which households can be productive and not just consumptive. To get to the heart of this contrast and to what we can do, we need to attend to mundane matters of home.

- Entertainment and leisure activity: Instead of purchasing the products of the entertainment industry, including television-watching, families could start playing games or making music together.
- Health (as noted in the "what can we do?" following chapter 7): Instead of the nursing homes of the medical industry, we could invest our time and talents in home care for elderly parents and hospice care for the terminally ill.
- Social Services (as we will consider at the end of chapter 10): Instead of assuming that social service agencies will take care of those in need of food and shelter, we could make steps to develop the kind of home life where we are able to show personal hospitality to the poor.

- Food (as noted in the "what can we do?" following chapter 5): Instead of depending entirely on the food industry and its processed and prepared foods, we could start gardening, cooking at home, make connections with local farmers, and join food cooperatives.
- Education: Instead of subcontracting education out to schools and assuming that someone else is taking care of it, parents and independent parent organizations could take responsibility, being actively engaged in and supplementing (if not simply providing directly) the education of their children.
- Other goods and services: Rather than running to the store or professionals, we can look for opportunities to share things (tools, labor) and trade things (products, manual and skilled labor) in an informal economy within neighborhoods and communities and among friends, apart from money and middlemen.

Each of these family and household-based alternatives will foster personal growth in our wisdom and skills for life, and they will no doubt enhance social participation and our ability to cooperate for the common good. These are mundane activities, but if practiced by a good number of households, neighborhoods will be transformed and, depending upon the number and depth of participation, whole towns and cities (perhaps the country) would be transformed as well.

9

Modern Economy
and the Social Order

DAVID M. MCCARTHY

The year 1891 marks the beginning of modern Catholic social teaching, when Pope Leo XIII issues an encyclical on the plight of the worker in the modern economy. In reality, Pope Leo's point of view draws on Catholic social thought that has been developing in Europe for almost a century, since the French Revolution.[1] As noted in chapter 4, the Latin title of the document, *Rerum Novarum*, points to "revolutionary changes" and "new things."[2] The new things, according to Leo XIII and Catholic social thought of the nineteenth century, are changes in political and economic life that left the industrial worker "isolated and defenseless" (*Rerum*, no. 2).

In the first paragraph of the document, the pope lists economic conditions that form the context of social conflict. By the nineteenth century, we see the industrial revolution (along with scientific inventions that mechanize production), labor understood as a market product, incredible wealth accumulated by individuals, and masses of working poor, whose social membership and identity are defined largely by their oppression. The urban poor are now members of the working class, which is assumed to have a natural antagonism to the new class of industrial capitalists.

Leo XIII admits that dealing with these changes is no easy task; indeed, he believes that dominant economic solutions (state socialism and unfettered capitalism) will produce more dangerous problems.[3] But he is convinced that a positive answer to the "new things" will be found if we take up the difficult task of defining "the relative rights [i.e., rights in the context of a social relationship] and mutual duties of the wealthy and of the poor, of capital and of labor" (Rerum, no. 1). Leo XIII does not offer a purely economic solution to economic problems. He calls for mutual social responsibility.[4] He argues that economic relationships, primarily between worker and employer, have to be put in a context of deeper social relationships, where each member fulfills social duties to the other and receives what he or she needs to live well.

The human being has a natural fulfillment which includes basic needs of life, food and shelter, health, intellectual and spiritual development, and putting one's mind and freedom to creating things and shaping a way of life—all of which are social activities—are set within relationships like family, economic institutions, religious bodies, and civic associations. In order to move our basic human capacities toward their fulfillment, people ought to have what the factory worker in the nineteenth century is being denied: the opportunity for work that is adequate to support a family, own property, and contribute to the good of others (nos. 34–35); good work along with suitable hours and healthy working conditions (nos. 16, 33); and free time to join in civic associations and to attend to religious obligations (no. 31).

The just wage is a good example of Catholic economic thinking. John Paul II calls it "the key problem of social ethics" (Laborum Exercens, no. 19). According to Catholic social teaching, it is appropriate that wages are significantly affected by the labor market, including factors such as the supply and demand for skilled labor, the health of a particular business, and the differences in regional economies. However, there is also a basis for a just wage in the nature of the human being. In Leo XIII's words, "The preservation of life is a bounden duty of each and all . . . [It] is a dictate of nature more imperious and more ancient than any bargain between man and man, that the remuneration must be enough to support the wage earner in reasonable and frugal comfort" (no. 34). Leo does not merely say that the preservation of life is a biological drive that individuals are bound to pursue. It is a biological drive, but also much more. Leo's phrase, "reasonable and frugal comfort," represents the distinctively human character of the life that is preserved. It is not simply physical or instinctual preservation, but what is needed to live with dignity, on the practical and moral level, as persons in community. The preservation of human dignity (in economic and social life) is a duty which binds each and all; that is to say, it is not an individual pursuit only, as much as it is the very fabric of social relationships which circumscribes the labor market and wage contract. In short, an ordering of social life to the good of the human being (to the common good) establishes the shape and limits of proper economic activity.

The Social Body or Economic Mechanism

Catholic social teaching challenges us precisely because it puts social relationships before economic theory. Leo XIII (and the Catholic social tradition as a whole) proposes that people with different but reciprocal roles, rights, and duties form a society as a social body, and that our interlocking social roles should form the foundation of economic relationships. The modern trend goes in the opposite direction.

Marxism holds that social relations are determined by the interests of economic classes, so that as the economy goes through its natural development, the society and the state ultimately coincide with the interests of the worker class. Writing about the monumental events of 1989—the fall of communism in the Soviet Union and eastern Europe—John Paul II notes that the failure of communism is, in part, because "it is not possible to understand man on the basis of economics alone, nor to define him simply on the basis of class membership" (*Centesimus Annus*, no. 24).

Capitalism, for the most part, also takes economic relationships as primary.[5] John Paul II calls this error "economism," where economic relationships subordinate personal relations, and capital and labor are considered "two impersonal forces" (*Laborem Exercens*, no. 13). Because we, the middle class in the United States, have been raised on the good of capitalism, this subordination of the social to the economic is sometimes hard to notice.

A good reference point (particularly in terms of Leo XIII) is Adam Smith's *Wealth of Nations*, published in 1776.[6] Smith treats the market as having a life of its own, as a mechanism that transcends the meaning of our personal intentions and actions.[7] More importantly, the mechanism of the market is separate from political relations, especially political authority and social constraints.[8] Smith, in contrast to Catholic social thought, treats the individual as separate from the social whole. The primary agents of his *Wealth of Nations* are the self-interested individual and the mechanisms of the economy. The impersonal forces are primary; they establish a law of self-interest, and it is a consistent theme in *Wealth of Nations* that it is foolish to resist. We succeed when we conform to them. If we seek our economic self-interest, then the competition of our individual interests will produce economic harmony and an orderly social life. If we take care of our own economic interests, the market, by spontaneous and unseen forces (an invisible hand), will take care of itself.

From the side of Catholic social thought this self-regulating mechanism of competition is illusory. According to the Catholic tradition, mechanisms of the economy have their source in personal choices. People make choices that create the structure of the economy, and too often these market mechanisms privilege those with the power to control the economic system. John Paul II summarizes the tradition well when he states that the "the guiding principle of Pope Leo's encyclical, and of all of the church's social doctrine, is *the correct view of the human person*" (*Centesimus Annus*, no. 11). In the time of Leo XIII, concerned Catholics become aware that the so-called "mechanism" of competition isolates workers, who are treated, not as persons-in-relationship to their employers, but as commodities on the labor market. The individualism of the market sets the industrialist's desire for high profits against the workers need for an adequate wage. The result is masses of urban poor, and even today the global labor market migrates to the newly urbanized poor in developing nations.[9] Social Catholicism proposes that the goals of the industrialist ought to include social responsibility, and only then will a healthy social and economic life be possible. When driven by economic interests alone, society becomes the "illusion of an animated body," fragmented, no longer an interplay of social roles, but "a lifeless mechanism, disorganized, lacking in inner harmony."[10]

The popularity of Smith's theory makes sense, as does the period when it emerges—the late eighteenth century. His science of the economy suits the emerging middle class of the eighteenth and nineteenth centuries, and I daresay it still suits us today: as individualism reigns among us, as the middle class is less likely than lower and upper classes to give to the poor, and increasingly our political involvement is not active participation, but monetary contributions. The modern economy and the middle class go together.

At the beginning of the modern era, the burgeoning trade helps create the middle class of merchants and tradesman, who are neither aristocrats nor peasants and laborers. They are in the middle of established positions in the old order of society, and they have no fixed or inherited social responsibility. The middle class falls between the established roles of nobility (who in the old order administers civil affairs), the vast majority of commoners, and the church. The middle class carves out its place primarily in terms of economic interests, and it does not take on a politically dominant role until the second half of the nineteenth century—and does so out of economic interest.[11] Smith's economic theory is well suited to this middle class of entrepreneurs because their place in society has been defined by their economic success, and Smith proposes that free economic competition provides its own mechanism of order and stability.[12] The pursuit of individual self-interest, by implication, is the best means to establish the contours of social life.

This relationship between the market and social roles (in terms of medieval social roles or modern mechanisms) is vital to Leo's account of human dignity and economic life. The premodern economy is primarily agricultural, marked by a limited production of food, the infrequent use of money, and a minimal amount of market exchange. During medieval times, for example, one third of the year is taken up with holiday leisure, and laborers worked about 50 percent less than their counterparts in nineteenth-century industry.[13] The point is that the economic exchange or the market is not fundamental to the structure of life. Most of agricultural life is set within the ancient manorial relationship between the lord of an estate and tenant-laborers, and both (with obvious differences) live off the land. One's place in society (largely inherited and immovable) is understood as a role and set of tasks for the good of all. Rather than classes with competing interests—aristocracy, proletariat, or bourgeoisie—medieval society is made up of interdependent stations or functions as part of a whole.

Amid this ancient and medieval agricultural economy, life is hard for the poor. Bishops and theologians frequently criticize the abuse of peasants and tenant-laborers by arguing in terms of the interdependent roles of social life—for the common purpose of private property (for the good of the laborer as well as the lord) and the duties of landowners to live modestly and to distribute excess goods to the poor. Some early Christian thinkers go as far as to say that living an extravagant life in the manor house is equivalent to stealing from the poor laborers. In any case, private ownership is understood in terms of the good of all, especially laborers who work a wealthy landowner's estate. Certainly, the theory does not always work out in practice, and bishops and their aristocratic families often are guilty of denying the poor the proper goods of life. The contrast to draw is between premodern and modern conceptions of social relations: how the justice and injustices of social and economic life are conceptualized.

Ancient and medieval theologians (as well as modern Catholic social teaching) draw on the biblical image of a body, where hand, foot, and head have different functions that are good for the whole (Rom. 12; 1 Cor. 12). This organic conception of social life fits with the inheritance of Greek philosophy where humans are considered social animals who are fulfilled in social life. A good modern analogy might be the family, and some social Catholics in the nineteenth century explicitly use the image of family when attempting to reform the relationship between the industrialist and the factory worker.[14] Relationships between parents and children have an established social form, and one of the purposes of parental income is to provide for children. Parents talk about income, property, and work in terms that include the good of the children. The point is that a prior social relationship, parents and children, gives structure to the use of wealth.

We moderns tend to set individual and society apart as competing entities: society limits my freedom to pursue my own interests because my self-interests, at a fundamental level, compete with the interests of others. The ancient and medieval conception is quite different. Personal interests are different but not fundamentally at odds. The individual person certainly is a distinct entity with desires and interests, but one of the higher (in the sense of distinctively human) desires of human life is a desire to freely, truthfully, and justly participate in the lives of others. We are fulfilled as human beings when we cooperate with others for our good and theirs. I am fulfilled, for example, in friendship, in enjoying the goodness that is another and seeking that person's good. On a broader social level, it is a common experience that people are fulfilled when they join with friends in doing good for the community or the poor. In the Catholic tradition, our fulfillment in the good of others is considered natural to the human being.

In *Rerum Novarum*, Leo XIII does not call for a return to the old order of aristocracy and commoners. Instead, he calls the new elite—the new class of industrialists and entrepreneurs—to accept the social responsibility of their dominant position in the economy. The old agrarian hierarchy (land owner/ patron and laborer) is not reasserted, but it is in the background.[15] Pope Leo holds that the new capitalists are part of a social whole and should not understand their relationship to laborers only in terms of impersonal market competition—paying only the pittance that any given labor market might require. The idea that the masses of urban factory workers share a free market with capitalists is simply self-deception (that is encouraged by modern individualism). The industrialist has a more secure and powerful position, and with that position comes social responsibility. Factory work (like manorial land in the medieval era) ought to form a bond rather than antagonism between worker and employers. The worker ought to give good work, and ought to receive what is needed to live well (not lavishly) and to contribute to the goods of social life (raising a family and participating in religious and civic associations).

Institutions and the Common Good

Modern Catholic social teaching can be understood as an attempt to assert the social nature of the human being in a world where the common good and reciprocal roles and duties are no longer taken for granted. As noted above, family becomes a sphere where shared endeavors and ends are sustained, and for this reason family relations are used as a common analogy for the social body. However, family in the modern world is increasingly narrowed and privatized, especially in the second half of the twentieth century. A typical problem for the contemporary American family is that it too is increasingly defined by individualism and a lack of shared endeavors. The same can be said for labor and civic associations. They are vitally important for Catholic thought, insofar as they provide a way for us to take on a role and place in the common work of a community. Often, however, our ideas about self-interest do not allow us to give full account of the role of labor and civic organizations in common life.

This thinning out of common life and the frequent social decline of family, labor, and civic associations also raises questions about the growing social dominance (beginning in the nineteenth century) of the modern state.

In Catholic thought, the common good is not the sum total of individual interests or majority rule; rather, it is the good that we human beings share in common that is the source of our fulfillment. In Catholic thought, the good of human life corresponds to human capacities for a good life with our neighbors. Theologically, our potential for fulfillment is conceptualized as the image of God. We are free and intelligent beings who have the capacity for common life, for making judgments about how to achieve what is good, how to give others what they deserve, even in the face of great adversity, and how to cultivate and enjoy the things of the earth. This sense of the common good does not determine the precise nature of public institutions and social roles. Rather, it is part of our human nature (the natural law) that we play a role in shaping the contours of common endeavors and social institutions. Pope John XXIII (in *Peace on Earth*, 1963) explains that "a well-ordered society requires that men recognize and observe their mutual rights and duties. It demands that each contribute generously to the establishment of a civic order in which rights and duties are more sincerely and effectively acknowledged and fulfilled" (no. 31).

Central to this civic order is family. (Recall the treatment of family in chapters 4 and 8.) Pope Leo XIII sees a threat to family in the industrial economy, and he connects the security of family to private property and a just wage. A wage to sustain one's life, and property to put to good use, are rights that exist apart from family, but these rights "are seen in a much stronger light if they are considered in relation to man's social and domestic obligations." Family, Leo XIII holds, is "a society limited indeed in numbers, but a true 'society', anterior to every kind of State or nation, with rights and duties of its own, totally independent of the commonwealth" (*Rerum*, no. 9). Socialism violates the right to private property which allows persons to sustain their lives and the social good by the free and intelligent use of their possessions. Likewise it intrudes on family, not only by denying private property, but also by its conception of an all-encompassing state (since the state is suppose to represent the will of a classless society). State socialism undermines the relationship between parents and children (*Rerum*, no. 11).

The dominant capitalist economy also undermines family. In economic theories akin to Smith's *Wealth of Nations*, the fate of families should be left to the impersonal laws of private property and competition. Working-class families will simply suffer or thrive according to the natural rise and fall of wages on the labor market.[16] In laissez-faire economics, the government is supposed to allow the market to regulate itself. As noted in the introduction, Catholic social thought holds that the market cannot be the only factor in determining wage. Wage is also determined by the needs of persons to live well (and living well here means not extravagance, but good in a social and moral sense). Following this point, the role of the government is to protect the vulnerable, especially the industrial worker who (amid the so-called competition of individual interests) has been rendered "isolated and defenseless."[17] If employers or workers reject their responsibilities to the other, the government "should intervene, to see that each obtains his own, but not under any other circumstance" (*Rerum*, no. 34).

Note that in the quotation above the role of civil government is limited; it is called to intervene in the relationship between employer and employee only when one or the other discards its social duties. The United State Conference of Catholic Bishops, for example, has been petitioning the government for a more adequate minimum wage and an extension of unemployment insurance during times of high unemployment.[18] John Paul II reflects this tradition well when he explains that economic exchange should be "circumscribed within a strong juridical framework which places it at the service of human freedom in its totality . . . the core of which is ethical and religious" (*Centesimus Annus*, no. 42). The government has a specific role of administering laws that establish boundaries of economic life, but does not have the right to take charge of it. In the words of Leo XIII, "the State must not absorb the individual and family; both should be allowed free and untrammeled action as far as is consistent with the common good and the interests of others . . . Rulers should anxiously safeguard the community and all its parts" (*Rerum*, no. 28).

The dominance of the state becomes a clearer problem by 1931 when Pope Pius XI issues *Quadragesimo Anno* on the fortieth anniversary of *Rerum Novarum*. "It is patent that in our days not alone [not only] is wealth accumulated, but immense power and despotic domination is concentrated in the hands of a few. . . . This accumulation of power, a characteristic note of the modern economic order, is a natural result of unrestrained free competition which permits the survival of those only who are the strongest" (nos. 105, 107). Pius XI indicates that this logic of economic power encourages the errors of state socialism. Socialism reacts against the disparities in wealth and poverty that laissez-faire capitalism produces. It proposes that the working class will and should "acquire the control of the State" (no. 108), which will then properly manage the economy.

On the other side of the ideological divide, the liberal state allows a free reign of economic individualism, which ironically gives greater power to the state. Individualism fragments the social body. In the words of Pope Pius, "The highly developed social life, which once flourished in a variety of prosperous and interdependent institutions, has been damaged and all but ruined, leaving virtually only individuals and the State, with no little harm to the latter" (*Quadragesimo Anno*, no. 77). The state is harmed because it is required to take on social responsibilities that are not its own; individuals and communities are harmed because their proper social roles, rights, and duties are undermined.

In response, Pius XI develops the concept of subsidiarity, the view that inter-mediate institutions—smaller social bodies in between individuals and the state—have particular roles in sustaining social life and the common good. Apart from economic questions, educational institutions are a good example. In his time, Pius XI resists the efforts of the modern state (particularly fascist Italy and Nazi Germany) to take control of schools and youth organizations. The state, according to Catholic social thought, ought to be limited, making room for local institutions and community organizations, as well as civic, religious, and labor associations.

In the economic sphere, Pius XI (like Leo before him and the popes after-ward) turns to labor associations as institutions that are vital to the common good. The view of labor relations in Catholic social teaching includes a critique of both socialism and labor unions as they are usually understood in capitalist philosophy. The worker class in socialism becomes equivalent to society itself, and in capitalism labor is a group which pursues its common self-interest. Pope Pius proposes that the recreation of functional groups in the economy may be the best way to resist the division of society into contending classes and to direct economic life to the common good. His model for these economic associations is the medieval and early modern guild which is understood as a fellowship or fraternity.[19] The guild is a community of tradesman or profes-sionals that develops and manages the line of work, regulates the labor mar-ket and wage, insures its members against hardships, and performs what we today would call charitable activities.[20] Pius XI imagines that a modern form of the guild would include both employers, employees, and what we think of as market competitors in an attempt to give structure to commerce in a way that serves the common good.

The modern economy sustains no clear analogue to trade guild. Like family, which is too often privatized, the common contemporary form of labor asso-ciation does not take on a role that can be set within the social metaphor of a body with many parts. Fortunately, many entrepreneurs and business people, like neighborhoods and fellowships of families, do take up community efforts and attempt to enrich common life. Rather than the constancy of institutions that Pius XI imagines, these social groups tend to have an improvised or ad hoc character. Family, for example, has no standard form in the contempo-rary world, so that families and neighborhoods must in a sense create forms of social cooperation from the ground up. Likewise with business and trade associations, persons use their ingenuity and expertise to create economic practices that enhance social responsibility.

This ad hoc character of intermediate institutions is signaled by John Paul II, who calls us to develop a disposition and habits of solidarity. In *Solicitudo Rei Socialis* (*On Social Concern*), he explains that solidarity is a way of un-derstanding our lives that recognizes our interdependence as individuals and peoples of the world (no. 38). We recognize our economic, cultural, political, and religious interdependence as moral categories. But we do not stop at this awareness. Solidarity "is not a feeling of vague compassion or shallow distress at the misfortunes of so many people, both near and far. On the contrary, it is *a firm and persevering determination* to commit oneself to the *common good*; that is to say, to the good of all and of each individual, because we are *all* really responsible *for all*" (no. 38). This is the social task of contemporary economic life, particularly in relationship to the poor (no. 42)—to create a social space, institutions and organizations directed to the common good, that circumscribes our economic activity.

Conclusion

This chapter has included a broad range of material, from Leo XIII's *Rerum Novarum* (1891) to John Paul II's *Centesimus Annus* (1991), but a single theme should be clear. Our social responsibilities ought to guide our economic activity. The economy does not have a life of its own, but is given its structure by human choices and actions. It is possible, if things were different, to direct our economic activity in a way that better serves the common good. The point is simple, but putting it into practice can seem almost impossible. We are immersed in a world of economic exchange that far outreaches our control. Nevertheless, we are called to work and make, buy and sell, in ways that preserve our dignity and the dignity of our neighbors. We might not be able to change the business world, but we can change how we do business.

Discussion

Fair Trade in an Economy of Anonymity

"The problem with capitalism is that there are not enough capitalists." This statement was made by G. K. Chesterton (1874–1936), who was a proponent of an early twentieth-century school of thought called "distributism." Chesterton and others developed distributism as a "third way" between capitalism and socialism. Socialism and capitalism were thought to be alike in the sense that both consolidate political and economic power: the former, big domineering socialist governments, and the latter, big domineering corporations and capitalists. The distributists criticized socialism because it undermines personal initiative and the personal and social goods that come from the ownership of property. The distributists pointed out that, ironically, capitalism does the same. In capitalism, money follows money. Economic power is amassed by a few who enlist the masses into their service through the payment of subsistence wages.

Today's global economy is not much different. In our world of information and high speed communication, various national and worldwide media are owned by a few conglomerates. We have access to pictures and video images across the world, but do we really see what the life of a poor farmer or factory laborer is like? In a world of free trade, of NAFTA and GATT, investment capital and corporate transactions are free to cross national borders, but labor is restricted and isolated. Capital markets are global, while poor laborers are seldom allowed to cross national borders. We Americans enjoy shirts and shoes at a good price because corporations can utilize the labor of the poor across the world.[21] Brand names have become identity markers: years ago labels moved from the tag inside the shirt to bold, large letters in front: Gap, Old Navy, Abercrombie and Fitch. Corporations have an identity and a relationship to us, but the labors are anonymous. I wear my Old Navy sweatshirt with little sense of who made it, how, or under what conditions. Indeed, mass production has virtually erased the laborers from view, even while we are wearing the things that they have made.

In response to this loss of the person in modern mass production, John Paul II has much to say.

> In the modern period, from the beginning of the industrial age, the Christian truth about work had to oppose the various trends of materialistic and economistic thought . . . [In] a one-sidely materialistic civilization . . . man is treated as an instrument of production, whereas he—he alone, independent of the work he does—ought to be treated as the effective subject of work and its true maker and creator. (*Laborum Exercens*, no. 7)

> One must denounce the existence of economic, financial, and social *mechanisms* which, although they are manipulated by people, often function almost automatically, thus accentuating the situation of wealth for some and poverty for the rest. These mechanisms, which are maneuvered directly or indirectly by the more developed countries, by their very functioning favor the interests of the people manipulating them. (*Sollicitudo Rei Socialis*, no. 16)

What Can We Do?

Fair Trade is a movement that has been growing for decades. The movement connects small farmers and craftspeople with consumers abroad. It gives a name and face to the laborer and bypasses corporate identity. The movement seeks to cultivate local economies and international trade. If you investigate the movement you will see that it follows John Paul II's idea of solidarity. It attempts to build markets between one local community and another; it develops a connection between persons along with the exchange of goods. The movement is small, and the products are limited; but the opportunities for common life are rich. The following are descriptions of the Fair Trade movement, one from a labeling (quality control) network and the other from Catholic Relief Services. Participation in the movement is worth discussing with our friends, neighbors, and parishes. Several families at St. Anthony Shrine Parish in Emmitsburg are just starting out with buying Fair Trade coffee. We want to go further, but it will be difficult. We might have to change how we live.

From Fair Trade Labeling Organizations International:

> Fair Trade is a trading partnership, based on dialogue, transparency and respect, that seeks greater equity in international trade. It contributes to sustainable development by offering better trading conditions to, and securing the rights of, disadvantaged producers and workers—especially in the South. Fair Trade organizations (backed by consumers) are actively engaged in supporting producers in awareness raising and in campaigning for changes in the rules and practices of conventional international trade.
>
> Fair Trade's strategic intent is:
> - Deliberately to work with marginalized producers and workers in order to help them move from a position of vulnerability to security and economic self-sufficiency.
> - To empower producers and workers as stakeholders in their own organizations.
> - Actively to play a wider role in the global arena to achieve greater equity in international trade.
>
> (www.fairtrade.net/about_fairtrade.html)

From Catholic Relief Services:

> The fair choice is the right choice. The daily decisions you make as a consumer can make a real, positive difference in the world. When you choose to buy fair trade products you are making a strong connection with hardworking, but impoverished workers around the world. Our CRS Fair Trade network guarantees fair wages to disadvantaged artisans, farmers and workers. It also provides the technical and financial assistance that poor people so desperately need but so rarely get in the conventional trading system. Team up with us. Buy fair trade products and you return human dignity to people just like you.
>
> (www.crsfairtrade.org)

10

Through the Needle's Eye

*The Catholic Worker Movement and the Challenge
of Voluntary Poverty*

KATHY DOW MAGNUS

Much of the church's concern for social justice centers on the question of how to reduce poverty and bring about a more just distribution of wealth among all peoples. In 1891 Pope Leo XIII spoke out for the rights of workers to receive a fair wage and to own private property. He insisted that employers have a responsibility to treat their workers with dignity.[1] Forty years later, Pope Pius XI criticized the social structures that promote poverty, arguing that the state must intervene to protect its people against the greed incited by capitalism. At the same time, he rejected communism and upheld the right to private property.[2] In 1967, however, Pope Paul VI urged that the right to private property be limited so that the disparity between rich and poor nations may be decreased, insisting that "the superfluous goods of wealthier nations ought to be placed at the disposal of poorer nations."[3]

In its quest for social justice, the church has aimed to promote the fair treatment of workers and it has sought to encourage a more equal distribution of goods, resources, and opportunities for wealth around the world; but it has never fundamentally called into question the basic right to own private property. This is not surprising, since hardly any of us can even begin to imagine what it might mean not to own anything. Before we learn to say our own names, we have mastered the art of possession and know how to insist that something is "mine." Indeed, we often identify so deeply with the things we own that to give up all of our possessions would mean to give up our very selves—our identity as we know it.

Yet there is a long-standing tradition in Christianity that does ask us to consider giving up our personal possessions. Indeed, we can easily trace this call to poverty back to the words of Jesus, as reported in the New Testament. When a rich young man asks Jesus what he should do to obtain eternal life, Jesus reminds him first of the great commandments. The young man replies that he keeps these commandments; yet he is vaguely aware that there is something he is still missing, "All these things I have kept; what am I still lacking?" he asks Jesus persistently. Jesus replies, "If you wish to be complete, go and sell your possessions and give to the poor, and you will have treasure in heaven; and come, follow Me" (Matt. 19:21). We are told that the man goes away very sad, for he had many possessions. Perhaps, we too feel sad and confused at hearing these words of Jesus. How can he possibly mean we are to give away all that we have? After the man leaves, Jesus emphasizes the point to his disciples, "Truly I say to you, it is hard for a rich man to enter the kingdom of heaven. Again I say to you, it is easier for a camel to go through the eye of a needle, than for a rich man to enter the kingdom of God" (Matt. 19:23–24).

Another translation of the same text cites Jesus as saying, "If thou wilst be perfect, go and sell your possessions. . . ." This might be a more comforting version of the text, if we come to understand and accept that we are imperfect. It seems that this task of entering into material poverty is not meant for everyone. (Whew! There is hope for me and you.) However, reference to the earlier Greek text and the linguistic context in which it was written shows that "perfection" was frequently understood in terms of completion. In Greek philosophy, for example, to be perfect is to be complete, to be fulfilled. So Jesus seems to be speaking to anyone who feels the dissatisfaction that is bound to come from a life that focuses on pursuing monetary security and material luxury. Such a life leaves us longing, leaves us incomplete. Like the young rich man who went away sad, we too may sense that material possessions alone cannot satisfy our true needs and desires and yet have trouble letting go of them. If we are wise, however, we can come to see periods of financial misfortune in our own lives as a gift from God and as an opportunity for spiritual growth. We can come to see periods of financial distress as God inviting us to let go of what stands in the way of our spiritual progress. During such periods it may be comforting to remember that Jesus calls us to a life of fulfillment that shuns the pursuit of material riches. This is a call that is easy to forget if we find ourselves in a period of financial prosperity. Yet it is precisely in those times of material abundance that we seem particularly obliged to ask questions. What exactly is it that hinders the rich man from passing through the gates of heaven? Why should we, imperfect as we are, still seriously consider the choice of voluntary poverty? In what ways might such a life be liberating? How might this kind of life lead to true happiness?

We may gain some insight into these questions if we consider that there are some very long-standing Catholic traditions that have espoused just this principle of voluntary poverty. The tradition goes back to Jesus and his disciples and continues in a number of the early church communities that held their possessions in common. It reappears throughout Christian history in numerous monastic clergies and religious societies whose members regularly take vows of poverty. But it also may be found among modern lay people. The Catholic Worker movement profoundly exemplifies this principle of voluntary poverty as it is practiced in contemporary society.

The Catholic Worker was founded by Dorothy Day, an American lay person, and Peter Maurin, a Frenchmen, in 1933. The organization was founded in order to promote social justice through nonviolent protests of injustice, the acceptance of voluntary poverty, and hospitality to the poor and dejected members of society. Today there are over 185 Catholic Worker homes, whose volunteers give the poor a place in their own communities and who actively protest all forms of violence and injustice. In this brief essay I would like to suggest that if we take a look at some of their practices, we may find insight into the paradoxical claim Jesus makes: that the rich, complete, abundant life is to be found in material poverty. By paying close attention to the words of the gospel and by seeing them embodied in the practices of the members of the Catholic Worker, we might come to a better understanding as to why some people—in this very day and age and in this highly consumerist society—make the voluntary choice to live in poverty.

In her autobiography, Dorothy Day tells the story of the great San Francisco earthquake she experienced as a child.[4] What impressed her more than anything else was the way that people came together to help each other in the time of desperation. What she learned from this experience was perhaps the true meaning of Jesus's words, "if you wish to be complete. . . ." The abundant life, she concludes, is found when one opens oneself up to the helpless. Ironically, our individual pursuits of economic security turn out to work against our ultimate happiness. True joy is found in a state of vulnerability that makes genuine community possible.

This belief served to found the Catholic Worker. The Catholic Worker volunteers quite literally opened their door to the poor. Visit the House of St. Joseph's on East First Street in New York City, for example, and you will find a host of talented, highly educated men and women, who not only devote themselves to feeding and clothing the poor, but who share their bedrooms and bathrooms with them. They do not have bedrooms and bathrooms of their own—these are open to the homeless, the drug addicted, the crippled, and the psychologically ill. In opening their community home to the poor, the workers open themselves up to the risks of dirt and disease. They give up the luxury of privacy and become truly vulnerable to the devastation of poverty. Yet they work tirelessly. Their work begins at the crack of dawn when they begin preparing the soup for over five hundred hungry visitors per day, and it continues through the night, as the tired, the cold, and the sick knock on their door. They have little to support themselves with besides the sale of the Catholic Worker newspaper (which still sells for a penny a copy) and outside donations. However, the volunteers speak of a joy and a peace that is not known to those of us who work for our own material luxury and who are caught in a never-ending search for just a little bit more.

What distinguishes the Catholic Worker from a number of other organizations that also aim to help the homeless and the hungry is that its members seek to live according to what the liberation theologians have called "a preferential option for the poor."[5] This entails two fundamental commitments. In the first place, Catholic Workers seek to identify with the poor. Though their relatively privileged backgrounds mark them as different from those they seek to help, the workers pledge to do more than give of their excess. They seek solidarity with the poor; that is, they seek to participate in the poor's experience of suffering.[6] This identification with them enables the volunteers to experience a genuine compassion with the other members of their community. Unlike the rich man who gives a small portion of his income to the poor, pats himself on the back and considers his duty done, those who truly identify with the poor do not indulge in self-congratulation. They run much less of a risk of becoming prideful as a result of all the "good" they are doing. Instead, they become humbled by the awareness of their own vulnerability and radical dependency upon God. They do not pity the poor; rather they suffer with them in their daily living. They do not look down upon those who are materially disadvantaged, but rather commit themselves to them in a way that makes a dignified relationship with them possible. Thus they enter into the experience of love in a most radical way. "The mystery of poverty," Dorothy Day explains, "is that by sharing in it, making ourselves poor in giving to others, we increase our knowledge and belief in love."[7]

The second major commitment involved in a preferential option for the poor entails becoming politically engaged in activities aimed at improving the situation of the poor and the disadvantaged. In this regard, the Catholic Worker movement advocates a range of nonviolent means of protesting the economic and social structures that promote violence and perpetuate poverty. Such actions include not paying taxes that fund wars, rejecting the military draft, setting up and participating in nonviolent strikes and protests, and holding vigils.[8] The workers also withdraw support from all organizations that promote social injustice, refusing, for example, to buy products from companies that do not pay their workers fair wages. As a result of such forms

of peaceful protest, many of the workers have suffered arrest and even im-
prisonment; but this does not discourage their commitment, for they see such
nonviolent means as the only hope for a more just society. Thus, while they
accept poverty for themselves, they also work to defeat the social conditions
that create poverty. Through such nonviolent practices, their solidarity with
the poor accrues a transformative mission.

Both of these commitments, which form the basis of the voluntary poverty
of the Catholic Worker (the identification with the poor and an active dedica-
tion to social justice), serve at the same time to promote a spirit of community.
Those who have taken on poverty voluntarily become strengthened in love and
compassion, and those who previously lacked food and shelter find their physical needs met in the context of a place they can truly call home. All members
are united through the sharing of their material needs and advantages and
in cooperating in the work that supports their community and advocates for
social change. Those who voluntarily enter into poverty, therefore, do not
seek poverty for its own sake; nor do they suffer with the poor for the sake of
suffering. They give up their possessions, not in order to go cold and hungry,
but in order to enter into a realm where the spiritual value of sharing becomes
the center of life, where one's own personal interests become identified with
the good of the whole community. In this kind of community, one shares
one's talents, one's ability to work, one's material advantages—one does not
possess them. The volunteers give up the right to call anything their own in
order to enter into a community of sharing, a community based upon the
radical love of Christ.

We already begin to see how such a life of voluntary poverty might be liberating. While most of us identify so closely with our possessions that we can
hardly even imagine giving them up, those who enter into voluntary poverty
become freed from the burdens of material possessions and find an identity
that embraces much, much more. They become liberated from a pursuit of
wealth that can never be satisfying. Because we are spiritual beings, material
goods can never fulfill our most important needs; they can never make us feel
complete. We might think that as soon as we own our own company, or have
our own house, or get the next new luxury car, we will be happy, but we find
that this happiness is short-lived and gives way to other desires. The more we
have, the more we want. We continue to feel something lacking and, if we
are caught up in the pursuit for money and material comfort, we assume that
what is lacking is of that order. We become blind to the real reason we feel
incomplete. Those who give up their possessions and the pursuit of material
wealth, however, escape from the bottomless pit of consumption. They begin
to see that all the money in the world cannot satisfy the hungry heart. They
no longer experience the constant desire for something more because they
have made room in their hearts for that which can truly satisfy—God. The
fact that they have given up the pointless race for material possessions makes

it possible for them to find themselves in the abundance of God's compassion and generosity. They lose the sense of themselves that was tied to what they owned and find themselves sharing in a greater, truer reality.

Is a share in this reality only possible for those who renounce all their possessions? Is such poverty the only way to true happiness? Does Jesus really demand this from all of us? We are told in the gospel that the disciples too were astounded by Jesus's call to poverty, and, aware that very few people would actually heed this call, they asked him, "'Then who can be saved?' Jesus said to them, 'With people this is impossible, but with God all things are possible'" (Matt. 19:25–26). Nothing is impossible with God; God can save even the rich person. Yet we remain cautioned: although not impossible for the rich person to get into heaven, it is extremely difficult. The passage remains obscure, for we are not told under what circumstances the rich person may be saved. We are left to conclude that our possessions are very apt to hinder us from entering into the most abundant life to which Jesus calls us. Why is it, then, that the rich man has so much trouble passing through the gates of heaven?

The ordinary middle-class citizen probably says to herself at this point, "This does not concern me; I am not rich." Strangely, instead of seeing all that we have, we see others who have more and call them rich. We forget the millions of people in the world who have less than we do, who would call us rich. What counts as rich seems to be wholly relative. (There are even millionaires who would not call themselves rich; from their perspective, they only have what they deserve while many others have much more.) But how, then, can Jesus's statement have any meaning at all? Who will admit to being rich? To whom is he speaking?

Here again, the philosophy of the Catholic Worker yields great insight. Striving to live out the works of mercy (Matt. 25:31–46), the Workers understand anything beyond what we immediately need as belonging to those in need. By this logic, any kind of material excess makes us rich enough that we should recognize Jesus as speaking to us when he refers to the camel trying to get through the needle's eye. Catholic Workers believe that we need to give of our excess "so that the poor can receive what is, in justice, theirs, the second coat in our closet, the spare room in our home, a place at our table."[9] The rich, then, are those who hold on to their possessions and refuse the experience of sharing with those in need, an experience that unites people together in God's love. Isolated in their own self-interest, they lose sight of others and of the greater purpose of life. It is a bit like a man who won't relinquish his luggage in order to get onto a plane. The door of the plane is narrow; it cannot fit all he wants to take, and there is no longer the option to check his luggage. If he refuses to leave his baggage behind, he loses sight of his own intention to take the trip. He holds himself back; he excludes himself from the happiness he thinks he is pursuing. He gets left behind, alone with his possessions.

The things he identifies with have become more important to him than the direction of his life.

As we have already seen, the members of the Catholic Worker who let go of their possessions open themselves up to the community at large and begin to experience the great depth of God's love. Conversely, then, when we hold fast to our possessions, we unknowingly set up divisions between ourselves and others and short-circuit the great mystery of love. We may even begin to see reality—including other people—in primarily material terms. (There are those who have nice cars and those who don't, those who live in the good area of town and those who live on the other side, etc.) Our possessions become our burdens when we try to move, grow, and stretch out to become something more than we are. They often hold us back and prevent us from developing in love with others. They give us ease and comfort, but they weigh down our souls and often keep us from the kind of action and interaction we really need. Like the computer game we can't get away from or the TV show we can't miss, they bind us and make us passive. Our souls become sluggish and reluctant to move beyond the immediate passing satisfactions the material world offers. As a result, we miss out on the more important and more joyful things of life. We are too distracted. The gates of heaven may be wide open for us, but we are too busy looking elsewhere—running through the mall or scanning the internet for just the right thing. We do not see the possibilities for greater joy that stand before us all the time. Sometimes we even make major life choices that set us on an entire course filled with nothing but distractions. For example, we may accept a financially rewarding job that demands our entire devotion. However, in performing such a job well, we may fail to attend to our own spiritual needs. We may fail to have any time for others. The depth and quality of our relationships suffer and we become isolated in our own monetary pursuit. Like mice on a treadmill, we become trapped in a self-propelled, endless circle, exhausting ourselves in an effort for a fulfillment we are not moving toward at all.

What this means, then, is that by excluding the needs of others from our consideration, we do injustice not only to them, but to ourselves as well. For this reason, we owe it to ourselves—and not just to the poor—to consider Jesus's call to poverty very seriously. If we do not find ourselves ready to make the kind of radical sacrifice Jesus recommends, and give away all of our possessions to the poor, we can still begin to take steps in this direction. By considering the example of the Catholic Worker, we can begin to see the meaning of Jesus's paradoxical claim that the fulfilled life is found not through material riches, but through a sharing of one's own possessions. The point is not to become poor for the sake of being poor, but rather to enter into a life of sharing, where the needs of others are as important as one's own needs. It is through such sharing that we can be freed from our own self-centered isolation and learn to recognize the greatness of God's love. It is through such sharing that we become aware of the ways in which the pursuit of material well-being often deters and distracts us from what is more important. It is through such sharing that we rise above the inertia of our material being and enter into a life of spiritual meaning and fulfillment.

So, if we are to take Jesus's words seriously, we need to make a commitment to examine our relationship to our possessions. We need to meditate on a whole series of questions. Do we identify ourselves so deeply with the things we possess that we cannot even imagine ourselves without them? Do we pride ourselves on status symbols and shun others who cannot fit the bill? Does our pursuit of material objects consume us and prevent us from participating in more enriching activities? Are we more concerned with having things than doing things? Does our concern for financial security lead us to make choices without considering the well-being of others? Do we spend more time pursuing material ease, comfort, and luxury than we do cultivating friendships and helping others in need? In short, do we possess our possessions, or do our possessions possess us?[10] Does our interest in having money shape and determine our lives? Do we fail to see any other values worth living for?

Surely, a certain amount of material means is necessary to sustain the human life that God created. But it makes all the difference how we relate to these material means. Do we live for them? Or do we put them to use for higher values? Jesus advises us to give away our possessions because he knows how they can distract and blind us to what is truly important and joyful in life. They can lull us into a comfort that is very deceiving. If we become rich, we are apt to gain a false sense of our own power and forget our fundamental need for God and for others. Jesus calls us to cultivate a kind of detachment from all the material resources that we have so that they may never become more important to us than our relationship to God and to others who stand in need of our help. Since this detachment is very difficult to cultivate as long as we have many possessions, we are best advised to give them away—or at least to begin to share them with those in need. Such sharing is what the church insists upon as well. In this sense the church seems to catch the spirit of Jesus's call, even though it does not demand that we all give up our personal possessions or our right to private property. What the church does demand is that we recognize the danger of greed running rampant in capitalistic societies, and that we seriously consider the needs of those who suffer from the poverty that is often produced as a direct result of our own material well-being. Those who have material excess must at least share with those who live in poverty.

Yet, if this turns out not to be enough for us, if we find ourselves still lacking, if we wish to be complete, we can still heed the more radical challenge of Jesus and enter into poverty ourselves. Naturally, as humans we fear the state of vulnerability we would find ourselves in if we really gave up all of our material security. However, according to Dorothy Day, it makes much more sense to put our trust in God than in our material possessions. As she teaches, only God can grant us real security and real fulfillment. Indeed, as she insists, if we surrender ourselves to God, he will provide for our material needs as well as our spiritual needs. It is "the natural law as well as the supernatural law,"[11] she proclaims. Throughout her life Dorothy Day witnessed this principle in action over and over again: God provides for our needs when we give ourselves over to Him. Echoing the words of one of her favorite priests, Father Roy, she retells a story that illustrates the point: "Suppose you want to go to California and it costs a hundred dollars. You have fifteen. It is not enough. So give it away, give it to the poor. Then you suddenly have twenty-five, and that is not enough and the only thing to do is give it away too. . . . You will get back one hundredfold. You will get what you need. Maybe it will come in graces. Maybe it will cover your spiritual needs, not just your physical. But sow, sow! As ye sow, so shall ye reap. He who sows sparingly, reaps sparingly."[12] Although our consumerist society teaches us to fear a state of financial weakness, Dorothy Day's life attests to the fact that it is actually and quite literally in giving to others that we receive. Through the act of sharing, material wealth often seems to multiply. Just as Jesus's sharing of the loaves of bread and fishes with the multitude led to a multiplication of resources until all were satisfied, our own sharing of our material means will lead to a life of abundance.

Discussion

Household Hospitality

Like Dorothy Day and Peter Maurin, Ivan Illich (1926–2002) worries that our bureaucratic institutions, conceptions of material progress, and our uncritical dependence on technology undermine personal relationships and responsibility. In an essay, "Hospitality and Pain," he outlines a shift from the medieval world to the modern West, when hospitality is institutionalized so that we, in the West, no longer welcome strangers. Illich retells a story told to him by Cardinal Jean Daniélou. "A Chinese friend of his, after becoming a Christian, made a pilgrimage from Peking to Rome on foot. In central Asia, he regularly found hospitality. As he got into the Slavonic nations, he was occasionally welcomed into someone's house. But when he arrived among the people of the western churches, he had to seek shelter in the poorhouses, since the doors of homes were closed to strangers and pilgrims."[13] I know that where I live we figure that some social service agency will do something for immigrants, travelers, and the needy. If Cardinal Daniélou's friend were to knock on our doors, we might call the police. At best, we would call the Department of Social Services and tell the traveler how to get there.

Our lives have become insular; we have trivialized the command to love our neighbors by working hard to live in places where our neighbors do not need any help. It is not likely that someone in need of shelter would manage to arrive in my suburban neighborhood. Ask any realtor: most of us are looking to live in homes and neighborhoods that provide protection from those in need. In her discussion of the Catholic Worker, Kathy Magnus notes that houses of hospitality are central to the vision of Peter Maurin and Dorothy Day. Faithful to this vision, Magnus describes the Catholic Worker's life of voluntary poverty and family-living with the poor, as well as the essential connection between this preferential option for the poor and following Christ.

Dorothy Day dares to ask ordinary Christian families to set aside a Christ room for taking in the homeless. She draws (like Illich) upon an ancient tradition: Christians in the Roman empire distinguished themselves by their love and hospitality.[14] The Christ room is an implied reference to Matthew 25:31–46. "Whatever you did for one of these least brothers of mine [the hungry, thirsty, ill-clothed, the stranger, and the imprisoned], you did for me" (25:40). This is Day's hope:

> When we succeed in persuading our readers to take the homeless into their homes, having a Christ room in the house as St. Jerome said, then we will be known as Christians because of the way we love one another. We should have hospices in all the poor parishes. We should have coffee lines to take care of the transients; we should have this help given sweetened by mutual forbearance and Christian charity. But we need more Christian homes where the poor are sheltered and cared for.[15]

You, like me, are likely to have objections. My wife and I have children to whom we have a responsibility to protect and nurture. Wouldn't we be irresponsible if we allowed strangers into our home? Wouldn't we be taking time and resources away from our children? Shouldn't we just work on being a family? Although the vision of the Catholic Worker is noble, it does not seem to be practical.

What Can We Do?

My objections above would probably frustrate Dorothy Day, as they are typical strategies of avoidance and inaction. Our best excuses for mediocrity tend to be our most noble aspirations.[16] Excuse #1: Yes, I would like to shelter the poor, but I have a greater duty to my children. Excuse #2: Yes, I do think that everything possible should be done for the needy, so I will call social services or a charitable organization because such agencies have everything that a person needs. I could only give a fraction of what could be given by professionals, so I am doing the person in need and my family a disservice by getting involved.

The first is the strategy of conflicting duties, and the second sets up a choice between all and nothing. In each we do nothing, but we can be happy with our good intentions and about the Catholic Workers and social workers because they give themselves to the poor.

Rather than inaction, we can overcome the all or nothing and conflicting duties strategies by taking small steps. First step: think about what we can do as an ordinary part of life. We tend to think about hospitality in terms of friendliness, but to offer another a place to stay does not mean that we will have to spend our days as companions in conversation. It means we are offering a bed and a meal. Because we no longer think about hospitality in terms of welcoming the stranger, our models for hospitality tend to be the dinner party and extended visits by relatives. On these occasions, our regular schedules (work, school, exercise, and so on) are put on hold. During most weekdays, my conversations with my wife tend to be functional: working out our schedules and raising our children. Such conversations are not enough for guests on holidays. But they are enough for someone to whom we are offering hospitality as a regular part of life. We are extending God's friendship, but we do not need to be friendly in a dinner-party sort of way. The first step is to think about how hospitality is a habit of life rather than a holiday.

Second step: set high standards. In her own dealings with the poor, Dorothy Day was well known for her high standards of good behavior. She was remarkably patient and compassionate toward those who were odd or deeply troubled. She would try to understand their gifts and help them understand how they could best contribute to the common work of the household. But she would not allow drunkenness, any threat of violence, or unruly behavior. Houses of hospitality have to be places of mutual care and peace, and to be truly hospitable we will have to ask some guests to leave, and in a few cases actually throw a person out of the house. To be hospitable a family will have to consider what it can do and for whom. If we have young children, we might show hospitality to someone who is elderly or sick, but we should not take in someone with a drinking problem.[17] We have to make tough choices. According to the all-or-nothing strategy, we don't want to reject anyone in particular, so we show hospitality only to our friends and family. We are so completely out of the habit of welcoming the stranger that we do not even consider whom we have the ability to welcome. The second step is to come in contact with enough people in need to be able to make good, practical choices about some little things that we can do.

Third step: think about how our houses would have to change to make hospitality practical. If we are going about our days as usual, we might be leaving a guest in the house alone, or the guest might get in the way of our household chores and duties. This worry is real. Do we give a stranger the run of the house? Doing so would be foolish and impractical. Again, we are back to the issue of friendliness. It is not unreasonable to ask a stranger to leave

the house when we leave and return when we return. But most of us would
think that it is rude, and in order to maintain proper friendliness we do not
befriend those in need. Ironic, isn't it? Ideally, we would structure our houses
so that a guest would not have direct access to the entire house—converting a
garage or basement into a Christ room. With such a space, we would be free
for a great deal of hospitality.

The fact of the matter is that when most of us move up in the world, we
buy houses that create greater distances between neighbors and have a greater
amount of space per person. We desire to have more unused space.[18] We
Christians should go in the opposite direction. When we have opportunity, we
should renovate our houses or buy new ones that give us greater opportunity
for hospitality. In doing so, our aspirations for following Christ would be
consistent with our aspirations for having a comfortable house. There is no
conflict of duties when we think about our homes, from the start, as places
where the stranger should have his or her own space, or when we think about
our houses as places that should provide the best, safest, and most frequent
opportunities to sit down for a meal with the stranger and the outcast. Imagine
how rich our lives would be. Imagine how close our families would be when
sharing common struggles of discipleship. Imagine how much our children
would learn about life and how to live without fear.

Easy Essays by Peter Maurin

Peter Maurin is famous for his easy essays, which he used to teach in the
streets and initiate conversation. The "Duty of Hospitality" and other easy
essays can be found at www.catholicworker.com/maurin.htm. When reading
the easy essay below, note that "Mahometan" is a term commonly used in the
early twentieth century for Muslim.

The Duty of Hospitality

People who are in need
and are not afraid to beg
give to people not in need
the occasion to do good
for goodness' sake.
Modern society calls the beggar
bum and panhandler
and gives him the bum's rush.
But the Greeks used to say
that people in need
are the ambassadors of the gods.
Although you may be called
bums and panhandlers

you are in fact the Ambassadors of God.
As God's Ambassadors
you should be given food,
clothing and shelter
by those who are able to give it.
Mahometan teachers tell us
that God commands hospitality,
and hospitality is still practiced
in Mahometan countries.
But the duty of hospitality
is neither taught nor practiced
in Christian countries.

PART FOUR

Moving Forward

11

The Challenge of Religious Liberty

RICHARD BUCK

Most democratic societies are characterized, in part, by religious pluralism: the existence of many different views about the nature of
G-d,[1] the afterlife, and the responsibilities each of us has to other human
beings and the natural world. In many cases, there are a few points of theological agreement among these traditions. For example, all Christians, Jews,
and Muslims believe that there is one G-d. However, there are clearly more
differences among these traditions than there are similarities. But in most
democratic societies, like the United States, Canada, and many countries
in Europe, South America, and Africa, the government does not compel its
citizens to affirm one religious faith, nor does it prohibit the public practice
of all but one faith. That is because there exists in these countries a legal right
to freedom of religion and religious worship. Assuming that one's religious
practices do not involve violations of the liberty of others, citizens in these
countries are free to believe and worship as they choose.

The legal guarantee of freedom of religion has led to a rich diversity of
religious practice in most democratic societies. Countries like the United States
and Great Britain embrace and support this diversity, rather than viewing it as
an unfortunate condition that should be overcome. It is not surprising, then,

that most of us take this freedom and the accompanying religious diversity for granted, but it raises interesting questions for Catholic theology. Specifically, the question is relevant whether the church should endorse a political system which guarantees by law the freedom of religious worship, because such freedom seems inconsistent with the view that the Catholic church is the one true church, and that, by extension, all other churches or faiths are at best approximations of the truth. The existence of a legal protection of freedom of religious worship seems to consciously make room for, if not implicitly to endorse the practice of, erroneous beliefs. The upshot of this is the fairly straightforward question: how can error have rights?[2]

Thesis and Hypothesis

Indeed, the church's position on the relationship between Catholicism and other faiths and, more importantly, on the relationship between church and state, was, up until the papacy of John XXIII, that error has no rights. The most important implication of this view, or thesis, was that the separation of church and state is untenable. If Catholicism is the one true faith, then it should be established as the state religion, and the state should be governed in accordance with the principles of the Catholic faith. But the political climate of the twentieth century was such that in most countries—especially those that guaranteed the freedom of religion—it was unlikely that Catholicism (or any other religion, for that matter) would ever be established as the state religion. In light of this, the church posited the hypothesis of Catholicism as the one true religion while also tolerating the separation of church and state and the right of non-Catholics to public practice and worship. This tolerance was required as a means to achieve the good of public peace. As such, religious tolerance is not a good in itself. Indeed, under some conditions (e.g., where religious pluralism does not exist), intolerance of other religions would be necessary to promote public peace.[3]

The thesis and hypothesis distinction has roots in *The Syllabus of Errors*, issued by Pope Pius IX in 1864. Of the many errors catalogued in this document, the most important for our purposes is what Pope Pius refers to as indifferentism, which claims that all religions are equally sound, and therefore there is no basis for the belief that Catholicism is the one true faith. If indifferentism is true, then religious intolerance is groundless and there is no rational basis for the establishment of a state religion. The thesis discussed above clearly endorses Pius IX's rejection of indifferentism. The hypothesis also holds, however, because as a practical matter the enforcement of one religion (and the legal intolerance of all others) would only lead to violence and bloodshed. Thus, the church made a concession to the existing political reality without compromising its core view that

Catholicism is the one true religion and there is no moral right to practice any other faith.

The Move toward Religious Freedom

Vatican II (1962–65) marked a significant change in the church's teaching on religious liberty. Indeed, the church focused on both maintaining its view that Catholicism was the one true faith, while at the same time promoting an openness and cooperation with other faiths—a view that was defended by some prominent Catholic theologians, among them the Jesuit John Courtney Murray. Rather than thinking of religious pluralism as a regrettable fact of contemporary social life, a condition rooted in the human failure to seek out and embrace the true faith, theologians like Murray viewed religious pluralism as a result of the natural development of human consciousness.[4] This development of human consciousness is the root of the modern demand for not only political freedom, but religious freedom as well. Furthermore, according to Murray both political and religious freedom are essential to the promotion of human flourishing. It is only when human beings are free that they can truly seek the truth and fully cultivate human talents.[5] For Murray then, political and personal freedom, as well as the religious freedom which personal freedom allows, are not simply contingent facts of the currently existing political reality. Such a view would be consistent with endorsing a different political reality in which Catholicism has been established as the state religion and there exists no freedom to affirm and practice any other faith. Indeed, this had been the view of the church since the time of Pius IX, and some of Murray's contemporaries continued to endorse this view. Rather, religious freedom is for Murray a "personal and political good," which means that religious freedom cannot be curtailed unless doing so was necessary to promote a more basic good, such as preserving public order and peace.[6]

As I have indicated, the view I described above and attributed to Murray marks a dramatic departure from the view held by the Catholic church until the middle part of the twentieth century. Thus, it would be important for Murray and those who supported this new view to show that religious freedom and a respect for religious pluralism are indeed consistent with fundamental principles of Catholic theology. Most importantly, it must be shown that identifying religious freedom as a human good does not compromise the belief that Catholicism is indeed the one true faith.

Religious Liberty, Human Dignity, and Revelation

Dignitatis Humanae, Vatican II's *Declaration on Religious Freedom*, promulgated in 1965, explains and defends religious liberty as a good of the person and political society that is rooted in and, therefore, fully consistent with the tenets of Catholicism.[7] But the *Declaration* also presents a defense of religious liberty rooted in the idea of human dignity. Dignity is often understood to mean an essential characteristic (or set of essential characteristics) that distinguishes us from nonhuman animals, which in other respects may be similar to us. The characteristic that is most relevant to religious liberty is the ability to make important choices throughout our lives. These choices range over many different aspects of our experience, and therefore require that we be free to live the kinds of lives we choose, so long as the choices we make are consistent with the same freedom for others. Naturally, the freedom to believe or affirm the religious beliefs of one's choice is the freedom of choice most relevant for religious liberty. In light of the church's position that Catholicism is the only true faith, it would appear to be very difficult to defend the choice to reject the Catholic faith. But if we look carefully at what it means to believe in a particular religion (what might be called an act of faith) we will see that the church can consistently defend religious liberty even if this entails the liberty to believe that the claims of Catholicism are false. The nature of the act of believing is such that a person cannot be forced to believe anything. While it certainly is possible to coerce someone into commission of a certain religious act—such as attending a religious service or even uttering a specific prayer or statement of allegiance—it is simply impossible to coerce a person into believing anything.[8] Authentic belief is always the result of a free choice. Religious freedom can, therefore, be properly understood as rooted in the very nature of human beings as beings with free will.

But our freedom to choose is bound by certain obligations. We see this, for example, in the civil laws that exist, even in those societies where there is extensive personal and political freedom. The existence of these laws, which restrict the choices we can make in our daily lives, is consistent with political freedom, because the very nature of a political society includes the idea of laws that place limits on the actions we can commit. Catholicism holds that the same is true for human beings: the nature of what it means to be human living in a world ordered by divine law suggests that we have certain moral obligations with regard to what we believe. In the *Declaration*, this is presented as a moral obligation to seek the truth, especially in religious matters.[9] So while human beings are free to affirm and act according to the religious view of their choice, they are morally obligated to seek knowledge of G-d through the Catholic church. But like all moral obligations, the obligation to seek the truth in religious matters cannot be satisfied except through an unforced affirmation of religious truth.

What the preceding discussion shows is that religious liberty, which is typically viewed as a freedom rooted in the constitutional history of particular nations, can also be viewed as a freedom that is tied to the very nature of human beings living in a world ordered by G-d. And such a freedom is consistent with Catholic theology, because it does not undermine the moral obligation which is binding on all persons to seek out and affirm the one true faith. And it is not only personal or individual religious liberty that can be supported this way. This liberty entails a parental right to provide a religious education to one's children. Support for this right falls to the civil government, which must make such opportunities reasonably available to parents and ensure that they are not forced to subject their children to instruction that is opposed to their religious beliefs. Freedom of religion also includes the right of religious groups to organize formally and promulgate their faith among their adherents, and even to those outside their religious community, so long as there is no attempt at coercive persuasion.[10]

What is perhaps most crucial to the grounding of religious liberty in human dignity is the idea that belief, and more important, the act of faith cannot be coerced. The notion that the act of faith must be free is essential in showing that religious liberty is grounded in divine revelation. Indeed, the gospel accounts of the life of Jesus and how he ministered to his disciples provide clear evidence that religious liberty is fully in accord with the nature of faith and the will of G-d. For example, while Jesus did criticize those who did not believe in G-d, he did not believe it was his or any other human being's role to compel religious faith. Rather, conversion was to be encouraged through the use of prayer and the power of G-d's word.[11] Any attempt at forced conversion was unworthy of the gospel, since the use of force would imply that the word of G-d and the ministry of Jesus were, by themselves, incapable of moving people to accept the sovereignty of G-d and the saving power of his son, Jesus Christ. To violate this freedom would be tantamount to rejecting the sacred liberty which was endowed to the church through the crucifixion of Jesus Christ.

Furthermore, the very aim of the church—the salvation of human beings—would be impossible in the absence of religious liberty. In defending religious liberty then, the church is actually furthering its own divine mission in the world. To be sure, the chief part of this mission is to spread the gospel throughout the world, and at first glance one might think that this mission would only be frustrated by the spread of religious freedom and the growth of the religious pluralism such freedom allows. But such a view overlooks the fact that the message of the gospel cannot be divorced from the manner in which the gospel is offered to the nations of the world. Religious liberty ensures that the love and respect for human beings that, it can be argued, is the core of the message of the gospel, are not violated in an attempt to compel adherence to its edicts.

Citizenship, Pluralism, and Religious Faith

Although I have only mentioned it briefly at this point, an important component of the church's position on religious freedom is the role of the state or civil government in ensuring not only that religious liberty is protected, but that opportunities exist for citizens to live meaningful religious lives. An extension of this idea is that citizens should be able to live and participate in the public life of their societies without hiding their religious identity or religious beliefs. For example, a person should not have to hide the fact that she is Roman Catholic in order to gain admission to a university or compete for a job. If a person's educational and employment opportunities could be affected by her religious identity, then in an important sense her religious freedom is restricted, since she is not able to live her faith commitments publicly without fear of discrimination.

To be sure, the examples I have just mentioned are not very controversial in contemporary democratic societies, though this has not always been the case. With few exceptions, religious discrimination in employment and education has all but disappeared. But there are other areas of public life in which the inclusion of religious beliefs and practices seems much more problematic. For example, in the United States there is still much resistance to bringing religious argument into the political arena. This is due, in part, to the legacy of a certain way of understanding the establishment clause of the First Amendment to the U.S. Constitution. An example of this resistance is the amount of attention given to the religious beliefs of candidates for elected office. Although these candidates often make frequent reference to their religious convictions during the course of an election—because they think that doing so will win them support among some segments of society—there is often great concern about electing a person who is a devout follower of any faith. One well-known example of this was the candidacy of John F. Kennedy, the first and only Catholic president of the United States. Many Americans were concerned that if elected, Kennedy would feel obligated to consult with the Vatican before making important domestic and foreign policy decisions. Such close involvement of the Catholic church, or any religious authority, was thought to be inconsistent with the First Amendment and a threat to religious liberty. Such worries persist today, even as an increasing number of candidates for elected office make their religious commitments an important part of their political platform.

All of this raises an important question: what role, if any, should a person's religious beliefs play in his or her political activity? As citizens we all have an obligation to participate to some extent in the political life of our societies. Should our religious convictions inform our political participation, whether in casting votes or, as an elected official, in drafting legislation that will be binding on all citizens? One might argue that it is inappropriate to bring our religious beliefs into political activity, since not all those who are affected by this activity will share those beliefs. On the other hand, how can a committed Catholic, for example, be expected to leave her religious beliefs out of her political deliberations, at whatever level of political activity?

The United States Conference of Catholic Bishops has published a document on political participation and responsibility that addresses some of these questions. The aim of this document, entitled *Faithful Citizenship: A Call to Political Responsibility* (2003), is to show that principles of Catholic theology should be brought into political life, and that this can be done in a way that is in keeping with religious freedom and a pluralistic society. According to the bishops, faithful citizenship requires that Catholics "see civic and political responsibilities through the eyes of faith and [bring] their moral convictions to public life."[12] Put simply, it is a Catholic citizen's responsibility not only to rely, when appropriate, on elements of Catholic doctrine to inform her political judgments, but also to do so even in the course of public debate with those who would not affirm the same doctrinal commitments. Given the fact that many public issues have moral dimensions, it would be impossible to engage in a serious consideration of these issues, privately or publicly, without bringing one's religious convictions to bear. Leaving aside one's religious convictions would therefore make meaningful political participation impossible and this would, according to the bishops, have grave theological repercussions. Political participation is essential to fulfilling Jesus's call for people to love one another and, in particular, to devote special attention to the poor, needy, and the otherwise vulnerable. This is part of the call to care for the common good, to build a culture of life. Thus, "responsible citizenship is a virtue and political participation a moral obligation."[13] But proper attunement to the issues most pertinent to fulfilling this call is virtually impossible without the guidance of the scriptures and religious doctrine.

In response to concerns about the effect of doctrinal commitments in the public square, the bishops contend that bringing one's faith into public political dialogue actually enhances, rather than threatens, pluralism, since it allows religiously committed citizens to bring their unique perspectives—perspectives which are almost always countercultural—into the public circle. But this can only happen when, in keeping with the position taken in *Declaration on Religious Liberty*, there is no attempt to impose sectarian doctrine.

The bishops have continued the argument of *Faithful Citizenship* in *Forming Consciences for Faithful Citizenship*, which was published in the fall of 2007 (see the discussion following chapter 6).[14] Here the bishops contend that the introduction of faith commitments into political life illuminates political discussion by "[helping] us to see more clearly the same truths that also come to us through the gift of human reason," thereby affirming our fundamental nature as beings capable of recognizing the deliverances of faith and reason.[15] Encouraging citizens to keep their faith commitments out of public life would, therefore, only diminish pluralism, since it would keep many citizens from a full and meaningful engagement in public life.

The church's position on religious liberty has changed dramatically in the last fifty years. As articulated in *Dignitatus Humanae* and in recent statements from the United States Council of Catholic Bishops, the defense of religious liberty clearly affirms core political values of contemporary democratic societies. But what is most important about the church's position is that it takes as its departure point fundamental truths about the nature of human beings.

Discussion

Violence and Truth

A central theme in Richard Buck's chapter on religious liberty is the relationship between freedom and the pursuit of truth. This connection between freedom and truth is a constant concern in the writings of John Paul II, who lived for many years under communist rule. The oppressive forces of totalitarian governments are clearly of concern in his World Day of Peace message in 1980. In "Truth, the Power of Peace," John Paul II makes a connection between "non-truth" and violence. He offers two examples.

> [One form of non-truth is] the practice of combating or silencing those who do not share the same views by labeling them as enemies, attributing to them hostile intentions and using skillful and constant propaganda to brand them as aggressors. . . . Another form of non-truth consists in refusing to recognize and respect the objectively legitimate and inalienable rights of those who refuse to accept a particular ideology, or who appeal to freedom of thought.[16]

Here the pope is unequivocal. Freedom of thought is essential to truth.

When speaking to the Western world, John Paul II maintains the same relationship of freedom and truth, but his concerns are different. Compare this quotation from *Centesimus Annus*, issued in 1991 (after the fall of the Soviet Union). The passage is from a section where John Paul II is referring to Pope Leo XIII and the tradition of Catholic social teaching:

> Particular mention must be made of the Encyclical *Libertas praestantissimum*, which called attention to the essential bond between human freedom and truth, so that freedom which refused to be bound to the truth would fall into arbitrariness and end up submitting itself to the vilest of passions, to the point of self-destruction. Indeed, what is the origin of all the evils to which *Rerum novarum* [*On the Condition of Labor*] wished to respond, if not a kind of freedom which, in the area of economic and social activity, cuts itself off from the truth about man?[17]

In sum, John Paul II approaches the relationship of freedom and truth from two different directions. Those who suppress freedom perpetuate lies and violence. Those who claim freedom as a right to reject questions of truth threaten to undermine the common good (the good we human beings share in common) and in so doing perpetuate non-truth as well. To make sense of these claims, one need only think of our freedom to fall into bad habits in, say, public speaking or musical performance. By claiming that we can speak, carry ourselves, project our voice, or hold an instrument however we want, we are limiting our freedom to communicate. When we are accountable to standards outside of ourselves (to common standards of communication and performance), we are likely to become freer to communicate, create, and share talents and ideas. In this sense, true freedom accords with the fulfillment of our capacities as human beings for common life. It is on this very point that the faith communities of the world find common cause. We share a commitment to truth. Even though we disagree on matters of truth, we share a rejection of the kind of freedom that perpetuates indifference and excludes questions about our common good as human beings.

In *Sollicitudo rei socialis* (*On Social Concern*, 1987), John Paul explains the point.

> The obligation to commit oneself to the development of peoples is . . . an im-
> perative which obliges each and every man and woman, as well as societies and
> nations. In particular, it obliges the Catholic Church and the other Churches
> and Ecclesial Communities, with which we are completely willing to collaborate
> in this field. In this sense, just as we Catholics invite our Christian brethren
> to share in our initiatives, so too we declare that we are ready to collaborate
> in theirs, and we welcome the invitations presented to us. In this pursuit of
> integral human development we can also do much with the members of other
> religions, as in fact is being done in various places. . . . Peoples or nations too
> have a right to their own full development, which while including—as already
> said—the economic and social aspects, should also include individual cultural
> identity and openness to the transcendent. Not even the need for development
> can be used as an excuse for imposing on others one's own way of life or own
> religious belief.[18]

Many people find these claims about truth, cooperation, and peace to be counterfactual. Isn't it the case that religions turn to violence precisely because they are committed to the truth? Certainly, religious violence is often covered in the news, and it is undeniable that some people seek religious justification for violence, but we should be careful with our arguments here. Usually we are letting a small but newsworthy minority speak for all. It is one thing to admit that some Christians, Jews, or Muslims seek religious justification for violence. It is an entirely different matter to claim that being Christian, Jewish, or Muslim inclines or requires one to be violent. The question for any faith is whether or not those who turn to violence are being consistent with their commitments to the truth. Each faith community has to work out these questions in terms of its theological traditions, sacred texts, and practices of worship.

In this volume, it is appropriate to consider how the Catholic church considers the issue of truth and violence as a theological question. Pope Benedict XVI, for instance, sees religious violence as a fundamental concern for our time. In a homily on September, 10, 2006, he uses the lectionary readings for the day, the healing of a man born deaf and mute (Mark 7:24–37) to propose that, in our concerns for justice, we need G-d's healing grace to open our ears and eyes. To those gathered for the Mass, he says this:

> Social issues and the Gospel are inseparable. When we bring people only knowledge, ability, technical competence and tools, we bring them too little. All too quickly the mechanisms of violence take over: the capacity to destroy and to kill becomes dominant, becomes the way to gain power—a power which at some point should bring law, but which will never be able to do so. Reconciliation, and a shared commitment to justice and love, recede into the distance.[19]

Benedict's claim about the gospel and peace is based on faith in Jesus Christ.[20]

> The world needs [G-d]. We need [G-d]. But what [G-d] do we need? In the first reading, the prophet tells a people suffering oppression that: 'He will come with vengeance' (Is. 35:4). We can easily suppose how the people imagined that vengeance. But the prophet himself goes on to reveal what it really is: the healing goodness of [G-d]. And the definitive explanation of the prophet's word is to be found in the one who died for us on the Cross: in Jesus, the Son of [G-d] incarnate, who here looks at us so closely. His 'vengeance' is the Cross: a 'No' to violence and a 'love to the end'. This is the [G-d] we need. We do not fail to show respect for other religions and cultures, we do not fail to show profound respect for their faith, when we proclaim clearly and uncompromisingly the [G-d] who has countered violence with his own suffering; who in the face of the power of evil exalts his mercy, in order that evil may be limited and overcome.[21]

What Can We Do?

John Paul II and Benedict XVI offer a striking claim. In terms of the Christian faith the problem with violence, injustice, and indifference to others is not caused by too much faith but too little. The truth of G-d's self-giving in Jesus Christ is a no to violence and love to the end—all the way to the cross. Our response, then, to Dr. Buck's chapter on religious liberty and the Catholic tradition should be a greater openness to discussions with other Christians, Jews, Muslims, Buddhists, and others about the truth of their faiths and our faith. It is interesting to note that the Catholic church (in the documents of Vatican II, for example) does not have, strictly speaking, a concept of religion. In the *Declaration on the Relation of the Church to Non-Christian Religions*, it is assumed that Catholics will share commonalities and differences with Hinduism, Buddhism, Islam, and Judaism in different sorts of ways.[22] Catholics do not have a relationship to other religions, but do have relationships with Jews, Zen Buddists, or Muslims. For example, John Paul II has made it a theme of his papacy to show the deep connections between Catholics and Jews. Benedict XVI, for his part, has raised difficult questions in relationship to violence and Islam. The response of the Islamic community has been to clarify for us what the Quran has to say about peace.

From a popular viewpoint, these conversations are dangerous. The popular view is that all religions are the same, and it is bad manners to talk about one's faith in terms of truth. But perhaps this concept of religion is a barrier that actually perpetuates a shallow understanding and misunderstandings of Judaism, Christianity, Islam, Buddhism, the faiths of India, and other parts of the world. The fear that difference may lead to violence is likely to lead to the indifference and misunderstandings that help perpetuate violence. Perhaps by facing up to our differences without fear, and in a peaceable way, we will also bring our common passion for truth, commitments to justice, and common love for the world. As John Paul II says in *Sollicitudo rei socialis*, it is in the "pursuit of integral human development" that we (Catholics) are obliged to join with other faiths. Of course, in doing so we risk failure. We Catholics will inevitably do or say the wrong thing. But rather than mounting the battlements for the sake of truth, we will have to join the saints in suffering and taking up the cross as the way of truth we confess through our faith in Jesus Christ. This way, according to John Paul II and Benedict XVI, requires us to witness to our faith, to seek greater understanding of other faiths, and to join with them in service to the world.

We will end with some examples. The United States Conference of Catholic Bishops has a standing committee (since 1968) on ecumenical and religious affairs. Within the subcommittee on interreligious dialogue, there is an ongoing consultation (since 1987) with the National Council of Synagogues. The consultation has accomplished a considerable amount of collaborative work:

- on the need for moral education in public schools;[23]
- on a critique of pornography and "the so-called 'ethic' of immediate sexual gratification [that is] fundamentally opposed to integral human growth and fulfillment;"[24]
- on a statement against those who deny the Holocaust;[25]
- on joint efforts to abolish the death penalty in the United States;[26]
- on common concerns about the environment and the effect of pollution and waste on the vulnerable in our society;[27]

• and on a common condemnation of anti-Semitism, hate crimes, and
  religious violence.[28]

We ought to take these efforts by Catholic and Jewish leaders as examples to
follow. Where we live and work, we are called to join with people of other faiths
and, in the words of John Paul II, to pursue "integral human development."

12

Compassion and Hospitality

TRUDY CONWAY

During the Nazi occupation of France, the people of the village of Le Chambon responded in a distinctive way to injustice and human suffering. They believed their Christian way of living called for a compassionate response to all persons who suffer, especially those who were not members of their own local faith community. At grave risk to themselves, the Chambonnais opened their homes to Holocaust refugees, not only taking in, but also welcoming, approximately five thousand strangers who were saved through their courageous efforts. While most accounts of the Chambonnais focus on their legendary acts of compassion, another distinctive virtue of this community merits consideration. Because of their respect for and love of God's people, they responded compassionately to the suffering of refugees and were called to acts of hospitality. The Chambonnais' actions are worth noting, for they exemplify what is required by hospitality, a virtue needed not only in dramatic circumstances in which strangers are at grave risk, but in the everyday interactions of persons within local communities. The Chambonnais provide a way of understanding how we might move from passive tolerance of others to a hospitable encountering of them that promotes both human well-being and the pursuit of truth.

The Compassionate Response of the Chambonnais to the At-Risk Other

The Le Chambon narrative offers a powerful account of the compassionate response to the suffering of other persons. According to the philosophical accounts of Aristotle, Rousseau, and Adam Smith on compassion, this basic social emotion is rooted in a triggering of a "fellow feeling," tied to both our recognition of the suffering of others and our judgment that our own life is also vulnerably open to the possibility of misfortune and suffering. Through the compassionate response, we feel the pain of the other, be it of family members, neighbors, distant strangers, and even enemies. Because of their own Huguenot history of persecution, the Chambonnais identified powerfully with the plight of the Jewish refugees arriving on their doorsteps. Because of this shared experience, they were able to enter imaginatively into their suffering. Compassion entails one's perceiving of the other's situation and being able to empathetically put oneself into the other's situation and envision his or her suffering.

Compassion connects persons to each other, allowing for the intermeshing of their lives. As Martha Nussbaum states, "It is conceived of as our species' way of hooking the interests of others to our own personal goods."[1] Herein I perceive the refugees' distress, uprootedness, loss of shelter and support, and affirm basic goods which would alleviate their condition. In doing so I recognize the other's good as my good. Aristotle argues that the powerful emotional response of compassion is deeply rooted in the basic awareness that, as a human subject, I am similarly at risk of suffering. The compassionate response of the Chambonnais to the plight of the refugee is rooted in their fundamental ability to recognize and respond to basic human needs, no matter how distant be the stranger at their doorstep. Compassion arises from the realization of a shared humanity, the recognition that we are all vulnerable beings dependent for our well-being on circumstances not fully under our control.

But the compassionate acts of the Chambonnais were deeply rooted in their understanding of their Christian vocation. *Justice in the World*, the 1971 publication of the World Synod of Catholic Bishops, and *Gaudium et Spes*, the 1965 Vatican II document, speak to this vocation. "Listening to the cry of those who suffer violence and are oppressed by unjust systems and structures, and hearing the appeal of a world that . . . contradicts the plan of its Creator," Christians are called both to see injustice and "to give authentic witness on behalf of justice."[2] Such Christian faith "needs to prove its fruitfulness by penetrating the believer's entire life . . . and by activating him toward justice and love, especially regarding the needy."[3] *Gaudium et Spes*, the *Pastoral Constitution on the Church in the Modern World*, emphasizes that "every social group must take account of the needs and legitimate aspirations of other groups, and even of the general welfare of the entire human family" (no. 26). The Chambonnais recognized that this entails a special obligation that "binds us to make ourselves the neighbor of every person without exception, and of actively helping him when he comes across our path" (*Gaudium*, no. 27). They also recognized that "this respect and love ought to be extended also to those who think or act differently than we do in social, political and even religious matters. In fact the more deeply we come to understand the ways of thinking through courtesy and love, the more easily will we be able to enter into dialogue with them" (*Gaudium*, no. 28). Because of the compassionate response of the Chambonnais, they were called to acts of hospitality, to the welcoming of strangers into their homes, captured in Madga Trocmé's "abrupt, ungrudging, raucous command issued through a wide-open door: 'Naturally, come in, and come in.'"[4]

The Hospitable Response of the Chambonnais to the Other

The compassionate response of the Chambonnais is highly commendable and explains the powerful effect of their story on listeners. But equally compelling are the details of their hospitable response. According to specifics developed in Philip Hallie's book, *Lest Innocent Blood Be Shed*, Pierre Sauvage's documentary *Weapons of the Spirit* (which chronicles his own experience as one of the harbored refugees), and discussions with members of the Chambonnais community, the hospitable response of the Chambonnais had the distinctive feature of affirming a human commonality expressed in difference. The Chambonnais recognized the refugees' suffering and welcomed them into their homes as fellow persons, sharing with them the meager goods they could manage in such trying times. At the same time, the Chambonnais were a people with a distinct, deeply rooted identity as French Huguenot Christians, members of a close-knit local religious community with deep faith commitments lived in distinctive practices. And yet the Chambonnais welcomed non-Christian foreigners into their homes, putting themselves at grave personal risk.

What comes across powerfully in the Le Chambon narratives is their welcoming of these refugees in a way that did not require them to abandon their own identity, beliefs, and practices. Their interaction with the refugees was powerfully characterized by a mutual respecting of other persons. Although their compassionate response was rooted in an awareness of a shared humanity traceable to a creator, their hospitable response clearly was affected by a recognition of irreducible difference. Because of this recognition they were able to offer hospitality to those who were different from themselves, respectfully acknowledging their variant convictions, beliefs, and practices. Rather than simply tolerating their guests' differences, they respected them, welcoming these non-Christians into their community, encouraging them to live as practicing Jews. They sought opportunities for interactions and advances in mutual understanding of their respective traditions, the meaning contexts of their belief and activity. In being hospitable they welcomed the refugees into their own homes, where daily ways were shaped by a specific tradition of belief and practice. They expected the refugees to honor the ways of their homes, while at the same time seeking to make these refugees feel at home, such that they could live their beliefs and practices in these strangers' homes. Andre Trocmé, the pastor of Le Chambon, was adamant that his parishioners not attempt to convert the refugees to their own strongly felt and lived convictions in such circumstances. The refugees had to be welcomed and respected as persons with robust identities and defining commitments. Interviews with refugees, decades after their stay in Le Chambon, reveal the power of this hospitable response. They describe welcoming invitations to Jews to attend Christian religious services and supportive efforts to ensure that these Jews could maintain their own religious rituals and daily practices. They realized what Pope Benedict XVI stresses, that "the accepting of hospitality is not just restricted to eating and drinking . . . but includes what is most precious to our neighbors: prayer and worship."[5] The Chambonnais sought to open a space within their community for the life of these committed Jews. The power of the Le Chambon story rests in these villagers' ability to recognize and affirm a common humanity expressed in difference.

Perhaps we can learn much from the hospitality of these people; perhaps their narrative offers us a model for interactions in multicultural and multi-religious communities. In recognizing and respecting other persons we must recognize and respect them both as human persons who share a common humanity with us, and as persons with robust, particular identities—as German Jews, French Huguenots, Iranian Muslims, Mexican Catholics, and so on. Elaine Scarry writes of the need for "generous imaginings" which enable us to interact with strangers, foreigners who are different from us.[6] In encountering such an "other," I recognize him or her to be another person who shares with me basic human needs, desires, and goals. I generously recognize our commonality and our need for circumstances of prosperity—external goods that promote human flourishing. I also recognize that these human needs, desires, and goals are addressed and pursued in the context of differing ways of being human. I recognize that I and the other were born into communities defined by distinctive beliefs, commitments, practices, and institutions that are passed down and sustained in the form of enduring traditions.

From Tolerance to Hospitality

The hospitable response of the Chambonnais may provide insight into what may be required in everyday contexts of diversity. Contemporary life is to a great extent distinguished by a recognition of diverse, pluralistic traditions and beliefs. Postmodern society is defined by both its recognition of diversity

and preoccupation with critiquing attempts to exclude, reduce, or conceal—
that is, to diminish—diversity, plurality, and difference. Recognizing that not
all beliefs, claims, and values can be harmoniously reconciled, pluralism gives
rise to a consideration of tolerance. Lack of unanimity creates conditions in
which tolerance becomes possible; we find ourselves at odds with the other, yet
refrain from interference in or suppression of such difference. But too often this
celebration of pluralism is characterized by a spirit of open-mindedness extol-
ling the virtue of tolerance. Yet at the same time, it appears to be grounded in
the acceptance of the groundlessness of all beliefs and claims. We are called to
respect the diversity of traditions, but only through recognizing their equally
contingent status free of justification. Herein the other's stand is recognized,
but only as equally arbitrary as one's own. One can neither justify one's own
stand nor provide reasons for convincing the other to embrace this stand.
With such an account, there is no motive for taking the other seriously, or even
oneself, for that matter. It seems the basis for such tolerance is diminished
esteem for one's own convictions and commitments. Rather than increasing
respect for other convictions, one's own and the other's are diminished in
esteem, and all becomes leveled out. Realizing the pernicious aspects of this
contemporary tendency, *Gaudium et Spes* rightly calls us to recognize that
respect for and goodwill toward the other "must in no way render us indifferent to truth and goodness" (no. 28).

Such tolerance produces an indifference toward the other. This spirit of
tolerance delivers a single universal appeal, namely, that we accept pluralism,
simply acknowledging its existence and the suffering caused by severe intolerance. Such a minimalistic account requires that we live and let live, removing
all impediments to and interference in another's way of life. We put up with
others so long as they do not disrupt our own way of life. Persons are left alone
to pursue their own differing ways. Tolerance offers no reason for attending to
the other, taking the other seriously, or welcoming the other into our community. Such tolerance is at best a negative, passive virtue that leads to a detached
indifference, providing no motivation for seeking exchange, dialogue, or the
open conversation enabled by the response of hospitality. Transformed into
mutual indifference, tolerance leaves us merely affirming pluralism, without
attempting any active engagement of our differences.

The people of Le Chambon provide a way of understanding how we might
move beyond tolerance to hospitality. They model a way of encountering the
other that is rooted in both the respecting of persons and the seeking of what
is good and true, goals central to liberal-arts learning. Such learning encourages an awareness of the embeddedness of the human subject in a tradition
among other traditions. All human understanding takes off from inherited
ways of making sense of this human world. These inherited judgments, which
form the scaffolding of one's thought, shape one's understanding of oneself
and the world. Without them there would be no understanding. All inquiry

takes off from a view of the world that shapes what can be taken seriously and affirmed. Such confidence and commitment to a tradition should not be mistaken for an arrogance that unreasonably presumes the exclusive superiority of one's tradition over all others. Rather, one stands confidently committed to the truth of the tradition into which one has been initiated and which shapes one's life.

Once one recognizes the centrality of beliefs, claims, and practices to the shared life of one's own community and tradition, one must reasonably extend such recognition to other communities and traditions. One may find oneself far from agreeing with, appreciating, or even outright disapproving of alien beliefs and practices. And yet from such a distance one may still acknowledge their centrality within the alien tradition. Tolerance is herein rooted in due respect for persons and traditions in their very diversity. But rather than resting with the mere respectful acknowledgement of such diversity, one is drawn toward engagement rather than disengagement, toward dialogue rather than indifference. Herein one seeks to understand the other, to reasonably explore differences, to engage in a dialogue defined by a distinctive spirit of hospitality. Such dialogue is taken seriously and sustained on the basis of respect for persons and the hope that such dialogue may further the disclosing of truth.

Such hospitable dialogue places demands on persons. Attending to the other requires that we mutually open ourselves to each other's claims in their very alterity. Such dialogue demands more than minimal recognition of the other, and becomes possible only if we practice a cluster of hermeneutic virtues: an openmindedness requiring that we be receptive to the disclosure of the other, seeking to understand and do justice to what is disclosed; an imaginative empathy allowing us to conceive of others in their differences; and a courage which allows us to reflectively examine judgments and beliefs. Rather than being preoccupied with discrediting the other or winning a debate, we seek to understand the other. The philosopher Hans-Georg Gadamer stresses that in such encounters the other's ideas may "become intelligible without our having to agree with them."[7]

Such dialogue is worthwhile on a number of levels. Encountering the other leads one to articulate and examine the tradition to which one belongs, thus encouraging self-understanding and a more reflective participation in that tradition. Encountering the other puts our fundamental beliefs into words and prevents us from lapsing into thoughtless conformity. Dialogue discloses our fundamental judgments, bringing us to reflect on our central truth claims and convictions. Dialogue also allows for the disclosure of the other's beliefs and judgments. Hospitality opens the possibility that we mutually attend to each other's claims, explicate our judgments, discover insight and oversights, agreements and disagreements, and disclose what was previously unseen. Hospitality opens the space of such dialogue. It requires mutual recognition of both commonality and difference. Without such commonality grounded in a shared humanity, there is no possibility of dialogue. Without significant difference, there is no compelling need for such dialogue. For dialogue to commence, the other must be recognized in both sameness and difference. For the dialogue to continue, the participants must neither rest content with the mere voicing of difference nor cancel differences in order to promote an artificial unanimity. Dialogue entails working to mutual understanding of our very differences.

Entering dialogue in such a spirit of hospitality, we stand both committed to our own truth claims and open to the equally committed claims of the other. Hospitable dialogue is distinguished by a certain intellectual humility whereby one maintains one's truth commitments, but takes seriously the other's truth claims as they bear on and question our own. Herein the other's views are courteously and civilly acknowledged and judiciously heard. Such respect does not require that we accept the other's claims, especially those fundamentally at odds with our own, but that we remain always open to the possible disclosure of truth through dialogue. We stand committed to the constellation of beliefs and claims that define our fundamental worldview, and at the same time open ourselves to dialogue, avoiding both an overconfident, close-minded dogmatism that refuses to subject itself to revision or expansion, and a skepticism that concedes all judgments as groundless. As Pope Benedict XVI has stated, the "height of development of a culture is shown in its openness, in its capacity to give and receive, in its power to develop further, to let itself be purified and thus to become adapted to the truth and to man."[8] Through critical dialogue that sifts out what is of worth, we maintain a commitment to revealing what is true and good.

Such dialogue requires a hospitable public space that values the articulation and engagement of our differences. Such hospitality toward the other is rooted in and restricted by the overarching requirement that we respect persons as holders of beliefs and truth claims, even when these differ from our own. It brings us to respectfully and critically consider the significance and worth of other points of views and ways of life. Intending dialogue in circumstances that risk misinterpretation and misunderstanding is a hopeful but realistic venture. It recognizes and addresses, rather than naively denying, the complexity and challenges. We commence dialogue with the other, acknowledging that it may not lead to unanimity or, as Aristotle says, "to our living together and enjoying the same things."[9] We realistically recognize that dialogue may end with our facing a non-reducible plurality of claims. But by engaging in dialogue we promote conversation and reasonable discourse, activities Aristotle described as fostering and sustaining friendship and civility.

The contemporary recognition of a plurality of rival traditions places great responsibilities upon us, especially as Americans and Christians living in a pluralistic society and diverse global world. It seems our times call for more than a passive, live-and-let-live tolerance to pluralism in which we prize our autonomy and noninterference with the other. Rather, such times call for an open hospitable dialogue engaging our differences, sensitive to both the strength and fragility of such dialogue. Such times demand that we recognize and work to eliminate situations and conditions that thwart and distort dialogue, cultivate the host of virtues bearing upon hospitality (humility, patience, civility, courtesy, respect for persons and truth), and work to envision and actualize ways of fostering dialogue. Herein we promote not tolerance as passive acquiescence to a regrettably inevitable pluralism, but hospitality that promotes the mutuality of respect which is distinctive of rational persons and civil societies at their very best. And thereby we may hopefully begin to understand and model the hospitality captured in the powerfully welcoming words of the Chambonnais to the strangers in their midst: "Naturally, come in, and come in."

It is regrettable that philosophers have failed to attend to the virtue of hospitality, as shown in its absence from their commentaries on the virtues. In contrast, religious traditions offer rich accounts of hospitality as a virtue to be cultivated in communities. When Job sought to evince his worth as a good man, he spoke of his hospitable response to strangers (Job 29:16). Matthew quotes Jesus as emphasizing that his way requires the feeding of the hungry, relieving the thirsty, and the welcoming of strangers into our midst (Matt. 25:34–5). Christ urges his followers to accept hospitality, as well as to offer it (Luke 10:5–9). He shows the importance and way of hospitality by demanding it of Zacchaeus, the tax collector, described by others as a sinner (Luke 19:1–10). Zacchaeus responds to this demand with joy, living out God's hospitality and thereby being recognized as a child of Abraham and bringing salvation upon his home. The Rule of St. Benedict requires that all arriving guests be received like Christ. Dante reserves a place in the lower levels of hell for those who violate Christian hospitality.

As Westerners we tend to think of hospitality as merely a private act tied to the demands of social etiquette, the welcoming of friends as reflecting a tacitly presumed code of social obligation. In contrast, in traditional Middle Eastern society hospitality, the welcoming and protection of the stranger, is acknowledged as the most esteemed virtue, disclosive of the moral character of an honorable agent. Expectations of hospitality are not limited to friend and kin; they extend to nonmembers who cross tribal borders and private households. Rural wayfarers in traditional Middle Eastern countries, without access to public accommodations and restaurants, could always count on the hospitable sharing of food and shelter. Such hospitality is neither decreed nor enforceable by law and is not formally codified in detailed rules of etiquette. It is the humane response to the social other that makes civil society possible and renders communities more livable.

Hospitality is simply the gracious welcoming of the other—the stranger and foreigner (and even one's enemy in some subcultures)—into one's civil community. The foreigner, as shown in its etymological root "foras," is defined as the one who comes from beyond, from outside the shared civic life of a community. In speaking a foreign tongue, the foreigner audibly announces that he or she comes from another ethos, community, or culture—a different way of living and thinking. Yet this foreigner is not viewed as the uncivilized barbarian who babbles incoherent nonsense. Rather, it is presumed that he or she comes from somewhere, some other community with variant manners, meanings, and mores whose members speak a different mother tongue. And yet as foreigner—particularly so—the other is allowed to enter households and is given hospitality, even refuge. The civil expectation is that foreigners will be treated with respect and be welcomed even before their origin, identity, or language is known. The code of honor requires that the foreign guest be always graciously welcomed. In many cases, the civil response to the other—the distinctly hospitable response—is placed over and above all other demands and expectations. Like the Chambonnais, such communities provide powerful examples of expectations in the hospitable response to the stranger. The practice of civility requires acting toward others with goodwill and gracious welcome. Correspondingly, the guest is expected to honor and respect the ways of the local household and community. Such mutual response allows for the extending of gracious and respectful relations beyond the kinship bonds of blood and heart. In doing so, hospitality is seen as making possible and extending civic life.

It may be the case that our postmodern world, so defined by its recognition and appreciation of pluralism, needs to attend to a virtue esteemed in more traditional societies and religious communities. Possibly this virtue offers what is needed for reconceiving how we might maintain the commitments that define our self and community while opening ourselves to those who do not share these same commitments. Ironically, the postmodern thinker Jacques Derrida turns to the premodern, religious resources identified by the Jewish philosopher Emmanuel Levinas in discussing what is most needed in our contemporary world. Drawing on the Torah that emphasizes fraternity, humanity, and hospitality, Derrida declares that "hospitality is culture itself and not simply one ethic amongst others."[10] He describes hospitality as an ethos, a fundamental way of dwelling in the world. Tied to such an ethos, ethics begins with the capacity to recognize, receive, and welcome the other. The Chambonnais saw such hospitality as the core of ethical living to which all persons are called by their creator. As Levinas stated, "That a people should accept those who come and settle among them—even though they are foreigners with their own customs and clothes, their own way of speaking, their own smell—that a people should give them an *akhsaniah*, such as a place at the inn, and the wherewithal to breathe and live—is a song to the glory of the God of Israel."[11] Drawing on this tradition, Derrida recognizes that hospitality is not a minor or insignificant virtue. It is central to human flourishing and harmonious social relations within and across cultures. Hospitality is what must be cultivated and passed on to future generations. Perhaps then what is most needed in our contemporary world is a move beyond tolerance to hospitality.

Cultivating Compassion and Hospitality

Christians like the Chambonnais help us learn to live the virtue of compassion as we encounter the suffering of near and distant persons. They also help us think through and live the virtue of hospitality, as we address the diversity increasingly encountered in our communities and world. *Gaudium et Spes* acknowledges this plurality of cultures, stating:

> Different styles of life and multiple scales of values arise from the diverse man-
> ner of using things, of laboring, of expressing oneself, of practicing religion,
> of forming customs, of establishing laws and juridic institutions, of cultivating
> the sciences, arts and beauty. Thus the customs handed down to it form the
> patrimony proper to each human community. It is also in this way that there
> is formed the definite, historical milieu which enfolds the man of every nation
> and age and from which he draws the values which permit him to promote
> civilization. (no. 53)

Both Paul VI and John Paul II called members of the church to enter into dialogue with diverse civilizations to further both their enrichment and that of the church. The words of *Gaudium et Spes*, encouraging dialogue within the church, provide a guideline for all human dialogue: persons "should always try to enlighten one another through honest discussion, preserving mutual charity and caring above all for the common good" (no. 43). The Chambonnais model well the commitment to which *Gaudium et Spes* calls all Christians, namely, the ongoing improvement of a social order "founded on truth, built on justice and animated by love" (no. 26). Both compassion and hospitality serve such an end, and for this reason should be emphasized and cultivated in our communities. Perhaps each of us needs to reflect on how, at many levels and in many ways, in our lives and our communities, we can actively further an ethos of compassion and hospitality toward the other.

Discussion

Hospitality in Action

Trudy Conway argues that hospitality provides an alternative to tolerance-as-indifference and entails a call to dialogue rooted in the desire for truth. For our discussion of the chapter, I will tell a story about Dr. Conway's work to abolish the death penalty in Maryland. Capital punishment is a divisive issue in our society and one upon which Pope John Paul II and the U.S. bishops have been clear.[12] They have stated that it ought to be abolished in the United States. Dr. Conway's experiences as an activist certainly fit with the themes of her chapter, and my interest in her story is to show how hospitality is at work in her activism. I will be citing a lecture, "Moving Beyond Vengeance," that Dr. Conway gave at a conference at Mount St. Mary's University called "Bearers of Hope and Healing."[13]

We begin with a scene in Trudy's kitchen. Her daughter, who was home from a college break, started a conversation while Trudy was whipping potatoes. She recalls that her daughter said something like this.

> Mom, you've always been against executions. But in all honesty, you've never done a single thing about them. I know you're busy and can't take on all issues that matter to you, but this passivity is wrong—since the state is executing persons in your name, with your tax support, and through your silence. If you don't voice your opposition, then you are part of the state's action. If everyone who opposed executions, acted on their conviction—the debate would move forward and, given the strength of the arguments, we would have abolition now rather than later. So with your silence, your hands are dirtied with each and every execution.[14]

As a parent, I can say that I might have been defensive or, worse, dismissive. I might have dismissed these strong statements as youthful passion ("Yes, my child, I used to think that way when I was young"). Trudy, however, listened and allowed her daughter's accusations to get under her skin and keep her up at night—a testimony to her hospitality, openness, and concern for truth.

Trudy's first act of hospitality was to allow herself to be judged by her daughter. The second was her openness to arguments about what is right and true. "After that kitchen conversation," Trudy explains, "like all academics, I started reading on the topic of the death penalty and found it to be philosophically interesting. It's a topic about which reasonable people can disagree because there is a complexity to it; it's a knotted complex of many issues. . . . In studying it, you soon realize some of the finest thinkers of the Western tradition have been divided on this issue."[15] Trudy notes that, in her view, the philosophical arguments against the death penalty are more persuasive, and the practical questions only add weight to the philosophical claims. The facts are that capital punishment is applied disproportionately to offenders who are poor and minorities, and the risks of executing innocent people are real (in recent years there has been "the exoneration of over one hundred twenty death row inmates"[16]). Even though Trudy was convinced, she was willing to give well considered counter-arguments their place in the conversation.

Next, Dr. Conway organized a series of programs at Mount St. Mary's University, developed and taught a course, and formed a Mount chapter of the Campaign to End the Death Penalty. Through her work in Maryland, she realized that faith-based programming was a particular need in the area, and she shaped the Mount's programs accordingly. She developed relationships with men on death row and victims' families. She did not do all these things alone. She invited people in, particularly students. Through several years of programming, student involvement, visitors from across the country, guest lecturers, and a statewide conference, the network of relationships has grown. She and members of the Mount community also have become connected with the organization Murder Victim's Families for Reconciliation (www.mvfr. org). She and fellow activists at the Mount have heard the stories of victim's families and death row inmates. Again, we see the work of hospitality. Trudy facilitated a community of compassion at the Mount and widened that community's connections to those who are personally and profoundly affected by capital crimes and the death penalty. Through her work she has encouraged dialogue on the practice of execution, pushing people beyond indifference to critical reflection on a significant moral issue of our time.

What Can We Do?

I refer the reader back to the discussion section at the end of chapter 6, and the seven themes of Catholic social teaching (as presented by the U.S. bishops[17]):

1. life and dignity of the person
2. a call to family, community, and participation
3. reciprocal rights and responsibilities in society
4. the option for the poor and vulnerable
5. the dignity of work and the rights of workers
6. solidarity and peacemaking
7. care for God's creation

What we can do is to become passionate and active in one of these areas. It will be helpful to investigate the website of the United States Conference of Catholic Bishops (USCCB). There are departments and programming areas (www.usccb.org/depts.shtml) from A to Z—from the Secretariat for African American Catholics to World Youth Day, with the National Pastoral Initiative on Marriage in between. The department of Social Development and World Peace is a good place to start. There are links for international and domestic issues as well as programming aids for parishes and educators. There is a host of options for what we can do.

The USCCB website provides opportunities and areas for becoming informed and involved in Catholic social teaching. A guide to how we are called to become active is provided by Dr. Conway's chapter on hospitality and by the story of her work to abolish the death penalty. Like Trudy, we can open ourselves to be judged and inspired by others. We can be hospitable to other points of view, not through an attitude of indifference but through respect and a desire to know and share the truth. We can give ourselves to the pursuit of justice and social change, and welcome others who join us. Each of these steps requires personal risks, but through these habits of hospitality we are likely to find ourselves, like Trudy Conway, amid a community that gives us joy and hope.

13

From Despot to Steward

The Greening of Catholic Social Teaching

BRIAN G. HENNING

The gradual depletion of the ozone layer and the related "greenhouse effect" has now reached crisis proportions as a consequence of industrial growth, massive urban concentrations and vastly increased energy needs. Industrial waste, the burning of fossil fuels, unrestricted deforestation, the use of certain types of herbicides, coolants and propellants, all of these are known to harm the atmosphere and the environment. The resulting meteorological and atmospheric changes range from damage to health to the possible future submersion of low-lying lands.[1]

Global warming, species extinction, massive deforestation, increased desertification, overpopulation, the salinization of fresh water, toxic waste disposal—it is problems such as these that have led many to conclude with the author of this passage that we are in the midst of an environmental crisis. Yet there continue to be surprisingly large groups of individuals who are dubious of the severity or even the existence of these so-called environmental problems. Many privately suspect that this "environmental crisis" is merely the fabrication of granola-eating, tree-hugging, sandal-wearing, ponytail-sporting, beatnik wannabes that care more about baby seals and redwoods than about fisherman and loggers. Besides, they often add, if any of these issues become problematic, we will surely be able to develop new technologies that will solve our problems. Environmental issues such as these, they conclude, are comparatively small matters of economics and technology, not morality and religion.

If you find yourself agreeing with this sort of assessment, you may be surprised to learn that the passage above was not written by an environmental activist. These words were part of a speech entitled "The Ecological Crisis: A Common Responsibility," delivered on January 1, 1990, by Pope John Paul II. In this speech the pope unequivocally declared not only that there is an ecological crisis, but that "the ecological crisis is a *moral issue*" (World Day of Peace, 1990, no. 15). Following in this tradition, Pope Benedict XVI's 2008 World Peace Day argued strongly that "we need to care for the environment: it has been entrusted to men and women to be protected and cultivated with responsible freedom, with the good of all as a constant guiding criterion."[2]

I am not primarily interested in following the ongoing political debates regarding whether there is in fact an environmental crisis. Taking our ecological crisis as given, I am more interested in examining the relationship, or lack thereof, between ecological awareness and Catholic social teaching. It is my contention that, historically speaking, Christianity bears some responsibility for having fostered a destructive and arrogant attitude toward the environment, but that properly understood a respect for nature is an essential part of Christian faith. Indeed, there is reason to believe that Catholic social teaching has the potential to make a unique contribution to contemporary discussions of environmental protection. However, before we can turn directly to this topic we must address the historical roots of our treatment and understanding of nature and the role that Christianity has played in informing this role.

Historical Roots of the Ecological Crisis

Many scholars seeking to explain the historical roots of the mounting ecological crisis point to a particular attitude that nature's sole purpose is to serve humans. This is what philosophers call an anthropocentric view of reality. In a sense, anthropocentrism simply means human-centered. In a sense, all thought is unavoidably anthropocentric in that it takes place from the perspective of human experience. Similarly, since only humans are complex enough to be conscious and free enough to be responsible, we might accurately say that all discussions of ethics—indeed, all branches of investigation—are unavoidably anthropocentric. However, an anthropocentric worldview goes beyond this basic orientation and concludes further that the natural world only has meaning

and value insofar as it is related to humans. It is this further assumption—
that nothing has value apart from its relationship to humans—that, scholars
argue, has justified and perpetuated a destructive attitude toward the natural
world.

In a now famous article entitled "The Historical Roots of Our Ecological Crisis," Lynn White Jr. argues that Christianity should take much of the
blame for creating and perpetuating this destructive attitude. White argues
that how people interact with their environment is "deeply conditioned by
beliefs about our nature and destiny—that is, by religion."[3] It is our most
basic beliefs that inform what we are allowed to do and not do to our natural
environment. Given this, White notes that in antiquity pagan animism held
that "every tree, every spring, every stream, every hill had its own *genius loci*,
its guardian spirit. . . . Before one cut a tree, mined a mountain, or dammed
a brook, it was important to placate the spirit in charge of that particular
situation, and to keep it placated."[4] Christianity, on the other hand, inherited
from the Judaic tradition a story of creation in which humans are uniquely
made in God's image and are given dominion over the created order. With the
supplanting of paganism, then, the spirits in nature "evaporate"; the once sacred grove becomes a mere stand of trees to be used for fuel and the once holy
mountain becomes a site for a new ski run or mine. "Christianity, in absolute
contrast to ancient paganism and Asia's religions . . . , not only established
a dualism of man and nature but also insisted that it is God's will that man
exploit nature for his proper ends."[5]

White concludes that Christianity, particularly in its Western form, is the
most anthropocentric religion the world has ever seen. "God planned all of
this explicitly for man's benefit and rule: no item in the physical creation
had any purpose save to serve man's purposes. And, although man's body is
made of clay, he is not simply part of nature: he is made in God's image."[6]
Thus, White continues, "Despite Copernicus, all the cosmos rotates around
our little globe. Despite Darwin, we are *not*, in our hearts, part of the natural
process. We are superior to nature, contemptuous of it, willing to use it for
our slightest whim."[7] After all, Genesis 1 clearly indicates that human beings
are to subdue the earth and to have dominion over every living creature (Gen.
1:28), right? According to this interpretation, in making humans divinely ap-
pointed despots over nature Christianity is responsible for having created the
underlying worldview that justifies the wasteful and indiscriminate destruction
of the natural world. There is only one conclusion to be drawn from this: "We
shall continue to have a worsening ecological crisis until we reject the Christian
axiom that nature has no reason for existence save to serve man."[8]

Now historically speaking, it is the case that many influenced by Christianity
have justified their exploitation of nature by explicitly or implicitly relying on
the account of creation in Genesis 1, wherein God gives humans dominion over
creation and orders us to subdue it. Historically, then, White's criticisms of

Christianity do have some weight. Christianity has historically encouraged an anthropocentric attitude which has fostered a very destructive understanding of our relationship to nature. What is less certain is the claim that Christianity is inherently or necessarily anthropocentric. Many contemporary theologians and philosophers are approaching this critical question by reexamining what it means to have dominion over creation.

Anne M. Clifford is representative of a growing body of theologians who are placing a renewed focus on the scriptural basis of humanity's relationship with the natural world. In her compelling essay, "Foundations for a Catholic Ecological Theology of God," Clifford agrees with White and others that "for much of the twentieth century, nonhuman nature has been treated by Christian theologians as a mere context in which human beings work out their salvation with the help of God's grace."[9] Yet, as Clifford goes on to note, there is nothing necessary in this interpretation. She begins by explicitly addressing White's claim that Christianity is inherently anthropocentric, arguing instead that if we properly understand our role within creation, we begin to recognize that the Bible is not anthropocentric or human-centered; it is primarily and essentially theocentric, or God-centered. It is only in God that the origin and meaning of all creatures is to be found.[10] This re-centering of the Bible has a potentially dramatic effect on how one interprets the creation stories in general, and the notion of dominion in particular.

Following several other contemporary scholars, Clifford argues that to understand properly the meaning of dominion, one must put it in the context of the story of the great flood.

> In Chapter 6 [of Genesis], we find God deeply grieved about the extent of the wickedness of humans, precipitating an ecological disaster of worldwide proportions. . . . God's directive [to build an ark for all animals] makes the meaning of having dominion clear—it is to see the survival of the other living creatures. . . . The Noahic covenant is a symbol of the unbreakable bond between all creatures and their Creator.[11]

Interpreting dominion in this context emphasizes two things. First, in a covenant God made not only with Noah but with "every living creature" (Gen. 9:9–10), we must remember that, although humans are unique, we are also a part of the interconnected web of nature. Properly understood, therefore, Christianity does not promote an absolute dualism between humans and creation. Although we are uniquely made in God's image, we are fundamentally a part of the natural world; there is only one creation. Second, as Clifford succinctly notes, God's command to build an ark for all animals "makes the meaning of having dominion clear—it is to see the survival of the other living creatures."[12] Understood within the context of the Noahic covenant, therefore, dominion does not give humans license to use nature with impunity. Rather, to be given dominion is to be charged with the grave responsibility to care for and protect God's creation for present and future generations. A properly theocentric conception of dominion entails responsible stewardship, not arrogant despotism. The earth has not been given to us to exploit for our most trivial desires; it has been entrusted to us to respect and protect.

> When humans abuse the charge of dominion given to them, taking upon themselves the domination of the rest of creation as their possession, instead of respecting the charge entrusted to them by God, all of creation suffers. There is no biblical basis for justifying this exploitation of the earth and its many forms of plant and animal life. Such behavior breaks God's covenant with creation and is a sin against the Creator. Because of such sin, a mournful dirge is heard throughout the land; all of creation suffers.[13]

It is for this reason, perhaps, that John Paul II argues that "Christians . . . [must] realize that their responsibility within creation and their duty towards nature and the Creator are an essential part of their faith" (World Day of Peace, 1990, no. 15). Thus, rather than seeing environmental awareness as a movement extrinsic to their own faith, many Christians are beginning to reawaken to what might be called the sacramental role of nature.[14] No longer should Christians see the natural environment as a mere resource to be disposed of as one pleases. Rather, nature provides a unique encounter with God. After all, "from the greatness and the beauty of created things their original author, by analogy, is seen" (Ws. 13:5).[15] As a unique overflowing of divine goodness, every creature is revelatory of God; every part of creation is an overflowing of divine goodness.[16]

In this renewed sacramental and scriptural light, not only is there ample reason to reject the view that Christianity inherently or necessarily entails a destructive anthropocentricism, the Christian faith in fact requires that the faithful take seriously their grave responsibility as stewards of creation. According to this model, human beings do not own the earth, but hold it in trust for both present and future generations. Benedict XVI puts this point rather forcefully, arguing that to truly respect the environment "means not selfishly considering nature to be at the complete disposal of our own interests, for future generations also have the right to reap its benefits and to exhibit towards nature the same responsible freedom that we claim for ourselves."[17] By continuing our unsustainable reliance on nonrenewable and heavily polluting energy sources, by continuing to undermine international efforts to curb global climate change, by continuing to ignore the dramatic increase in species extinctions, we are hurting not only ourselves, but also bequeathing to future generations a poorer quality of life than we have inherited.

A tangible sign of this "greening" of Catholic social teaching may be seen in the U.S. Conference of Bishops' creation of an "Environmental

Justice Program."[18] As its name suggests, this program focuses on the often neglected connection between the care for the poor and the care for the earth. Many scholars, both secular and religious, have begun to focus on the fact that poor, minority (e.g., African Americans, Appalachians, Pacific Islanders, Hispanics, and Native Americans), and indigenous people bear disproportionate environmental risk from, among other things, resource depletion, runaway development, environmental pollution, hazardous waste facilities, contaminated food, and pesticides. Both in this country and around the world, the most vulnerable individuals among us are more likely to drink polluted water, breathe polluted air, eat contaminated food, and be less politically empowered to do something about it. This is environmental injustice.

It is this critical connection between social justice and environmental protection that is potentially the most important contribution that Catholic social teaching can make to contemporary discussions of environmental ethics. Any viable solution to our environmental crisis must put at its heart the focus on social justice. As the U.S. bishops put it very eloquently, "A just and sustainable society and world are not an optional ideal, but a moral and practical necessity. Without justice, a sustainable economy will be beyond reach. Without an ecologically responsible world economy, justice will be unachievable."[19] In this light, we begin to see that environmental stewardship is a fundamental part of the Catholic church's commitment to social justice. Indeed, environmental protection is a necessary condition for the achievement of a truly just society dedicated to the protection of life.[20]

In addition to emphasizing the link between environmental and social justice, this conclusion also points to the fact that a consistent respect for life requires the protection of both human and nonhuman forms of life. In John Paul II's words, "Respect for life and for the dignity of the human person extends also to the rest of creation, which are called to join man in praising God" (World Day of Peace, 1990, no. 16). Thus, respect for and protection of nonhuman forms of life is an important part of the culture of life that Catholics seek to foster. Drew Christiansen and Walter Grazer make this important point very aptly:

> In striving to protect the dignity of every person and promote the common good of the human family, particularly the most vulnerable among us, the Church champions the rights of the unborn, helping to lead the national effort to oppose abortion; it endeavors to bring dignity to the poor and help them become full partners in our society; it works to overcome the scourge of racism and bring everyone to the table of the human family; it welcomes the stranger among us; and in all cases, it promotes the family as the center of human culture and moral development. Now, the Church is recognizing that the web of life and the promotion of human dignity are linked to the protection of God's gift of creation.[21]

The U.S. bishops are surprisingly forceful in their inclusion of the respect for nature, going so far as to claim that mistreatment of the natural world not only "diminishes our own dignity and sacredness" and destroys resources needed by future generations, but in fact "contradict[s] what it means to be human. . . . Our tradition," they continue, "calls us to protect the life and dignity of the human person, and it is increasingly clear that this task cannot be separated from the care and defense of all of creation."[22]

As John Paul II noted, our relationship to and treatment of the natural world is of critical importance. "While in some cases the damage already done may well be irreversible, in many other cases it can still be halted. It is necessary, however, that the entire human community—individuals, States and international bodies—take seriously the responsibility that is theirs" (World Day of Peace, 1990, no. 6). John Paul II's call for each of us to take responsibility for our treatment of the earth provides a natural transition to the last part of my comments which, in the spirit of taking responsibility for our treatment of nature, focuses on some very specific things that those of us at colleges and universities can do.

Becoming a responsible environmental steward involves no magic, no mystery. The first step is to become ecologically aware of the impact of your actions, particularly your consumption patterns. The difficult truth is that much of our consumption, particularly in a wealthy country like the United States, is wasteful and unnecessary.[23] Though our population is relatively small, as a nation our ecological footprint is enormous.[24] The first step to diminishing our resource use is to consume less. Walk more and drive less. Turn up your thermostat a few degrees in the summer and turn it down a few degrees in the winter. Use natural light when possible. Drink tap water instead of buying bottled water or soda. Recycle as much as possible, but don't forget the "neglected R's": reduce and reuse.

Being a responsible environmental steward doesn't require that you sell off everything you own and live in a cabin in the woods. Though Americans in particular can and should decrease wasteful consumption, what is also needed is a shift in what we buy. For instance, buying local products not only decreases the pollution caused by transporting items from long distances (e.g., buying fruit grown in Pennsylvania rather than in Chile), it has the added benefit of supporting the local economy. Rather than going to a big-box retailer, visit your local farmer's market. Similarly, buying organic decreases the destructive impact of pesticides and herbicides; it allows farmers to sell their produce at a premium, and it may be healthier to boot. While buying local and organic may cost a few dollars more, buying efficient products often pays for itself. Whether buying a car or a lightbulb, seek out the most efficient products available. All of these examples point to the same conclusion: in our integrated global economy one of the easiest and most potent ways of effecting change is to vote with your dollars.

Yet for college students living in residence halls and eating in dining halls, this is not always easy to do. Nevertheless, there are many things that you can do as a college student to become more environmentally responsible. Perhaps the most important first step is to educate yourself by participating in or organizing curricular and cocurricular activities that will help you and your community become more ecologically aware.[25] For instance, you can enroll in environmental studies or environmental science classes and learn more about subjects such as global warming, conservation biology, or environmental politics. Join or start an environmental stewardship club on campus and organize events that help to focus the community's attention on becoming more environmentally responsible. As you approach graduation, consider taking the "graduation pledge" and commit to explore and take into account the social and environmental consequences of any job you consider and try to improve these aspects of any organization for which you work.[26]

As the passage at the start of this essay noted, the stakes are very high. As the U.S. bishops presciently noted in 1991, "Humanity is at a crossroads. . . . We can either ignore the harm we see and witness further damage, or we can take up our responsibilities to the Creator and creation with renewed courage and commitment."[27] The choice before us is clear: we can continue to maintain our despotic delusion or we can humbly accept the burden of responsible stewardship.

Discussion

Common Cause or Someone Else's Problem

By introducing us to the "greening" of Catholic social teaching, Brian Henning calls us to action. Dr. Henning tells me that we understand enough about climate change to act—evidence that global warming is serious, that human industry and habits of consumption make significant contributions to the problem, and that changes on our part will make a difference. However, he also explains that the facts of global climate change and the consensus among scientists are often exaggerated and usually given more certainty than the scientific method is able to achieve. There are reputable scientists who argue that the link between global warming and human activities (e.g., our dependence on fossil fuels) is not completely obvious. Dr. Henning suspects that we exaggerate the evidence in order to move people to act in a world that hopes for scientific absolutes. It is assumed that only infallible proof will lead to decisive action. Note, however, that Dr. Henning's approach, as well as the framework of Catholic social thought, is different. His chapter develops an understanding of our relationship to the earth and the responsibilities that are inherent in that relationship.[28] It is our relationship to creation that shapes our convictions and actions.

Global climate change raises an interesting set of questions about what moves people to change their lives. A recent study of American attitudes toward global warming is both enlightening and troubling. The study finds that the more informed Americans are about the causes of global warming the less likely we are to take responsibility. It is a common-sense view that information facilitates action. The study, "Personal Efficacy, the Information Environment, and Attitudes Toward Global Warming and Climate Change in the United States," finds the opposite.[29] "Respondents who are better informed about the issue [of global warming] feel less (not more) responsible for it."[30]

According to the study, the more a person trusts the findings of scientists, (1) the more he or she is likely to hope that scientists will find a technological solution, and (2) the more the person is aware that individual actions alone will make little difference. Consider the study's conclusion on the first point.

> Respondents who showed a great deal of confidence that scientists understand global warming and climate change showed significantly *less* concern for the risks of global warming than did those who have lower trust in scientists. Though this effect differs from our expectations, it is consistent with the notion that people trust that scientists will be able, somehow, to devise technical solutions to any problems that arise because of global warming and climate change.[31]

The following quotation pertains to the second point—what seems to be despair about the difference an individual can make.

> As the level of self-reported knowledge increases, the perceived ability to affect global warming outcomes decreases. This is a reasonable finding. Global warming is an extreme collective action dilemma, with the actions of one person having a negligible effect in the aggregate. Informed persons appear to realize this objective fact. Therefore, informed persons can be highly concerned and reasonably pessimistic about their ability to change climate outcomes.[32]

Both findings (points 1 and 2) suggest that knowledge about global warming perpetuates inaction and fits comfortably with the conviction that someone else is going to have to fix it.

The study has striking implications. It is not only those who deny the evidence of global climate change that are inhibiting common efforts for change—change is also stalled by those who are convinced by the evidence. The problem is at least twofold. First, our dependence on technology, which is part of the cause of global warming, is also why we don't think that we need to change the way we live. Technology will provide. Second, most of us are not able to imagine and hope for the widespread cooperation and collective action that are required. Both problems are not unique to our current environmental crisis: consider how often this book has called for communal and social interdependence, rather than technological expertise, and how often it has appealed to our common responsibilities to the common good. Global warming is a test case for Catholic social teaching. It requires convictions about our duties and our place in relationship to God, our neighbors, and God's creation, cooperation for the good of all, and a commitment to change how we live.

What Can We Do?

Many city, towns, and parishes are trying to change their habits of life. For example, go to the website of Old St. Patrick's Church in Chicago (www.oldstpats. org). On the right hand menu, choose "season for social justice" and then the option, "what can you do?" The first imperatives that you will see are: "individually—reduce, reuse, recycle; collectively—advocate." The list of how we can reduce, reuse, and recycle is lengthy. It is likely that you have seen a similar list about energy and water conservation. There is much on St. Pat's list that we can and should do. My one worry is that, at certain points, its call to reduce, reuse, and recycle reads like merely a strategy—another technique for keeping our lives the same (even if using less energy and resources). I do not mean to accuse the people of St. Pat's of anything. It is only that what I assume are a vibrant liturgy and community life are missing from the list of "what we can do?"

The same holds for its call to advocacy. To be an advocate means to promote and support a vision of life, people, and a common course of action. Advocacy in its fullest sense is what Trudy Conway, in chapter 12, calls hospitality; it is a commitment to living truthfully in a way that reconciles people, develops relationships, and sustains a community as it becomes ever more passionate about the truth. If our environmental concerns are reduced to conservation techniques (and to keeping our lives basically the same), they will become a joyless burden. Advocacy as lobbying our legislators is important (as Old St. Patrick's website rightly proposes). But advocacy begins with hospitality. Without a transformed community life, environmentally friendly changes in our lives and the laws that might require change will be like fat-free desserts—a sad imitation of the kind of consumption we really desire. Our efforts to be responsible with our resources and to advocate for collective action require risks of love. The main goal of environmental ethics (within the Catholic frame) is to change how we live in relationship to God, neighbor, and creation—decreasing technological dependence, staying closer to and experiencing the intimacy of home, and increasing our time to live well in friendship with God and neighbor.

Following Pope Benedict XVI, we ought to see environmental issues as a call to community. The following excerpt is from his World Day of Peace address, January 1, 2008 (no. 7).

The family needs a home, a fit environment in which to develop its proper relationships. *For the human family, this home is the earth*, the environment that God the Creator has given us to inhabit with creativity and responsibility . . . not selfishly considering nature to be at the complete disposal of our own interests. . . . Nor must we overlook the poor, who are excluded in many cases from the goods of creation destined for all . . . it means being committed to making joint decisions after pondering responsibly the road to be taken, decisions aimed at strengthening that covenant between human beings and the environment, which should mirror the creative love of God, from whom we come and towards whom we are journeying.

Notes

Introduction

1. Encyclicals and addresses by Pope Leo XIII, Pius XI, John Paul II, and Benedict XVI can be found on the Vatican website, www.vatican.va/holy_father/index.html. The documents of Vatican II, namely *Gaudium et Spes: The Church in the Modern World*, can be found on www.vatican.va/archive/hist_councils/ii_vatican_council.

"Justice in the World" by the Synod of Bishops (1971) can be found on the website of the Office of Social Justice Archdiocese of St. Paul and Minneapolis, www.osjspm.org/majordoc_justicia_in_mundo_offical_test.aspx.

The standard collection of documents in print is edited by David J. O'Brien and Thomas A. Shannon, *Catholic Social Thought: The Documentary Heritage* (Maryknoll, NY: Orbis, 1992).

When encyclicals are cited, the number refers, not to a page, but to a paragraph number, which is standard on all editions of the documents. With the paragraph numbers, one can consult either the collection edited by O'Brien and Shannon or the Vatican website.

The numbers in the notes for the following chapters refer to these paragraph numbers. The page numbers for the documents in *Catholic Social Thought*, ed. O'Brien and Shannon, are: *Rerum Novarum*, 14–39; *Quadragesimo Anno*, 42–80; *Pacem in Terris*, 131–62; *Gaudium et Spes*, 164–237; *Justice in the World*, 287–300; *Laborum Exercens*, 352–92; *Sollicitudo Rei Socialis*, 395–436; *Centesimus Annus*, 439–88.

Chapter 1   Biblical Justice

1. This pledge is the property offered as collateral by the borrower to the lender, and held by the lender until the loan has been fully repaid. If you have ever played the game Monopoly and have mortgaged one of the properties you owned, you have experienced this. When you mortgage a property, you are required to turn the deed face down, and you may not collect any rent when another player lands on the property while it is still mortgaged to the bank. Only when you have repaid the bank loan may you turn the deed face up, and begin once more to collect rent from other players unfortunate enough to land on your property. So it was in the ancient world, and still is in the modern world, whenever anyone pawns a piece of property in return for a loan. The property is not available to the borrower while money is still owed to the lender.

Chapter 2 The Liturgy as a Source of Formation in Catholic Social Teaching

1. *Rites of the Catholic Church*, The Roman Ritual revised by decree of the Second Vatican Council and published with authority of Pope Paul VI, approved for use in the Dioceses of the United States of America by the National Conference of Catholic Bishops and confirmed by the Apostolic See, prepared by the International Commission on English in the Liturgy: a Joint Commission of Catholic Bishops' Conferences (New York: Pueblo Publishing Company, 1990), 395.

2. Dorothy Day, *Loaves and Fishes* (Maryknoll, NY: Orbis, 1997), 176.

3. *Catechism of the Catholic Church*, 2nd ed., rev. in accordance with the official Latin text promulgated by Pope John Paul II (Washington, DC: United States Catholic Conference, 2000), 588.

4. M. Therese Lysaught notes that "Christians dwell with God no longer in the last day of creation, but in the first day of the new creation in the eschatological time of resurrection." "Love and Liturgy," *Gathered for the Journey*, eds. David Matzko McCarthy and M. Therese Lysaught (Grand Rapids: Eerdmans, 2007), 32.

5. *Rites of the Catholic Church*, 404.

6. Ibid.

7. Ibid.

8. James L. Empereur and Christopher G. Kiesling, *The Liturgy that Does Justice* (Collegeville, MN: Liturgical, 1990), 51–52.

9. *Catechism of the Catholic Church*, 588. The *Catechism* describes various forms of human misery—material deprivation, unjust oppression, physical and psychological illness and death—and notes that "those who are oppressed by poverty are the object of *a preferential love* on the part of the Church which, since her origin and in spite of the failings of many of her members, has not ceased to work for their relief, defense, and liberation through numerous works of charity which remain indispensable always and everywhere" (no. 2448).

10. Paul VI, *Apostolic Constitution on the Sacrament of Confirmation*, *Rites of the Catholic Church*, 472.

11. Ibid., 479.

12. Ibid., 488.

13. Ibid., 499.

14. Ibid., 508.

15. Ibid., 509.

16. Ibid., 4.

17. *Dogmatic Constitution on the Church (Lumen Gentium)* in *Decrees of the Ecumenical Councils*, ed. Norman P. Tanner, trans. Edward Yarnold (Washington, DC: Georgetown University Press, 1980), 849–900.

18. Daniel C. Maguire, "The Abnormality of War: Dissecting the 'Just War' Euphemisms and Building an Ethics of Peace," *Horizons* 33 (Spring 2006): 123–25.

19. "Eucharist Prayer IV: Jesus, the Compassion of God," *Eucharistic Prayer for Masses for Various Needs and Occasions*, approved for use in the Dioceses of the United States of America by the National Conference of Catholic Bishops and confirmed by the Apostolic See, English translation prepared by the International Commission on English in the Liturgy (Totowa, NJ: Catholic Book Publishing, 1996), 56.

Chapter 3 Eucharist and Social Justice

1. David Power, *Love without Calculation: A Reflection on Divine Kenosis* (New York: Crossroad, 2005), 6.

2. Ibid.

3. Ibid.

4. Ibid., 7.

5. Ibid.

6. Ibid.

7. Ibid., 8.

8. Nathan Mitchell, *Real Presence* (Chicago: Liturgical Training Publications, 1998), 51–52.

9. Ibid., 53.

10. "Liturgical Role of Silence" in *The New Dictionary of Sacramental Worship*, ed. Peter Fink (Collegeville, MN: Liturgical, 1990), 1189.

11. Augustine, Sermon 272, in *Sermons (Works of St. Augustine)*, ed. John E. Rotelle, OSA, trans. Edmund Hill, OP (Hyde Park, NY: New City Press, 1993), pt. 3, vol. 7, 300–301.

12. Rodica Stoicoiu, "Consecration or Communion: Identifying Ourselves as a Eucharistic People," in *New Theological Review* 15 (2002): 74–78.

13. Benedict XVI, *Deus Caritas Est*, 14, www.vatican.va/holy_father/benedict_xvi/encyclicals/documents/hf_ben-xvi_enc_20051225_deus-caritas-est_en.html.

14. John Chrysostom, *In Evangelium S. Matthaei, hom.* 50:3–4: PG 58, 508–509 is cited in *Ecclesia de Eucharisti*, 20n34, www.vatican.va/holy_father/john_paul_ii/encyclicals/documents/hf_jp-ii_enc_17042003_ecclesia-de-eucharistia_en.html.

15. *Ecclesia de Eucharisti*, 20.

16. Robert J. Karris, OFM, *Eating Your Way Through Luke's Gospel* (Collegeville, MN: Liturgical, 2006), 97.

17. Ibid., 3–13.

18. Ibid., 55–56.

19. John Sniegocki, "Implementing Catholic Social Teaching," in *Faith in Public Life*, The Annual Volume of the College Theology Society 2007, ed. William J. Collinge (Maryknoll, NY: Orbis, forthcoming), 53.

20. Jeremy Rifkin traces our culture of meat consumption in *Beyond Beef: The Rise and Fall of the Cattle Culture* (New York: Plume, 1993).

21. US Department of Agriculture, *Food Consumption*, www.ers.usda.gov/Briefing/Consumption.

22. See Michael Pollan, "Unhappy Meals," *New York Times Magazine,* January 28, 2007, www.michaelpollan.com/article.php?id=87.

23. Ibid.

24. Sniegocki, "Implementing Catholic Social Teaching," 60–61.

25. Ibid., 60–61, cites the UN Food and Agriculture Organization (FAO), "Livestock a Major Threat to Environment," www.fao.org/newsroom/en/news/2006/1000448/index.html.

26. Sniegocki, 60–61, refers us to John Robbins, *The Food Revolution: How Your Diet Can Help Save Your Life and the World* (Berkeley: Conari Press, 2001); Michael Jacobsen, *Six Arguments for a Greener Diet: How a More Plant-Based Diet Could Save Your Health and the Environment* (Washington, DC: Center for Science in the Public Interest, 2006).

Chapter 4 Pope Leo XIII and a Century of Catholic Social Teaching

1. This quotation is taken from the translation of *Rerum Novarum* in David J. O'Brien and Thomas A. Shannon, eds., *Catholic Social Thought: The Documentary Heritage* (Maryknoll, NY: Orbis, 1992).

2. The philosopher of religion Robert Neville has a very interesting paper entitled "Political Tolerance in an Age of Renewed Religious Warfare," in *Philosophy, Religion, and the Question of Intolerance*, ed. David Ambuel and Mehi Amin Razavi (Albany, NY: SUNY Press, 1997). Its first two pages simply name important sociopolitical events in the last quarter century. Its conclusion is that the notion that religion is a private and personal matter is an empirically false claim.

3. John Paul II, *Centesimus Annus* (1991), 3, www.vatican.va/holy_father/john_paul_ii/encyclicals/documents/hf_jp-ii_enc_01051991_centesimus-annus_en.html. Emphasis in original.

4. "As he was walking by the Sea of Galilee he saw two brothers, Simon who was called Peter and his brother Andrew; they were making a cast in the lake with their net for they were fishermen. He said to them 'Follow me and I will make you fishers of men'" (Matt. 4:19).

5. O'Brien and Shannon, *Catholic Social Thought*, 13.

6. John Locke, *Second Treatise of Civil Government*, ed. J. W. Gough (Oxford: Blackwell, 1948), no. 4.

7. See "Of Property" in Locke's *Second Treatise of Civil Government*, for a classic articulation of the dual role that property plays in the origin of modern rights theory.

8. From this point on, citations and numbering of *Rerum Novarum* are from the translation on the Vatican website: www.vatican.va/holy_father/leo_xiii/encyclicals/documents/hf_l-xiii_enc_15051891_rerum-novarum_en.html.

9. It is interesting in this regard that in medieval—Christianized—Europe, the poor and even the sick have a place and role in relationship to others.

10. See John XXIII, *Pacem in Terris* (1963), 8–38, www.vatican.va/holy_father/john_xxiii/encyclicals/documents/hf_j-xxiii_enc_11041963_pacem_en.html.

11. At the end of our discussion we came to an interesting insight. Mr. Adams did not think of his company's contribution to society in terms of volunteer work, even though it is important to society. He assumes rather that his business's contribution is primarily in how it does business.

Chapter 5 Saint Augustine of Hippo

1. See bk. 1 of *De libero arbitrio*.

2. *De doctrina christiana* 1.27.28. I am using the translation by D. W. Robertson, *On Christian Doctrine* (Indianapolis: Bobbs-Merrill, 1958), with slight alterations, chiefly in the interest of inclusive language.

3. Ibid., 1.33.37.

4. Ibid., 3.10.16.

5. Ibid., 3.10.15.

6. Ibid., 1.26.27.

7. Imagine you were captured by a terrorist. Now imagine how things would change if you discovered you were both Red Sox fans.

8. Augustine's *Confessions* comprises thirteen books, a book being roughly equal to what might be called a chapter today. Bks. 1–9 are mainly autobiographical, while bks. 10–13 consist mainly of biblical interpretation and theological speculation.

9. Ibid., 2.9.17.

10. Ibid., 4.4.9.

11. Ibid., 4.8.13.

12. Ibid.

13. Ibid.

14. See J. Kevin Coyle, "Mani, Manichaeism," in *Augustine through the Ages: An Encyclopedia*, ed. Allan D. Fitzgerald (Grand Rapids: Eerdmans, 1999), 520–25.

15. *Confessions* 4.4.7.

16. Ibid.

17. Augustine (or the Latin translation of Acts he is using) adds "toward God" to the end of this passage.

18. Frederick J. Crosson, "Structure and Meaning in St. Augustine's *Confessions*," in *The Augustinian Tradition*, ed. Gareth B. Matthews (Berkeley: University of California Press, 1999), 30.

19. See Robert A. Markus, "Donatus, Donatism," in *Augustine through the Ages*, ed. Fitzgerald, 284–87.

20. *Ten Homilies on the First Epistle of St. John* 2.3, in *Augustine: Later Works*, vol. 8 of *The Library of Christian Classics*, trans. John Burnaby (Philadelphia: Westminster, 1955).

21. *Ten Homilies,* 6.10.

22. Augustine often makes use of these images, drawn, respectively, from Matt. 13:24–30 and 25:31–46.

23. Augustine, *Confessions*, 8.5.10.

24. See Gerald M. Bonner, *Freedom and Necessity: St. Augustine's Teaching on Divine Power and Human Freedom* (Washington, DC: Catholic University of America Press, 2007).

25. To take a single instance, "A number of people produce at will such musical sounds from their behind (without any stink) that they seem to be singing from that region." *City of God* 14.24, trans. Henry Bettenson (Harmondsworth, Middlesex: Penguin, 1972).

26. Augustine, *City of God*, 14.28.

27. Ibid., 15.1.

28. Ibid., 19.13.

29. Ibid., 19.17 (Bettenson translation slightly altered).

30. Ibid.

31. Ibid., 19.14. Augustine is sometimes taken to be saying in *The City of God* that government is a result of the Fall and would not exist among a sinless humanity, but this is not accurate. For him humans, whether or not they had sinned, would by nature belong to families, and in the absence of sin political communities would be like (ideal) families, in which orders are given "from a dutiful concern for the interests of others, not with pride in taking precedence over others, but with compassion in taking care of others" (*City of God*, 19.14). Augustine contrasts the institution of the family with that of slavery, which he accepts as normal within fallen human society, but which would not exist in a sinless world. What sin introduces into the political order is what makes it resemble slavery: the need to preserve peace and order by coercion, not by cooperation (*City of God*, 19.15).

32. Ibid., 19.17.

33. On this subject, see Robert A. Markus, *Christianity and the Secular* (Notre Dame, IN: University of Notre Dame Press, 2006), and his earlier *Saeculum: History and Society in the Theology of St. Augustine,* 2nd ed. (Cambridge: Cambridge University Press, 1989).

34. Augustine, *City of God*, 19.17.

35. The citations from the *Pastoral Constitution on the Church in the Modern World* are taken from the Vatican website, www.vatican.va/archive/hist_councils/ii_vatican_council/documents/vat-ii_cons_19651207_gaudium-et-spes_en.html.

36. The two encyclicals cited in the document were promulgated shortly before Vatican II by John XXIII, *Mater et Magistra: Christianity and Social Progress* (1961) and *Pacem in terris: Peace on Earth* (1963). Both can be found at www.vatican.va/holy_father/john_xxiii/encyclicals/index.html.

37. The seven principles of food cooperatives are: "Membership to the co-op is open and voluntary. The co-op is democratically controlled by its Member-Owners. There is member-owner economic participation. The co-op is autonomous and independent. The co-op provides education, training and information. There is cooperation among cooperatives. The co-op has a genuine concern for the community," www.commonmarket.com/coop_difference.html.

38. "Our goal is to provide a unique shopping experience that is fun, personal and educational for all our customers. The main duty of all Common Market employees is exemplary customer service to all and we are always looking for individuals who have upbeat attitudes, love good, fresh food, like to learn and most importantly love serving people! We value the knowledge and input of our employees and have a strong commitment to developing the skills that will help them become both our future leaders and leaders in our community," www.commonmarket.com/employment.html.

Chapter 6 A Contemporary Augustinian Approach to Love and Politics

1. Published as *Volk und Haus Gottes in Augustins Lehre von der Kirche (The People and House of God in Augustine's Doctrine of the Church)* (Munich: K. Zink, 1954).

2. Benedict XVI, *Deus Caritas Est* (December 25, 2005), www.vatican.va/holy_father/benedict_xvi/encyclicals/documents/hf_ben-xvi_enc_20051225_deus-caritas-est_en.html. I will refer to this document by section number and incorporate references to it into my text. I have occasionally modified the spelling and punctuation to accord with American conventions. The second encyclical is *Spe Salvi, In Hope We Are Saved*, and is also available at www.vatican.va.

3. Probably against the Swedish Lutheran theologian Anders Nygren (1890–1978), though no opponent is named.

4. See Collinge's discussion of Augustine in the section on "The Church," in chap. 5.

5. "Whoever is without love does not know God, for God is love"(1 John 4.8).

6. *De Trinitate* 8.8.12, probably roughly contemporary with the homilies on 1 John and similar in theme.

7. Synod of Bishops, "Justice in the World" (1971), *Catholic Social Thought: The Documentary Heritage*, ed. David J. O'Brien and Thomas A. Shannon (Maryknoll, NY: Orbis, 1992), 6.

8. See Charles M. Murphy, "Charity, not Justice, as Constitutive of the Church's Mission," *Theological Studies* 68 (2007): 274–86.

9. Liberation theology is a movement that originated in Latin America in the late 1960s. It emphasized the duty of Christians to transform social structures that oppress the poor, and it saw this as part of the general Christian project of liberating humanity from sin and its effects. It often used terms and concepts drawn from Marxism. It had considerable influence on the 1971 Synod of Bishops' document *Justice in the World*, but it was criticized in two documents in 1984 and 1986 from the Congregation for the Doctrine of the Faith, the Vatican's doctrinal office, then headed by Joseph Ratzinger.

10. "Proper" here means "belonging specifically to," as opposed to "common." It is common to all fielders in baseball that they catch the ball, but proper that the catcher catch the ball when the pitcher throws it to the batter—that is how the catcher is distinguished from the other fielders.

11. Benedict does not mention it, but this point presumably applies to clergy as well, to the extent that they are allowed to participate in politics—for instance, to priests when they vote or when they serve on the boards of community organizations.

12. Augustine, *City of God*, 19.17.

13. Ibid., 19.21.

14. Ibid., quoting Scipio in Cicero's *De re publica* 1.25.39.

15. Ibid., 19.24.

16. Ibid.

17. O'Brien and Shannon, *Catholic Social Thought*, 40.

18. Ibid., 41–46.

19. Ibid., 47–48.

20. This information comes from the copyright page of the 1999 document, *Faithful Citizenship: Civic Responsibility for a New Millennium* (Washington, DC: United States Catholic Conference, 1999).

21. *Forming Consciences for Faithful Citizenship: A Call to Political Responsibility from the Bishops of the United States*, www.usccb.org/faithfulcitizenship.

22. www.vatican.va/holy_father/benedict_xvi/encyclicals/documents/hf_ben-xvi_enc_20051225_deus-caritas-est_en.html.

23. *Deus Caritas Est*, 29. The internal quotations are from, respectively, Pope John Paul II, Post-Synodal Apostolic Exhortation *Christifideles Laici* (December 30, 1988), 42, and *Catechism of the Catholic Church*, 1939.

24. "The Challenge of Forming Consciences for Faithful Citizenship" (Washington, DC: USCCB Publishing, 2007), 2.

25. The Peace Light Memorial was proposed by Union and Confederate veterans during the 50th anniversary (1913) of the Battle at Gettysburg and finally dedicated on July 3, 1938, during the 75th anniversary celebration, www.nps.gov/archive/gett/getttour/tstops/tstd-03.html.

26. William Collinge was kind enough to answer my questions about the Heritage Festival on February 10, 2008.

Chapter 7 Modern Politics and Catholic Social Teaching

1. The classic exponents of the social-contract theory of government are Thomas Hobbes, John Locke, and Jean-Jacques Rousseau, all of whom assumed that such an account of the source of the state's power provided an alternative to claims of arbitrary or divine authority, usually in the form of monarchy.

2. See, for example, Hobbes, *Leviathan*, esp. pt. 1, chap. 14, and Locke, *Two Treatises of Government*, esp. Second Treatise, chaps. 2–3. The theorists differ on the character or the state of nature, but they each presume it as a prelude to the formation of society.

3. In the time of Hobbes and Locke, such an alternative took the form of monarchy, whose orderly powers descended from divine right, such that individuals owed their lives in service to God and to the king. See, for example, a 1610 address from King James I, where he states: "Kings are justly called gods for that they exercise a manner or resemblance of divine power upon earth. . . . God has power to create, or destroy, make, or unmake at his pleasure, to give life, or send death, . . . and the like power have kings. They make and unmake their subjects; they have the power of raising up and casting down, of life and of death; . . . and to the king is due both the affections of the soul and the service of the body of his subjects." King James I, "A Speech to the Lords and Commons of the Parliament at Whitehall," in *The Bedford Companion to Shakespeare*, 2nd ed., ed. Russ McDonald (Boston: St. Martin's, 2001), 328–29.

4. Pope John Paul II denies that the church's social doctrine is a "third way" in *Solicitudio Rei Socialis* (December 30, 1987), 4. Catholic social thought provides not, strictly speaking, a system of government but rather "the accurate formulation of the results of a careful reflection on the complex realities of human existence, in society and in the international order, in the light of faith and of the church's tradition." Thus it is anthropology, not political science. But while these can and should be distinguished, they cannot be wholly separated. Using the language of "third way" here is pedagogically helpful in distinguishing the teaching strongly from the theories of capitalism and socialism. As far back as the end of the nineteenth century (and the Encyclicals of Leo XIII), Catholic social teaching was thought to offer a third way between these dominant ideologies. One of the most prominent exponents of this understanding of the third way is G. K. Chesterton (and his fellow distributists). See Chesterton's *What's Wrong with the World* (1910) or *The Outline of Sanity* (1926). Pope John Paul II may want to distinguish Catholic Social thought from the "third way" because the term has also been used to refer to the likes of former prime minister of the United Kingdom, Tony Blair ("Blair's Third Way," *The Guardian*, May 8, 2005, www.guardian.co.uk/news/2005/may/08/leaders.labour).

5. For example, in the earlier encyclicals, which dealt primarily with strife between workers and owners, the idea of class conflict was flatly rejected. See Leo XIII *Rerum Novarum* (May 15, 1891), 15. Ditto with *Rerum*, and all the sources in the following notes 6–11. In later encyclicals this concern is expressed on a more global scale, in terms of the relationship between developed and less developed nations (which, in light of the globalization of capital, is a new version of the prior conflict). See *Solicitudio*, 39.

6. *Gaudium et Spes: Pastoral Constitution on the Church in the Modern World*, in *Catholic Social Thought: The Documentary Heritage*, ed. David J. O'Brien and Thomas A. Shannon (Maryknoll, NY: Orbis, 1992), 24.

7. Ibid., 25.

8. John Paul II, *Centesimus Annus*, in *Catholic Social Thought*, ed. O'Brien and Shannon, 47.

9. Pius XI, *Quadragesimo Anno*, in *Catholic Social Thought*, ed. O'Brien and Shannon, 81.

10. Ibid., 84–85.

11. *Solicitudio Rei Socialis*, 38.

12. M. Blatte, J. Carney, and L. Gottlieb, "Hands Across America" (soundrecording), EMI America Records, 1986.

13. *Centesimus Annus*, 13. The origins of subsidiarity are traced to *Quadragesimo Anno*, 79, which states that "it is an injustice and at the same time a grave evil and a disturbance of right order to transfer to the larger and higher collectivity functions which can be performed and provided for by lesser and subordinate bodies."

14. And insofar as Katrina's devastation is related to global warming, which itself arises from greed and competition among people and nations, the point is all the stronger. Cooperation is not something just for emergencies. It is meant to be a daily way of life.

15. *Centesimus Annus*, 49.

16. Wendell Berry, "Does Community Have a Value?" in *Home Economics* (New York: North Point Press, 1987), 179.

17. *Gaudium et Spes*, 74.

18. Virgil Michel, OSB, *The Social Question* (Collegeville, MN: St. John's University Press, 1987), 26.

19. Ibid., 26.

20. This follows from the basic Catholic teaching on the universal destination of goods. See *Centesimus Annus*, 30, quoting *Rerum Novarum*, 18–19.

21. *Centesimus Annus*, 25.

22. Michel, *The Social Question*, 26.

23. Ibid., 27.

24. *Solicitudio Rei Socialis*, 36.

25. See, for example, "Discourse on the Origin and Foundations of Inequality Among Men," in *Rousseau's Political Writings*, eds. Alan Ritter and Julia Conaway Bondanella (New York: W. W. Norton, 1988), 9, 33–45.

26. See, for example, "The *Grundrisse*," in *The Marx-Engels Reader*, 2nd ed., ed. Robert C. Tucker (New York: W. W. Norton, 1978), 292–93.

27. *Centesimus Annus*, 41.

28. Ibid.

29. Ibid., 39.

30. *Solicitudio Rei Socialis*, 37.

31. *Rerum Novarum*, 25.

32. Wendell Berry, "Out of Your Car, Off Your Horse," in *Sex, Economy, Freedom, and Community* (New York: Pantheon, 1993), 24–25.

33. "The High Cost of Health Care," *The New York Times*, November 25, 2007, 9.

34. National Coalition on Health Care, "Health Insurance Cost" (2007), www.nchc.org/facts/cost.shtml.

35. Statistics on health insurance are found at www.census.gov/hhes/www/hlthins/hlthin06.html.

36. USCCB, "A Framework for Comprehensive Health Care Reform" (Washington, DC: USCCB Publishing, 1993).

37. Michael Tanner, "Health Care Reform: The Good, the Bad, and the Ugly," *Cato Institute* (November 24, 1992), www.cato.org.

38. Daniel J. DeNoon, "Many Parents Don't Know Cold Facts: False beliefs about colds lead to unnecessary doc visits, misuse of antibiotics," *WebMD Medical News* (February 3, 2003), www.webmd.com/allergies/news/20030203/many-parents-dont-know-cold-facts.

39. Dan Ullrich, "End-of-Life Care Costs Under Scrutiny," *Health Link, Medical College of Wisconsin* (December 12, 2006), http://healthlink.mcw.edu/article/1031002700.html.

Chapter 8 Natural Law

1. Sophocles, *Antigone*, lines 450–57, trans. Ian Johnston (Vancouver Island University), http://records.viu.ca/~johnston/sophocles/antigone.htm.

2. There are those who find in Sophocles' play more ambiguity about the moral status of Antigone and Creon. It is true that Sophocles exploits parallels between the two strong-willed characters, but to relativize their choices is to ignore the difference between that which each one wills. It is significant that Antigone embraces her fate with clear-eyed anticipation; her resolve to do what is right never wavers. Creon, by contrast, is blind, and once his fate is clear to him—too late—he regrets his actions.

3. Leo XIII's *Aeterni Patris* (1879) is "on the restoration of Christian philosophy according to the mind of St. Thomas Aquinas." Cf. John Paul II's *Fides et Ratio* (1996), secs. 43–44 and 78: "The Magisterium's intention has always been to show how Saint Thomas is an authentic model for all who seek the truth. In his thinking, the demands of reason and the power of faith found the most elevated synthesis ever attained by human thought, for he could defend the radical newness introduced by Revelation without ever demeaning the venture proper to reason."

4. A. G. Sertillanges, *Foundations of Thomistic Philosophy*, trans. Godfrey Anstruther (London: Herder, 1931), 9.

5. Otto Willmann, in his *Geschichte des Idealismus*, vol. 3 (Braunschweig: Friedrich Vieweg & Sohn, 1897), 458, quoted in Francesco Olgiati, *Key to the Study of St. Thomas*, trans. John S. Zybura (London: Herder, 1925; rev., 1929), 1.

6. G. K. Chesterton, *Saint Thomas Aquinas* (London: Sheed & Ward, 1933), 175. This book has been often reprinted, and sometimes subtitled "The Dumb Ox." There are many books that aim to introduce the life and thought of Aquinas, but this brilliant classic stands alone.

7. One of the best books about natural law is C. S. Lewis, *The Abolition of Man* (1944). To draw attention to the fact that both the general idea of natural law, and particular natural law teachings transcend culture, Lewis chooses to refer to natural law by an Eastern name, calling it the Tao. The book contains an insightful appendix of different expressions of natural law from various cultures and times.

8. Aristotle, *Rhetoric*, I.13 (1373b); cf. I.15 (1374a), which also quotes Sophocles in reference to law that is *kata phusin* (based on nature or according to nature).

9. What is sometimes referred to as Aquinas's "treatise on law" is in fact a part of the larger theological work, his *Summa Theologiae* (I–II, qq. 90–108). But the reflections about the role of reason in Aquinas mean that it is not entirely inappropriate to regard at least large portions of the theory as philosophical. On the history of natural law theory, and Aquinas's place in it, see Heinrich A. Rommen, *The Natural Law: A Study in Legal and Social History and Philosophy* (Indianapolis: Liberty Ford, 1988); Yves Simon, *The Tradition of Natural Law* (New York: Fordham University Press, 1965; repr., 1992); and Howard P. Kainz, *Natural Law: An Introduction and Re-examination* (Chicago: Open Court, 2004).

10. Cf. *Summa Theologiae*, I, qq. 22 and 103.

11. *Summa Theologiae*, I–II, q. 91, a. 2.

12. On the parts of the definition of law, see the four articles of *Summa Theologiae*, I–II, q. 90.

13. For an exploration of the significance of this conception of law, see Russell Hittinger, *Thomas Aquinas and the Rule of Law* (Catanzaro: Rubbettino, 2007).

14. On the role of God in natural law theory, see Fulvio DiBlasi, *God and the Natural Law: A Rereading of Thomas Aquinas* (South Bend, IN: St. Augustine's Press, 2006).

15. The emphasis on the role of intellect in discerning the natural law is not meant to obscure the role of the affections, appetite, or will. Prudence, the intellectual virtue by which the mind

discerns moral truth, presumes moral virtue as well, and it is important to remember the role of moral disposition—the orientation of the will—in grasping the natural law. On this see the excellent essay by Kevin E. O'Reilly, "The Vision of Virtue and Knowledge in the Natural Law of Thomas Aquinas," *Nova et Vetera* 5 (2007): 41–65.

16. Cf. the appendix to Lewis's *Abolition of Man*, which finds in diverse cultures common illustrations of the Tao on such matters as beneficence, familial duties, justice, truthfulness, mercy, and self-sacrifice.

17. Think of the blindness suffered by those who have dwelt in the darkness of Plato's Cave; or think of those described in Paul's Letter to the Romans, who were responsible for knowing and acting on the truth but whose sinful behavior leads to vain imagination, darkened hearts, and reprobate minds.

18. A recent, alternative account of Catholic natural law theory is somewhat more indebted to Kant than to Aquinas; it develops a different account of practical reason, within a different metaphysical framework. For a Thomistic criticism of this alternative theory, see Russell Hittinger, *A Critique of the New Natural Law Theory* (Notre Dame, IN: University of Notre Dame Press, 1987), and Stephen A. Long, "Natural Law or Autonomous Practical Reason: Problems for the New Natural Law Theory," in *St. Thomas Aquinas and the Natural Law Tradition: Contemporary Perspectives*, ed. John Goyette, Mark S. Latkovic, and Richard S. Myers (Washington, DC: Catholic University of America Press, 2004), 165–93.

19. Martin Luther King Jr., *Letter from Birmingham Jail* (Copyright: The Estate of Martin Luther King Jr.), 1–11, www.stanford.edu/group/King/frequentdocs/birmingham.pdf. The quotation is on p. 4 of this version.

20. Ibid., 4.

21. John Paul II, *Veritatis Splendor* (August 6, 1993), 6–27, www.vatican.va/holy_father/john_paul_ii/encyclicals/documents/hf_jp-ii_enc_06081993_veritatis-splendor_en.html. Compare John Paul II's encyclical on faith and reason, *Fides et Ratio*, 33.

22. Pius XI, *Quadragesimo Anno* (May 15, 1931), 79, www.vatican.va/holy_father/pius_xi/encyclicals/documents/hf_p-xi_enc_19310515_quadragesimo-anno_en.html.

23. John Paul II, *Centesimus Annus* (May 1, 1991), 48, www.vatican.va/holy_father/john_paul_ii/encyclicals/documents/hf_jp-ii_enc_01051991_centesimus-annus_en.html. Compare *Catechism of the Catholic Church*, no. 1883, www.vatican.va/archive/catechism/ccc_toc.html.

24. Good general introductions to subsidiarity are Thomas C. Kohler, "In Praise of Little Platoons," in *Building the Free Society: Democracy, Capitalism, and Catholic Social Teaching*, ed. George Weigel and Robert Royal (Grand Rapids: Eerdmans, 1993), and Benjamin S. Llamzon, "Subsidiarity: The Term, Its Metaphysics and Use," *Aquinas* 21 (1978): 44–62.

25. Nor is this a specifically Catholic insight. For other expressions of what the Catholic tradition calls subsidiarity, compare the writings of Calvinist Abraham Kuyper (*Calvinism: Six Stone Foundation Lectures* [Grand Rapids: Eerdmans, 1943]), and the Swiss Protestant Emil Brunner (*Justice and the Social Order*, trans. Mary Hottinger [New York: Harper & Brothers, 1945]).

26. Christopher Wolfe, "Subsidiarity: The 'Other' Ground of Limited Government," in *Catholicism, Liberalism, and Communitarianism: The Catholic Intellectual Tradition and the Moral Foundations of Democracy*, ed. Kenneth L. Grasso, Gerard V. Bradley, and Robert P. Hunt (Lanham, MD: Rowman & Littlefield, 1995). See also Christopher Wolfe, "Thomistic Natural Law and the American Natural Law Tradition," in *St. Thomas Aquinas*, ed. Goyette, et al., 197–228.

27. Russell Hittinger, "Social Roles and Ruling Virtues in Catholic Social Doctrine," *Annales Theologici* 16 (2002): 295–318. "The notion of the *munus* unifies two things which are so often split apart in modern political and social thought: first, what man claims as his own, and second, what man has to give as a gift of service" (301). The term *munus* "holds together the Aristotelian notion of an *ergon* or characteristic function with the more biblical concept of [a divinely given] vocation or mission" (302).

28. On the origin and meaning of the term, see Normand J. Paulhus, "Uses and Misuses of the Term 'Social Justice' in the Roman Catholic Tradition," *Journal of Religious Ethics* 15 (1987): 261–82. The term was coined by a 19th century Thomist, who used it in an 1840 treatise on natural law. See Thomas C. Behr, "Luigi Taparelli D'Azeglio, SJ (1793–1862) and the Development of Scholastic Natural-Law Thought As a Science of Society and Politics," *Journal of Markets and Morality* 6 (2003): 99–116.

29. Paulhus, "Uses and Misuses," 275–76.

30. "For Pius XI, social justice is nothing other than the manifold organicity of the common good; or, to put it another way, it is the demand that the common good be brought about through organizations, institutions, and groups" (Hittinger, "Social Roles and Ruling Virtues," 303).

31. *Summa Theologiae*, II–II, q. 58, a. 6.

32. The quotations from *Rerum Novarum* are cited from www.vatican.va/holy_father/leo_xiii/encyclicals/documents/hf_l-xiii_enc_15051891_rerum-novarum_en.html.

33. Pius XI, *Quadragesimo Anno*, 80.

34. John Paul II, *Letter to Families* (1994), www.vatican.va/holy_father/john_paul_ii/letters/documents/hf_jp-ii_let_02021994_families_en.html.

Chapter 9 Modern Economy and the Social Order

1. Paul Misner, *Social Catholicism in Europe* (New York: Crossroad, 1991), 35–55.

2. *Rerum Novarum* and other encyclicals are cited in David J. O'Brien and Thomas A. Shannon, eds., *Catholic Social Thought: The Documentary Heritage* (Maryknoll, NY: Orbis, 1992).

3. Another term for unfettered capitalism might be laissez-faire capitalism, but historians of the modern economy disagree on the proper use of the term. By unfettered capitalism I mean a view that economic exchange provides its own self-regulation and does not need social or legal controls.

4. Misner, *Social Catholicism*, 189–212.

5. I add, "for the most part," because both capitalism and socialism are fluid terms. There are many capitalisms and socialisms. Most capitalisms, like most socialisms, are tied to modern philosophical and political thought that imagines a presocial individual. A contrast would be G. K. Chesterton (1874–1936) and the distributist school of thought. Because capitalism too often narrows economic relations to the use of capital, John Paul II prefers the term "free market" or "market economy" in *Centesimus Annus*, 42.

6. Adam Smith, *An Inquiry into the Nature and Causes of the Wealth of Nations*, ed. C. J. Bullock (New York: P. F. Collier & Sons, 1909).

7. In the famous invisible hand passage of the *Wealth of Nations*, Smith holds that when an individual seeks his or her economic self-interest, "he intends only his own gain, and he is in this, as in many other cases, led by an invisible hand to promote an end which was no part of his intention" (351–52). Like many modern social scientists, he holds that the natural mechanisms of economic life determine individual behavior. At various points Smith suggests that the poor, because they lack economic means, are more determined by economic mechanisms. The rich, because they enjoy economic freedom, are free from economic determination (see bk. 1, chap. 8, "On the Wages of Labor").

8. Part of Smith's argument in *Wealth of Nations*, bk. 2, chap. 3, "On the Accumulation of Capital," is that the effort of individuals seeking their own gain is often enough to overcome the "extravagance of government" and "the errors of administration" (283). Smith's overall argument is that the economy has a natural course apart from, but shaped within, particular societies and the imposition of social policy. The economy has a natural, universal course of development which is instantiated at various stages and in different dress in various cultures and places in the world.

9. Ellen Israel Rosen, "The Wal-Mart Effect: The World Trade Organization and the Race to the Bottom," *Chapman Law Review* 8 (Spring 2005): 261–82; Stephen F. Diamond, "The PetroChina Syndrome: Regulating Capital Markets in the Anti-Globalization Era," *Iowa Journal of Corporate Law* 29, no. 41 (2003): 39–102.

10. Normand J. Paulhus, "Social Catholicism and the Fribourg Union," *Annual of the Society of Christian Ethics* (Society of Christian Ethics, 1980), 78.

11. Hannah Arendt, *Origins of Totalitarianism* (New York: Schocken Books, 2004), 167–209.

12. See Smith, *Wealth of Nations*, bk. 3, chap. 4.

13. Juliet B. Schor, *The Overworked American: The Unexpected Decline of Leisure* (New York: Basic Books, 1992), 43–48.

14. Paulhus, *Social Catholicism*, 81–82.

15. The organic conception (in Leo XIII) is also hierarchical, as one of the necessary social functions (at various levels of life) is authority. I mention this point in contrast to Adam Smith. Ancient and medieval thinkers believe that the ordering of society is objective (drawing from the natural fulfillment of the human being) and that various forms of authority are needed to properly order social relationships. Smith, in contrast, imagines that a harmonious order will be produced by a mechanism of the market—the competition of individual self-interests—not by duties determined by the common good.

16. See Smith's discussion of the infant mortality rate in *Wealth of Nations*, bk. 1, chap. 8, "On the Wages of Labor."

17. "It is in the power of a ruler to benefit every order of the State, and amongst the rest to promote in the highest degree the interests of the poor; and this by virtue of his office, and without being exposed to any suspicion of undue interference—for it is the province of the commonwealth to consult for the common good" (*Rerum Novarum*, no. 26).

18. A just wage cannot be specified on a national level, given that the cost of living and the economy differs from region to region. But a minimum wage can set a base standard and should not be confused with a just wage, which is primarily the responsibility of an employer and employees (who ought not demand a wage that is so high that it is unjust to the employer).

See the U.S. bishops' website on the minimum wage: www.usccb.org/sdwp/national/min.shtml.

19. John Bossy, *Christianity in the West, 1400–1700* (New York: Oxford University Press, 1985), 57–63.

20. Ibid., 62–63.

21. The benefits of worldwide globalization are a matter of debate. See Luciana Melchert Saguas Presas, "De-globalisation or Further Globalisation," *British Journal of Politics and International Relations* 5, no. 3 (August 2003), 455–66.

Chapter 10 Through the Needle's Eye

1. Leo XIII, *Rerum Novarum, On the Condition of Labor* (1891). See the treatment of *Rerum Novarum* in chaps. 4, 8, and 9.

2. Pius XI, *Quadragesimo Anno* (1931), www.vatican.va/holy_father/pius_xi/encyclicals/documents/hf_p-xi_enc_19310515_quadragesimo-anno_en.html.

3. Paul VI, *Populorum Progressio* (1967), 49, www.vatican.va/holy_father/paul_vi/encyclicals/documents/hf_p-vi_enc_26031967_populorum_en.html.

4. Dorothy Day, *The Long Loneliness* (New York: Harper and Row, 1952), 44.

5. "The Aims and Means of the Catholic Worker," reprinted from *The Catholic Worker* newspaper, May 2000, www.catholicworker.com/cwo015.html.

6. Donal Dorr, "Prefential Option for Poor," *The New Dictionary of Catholic Social Thought*, ed. Judith A. Dwyer and Elizabeth L. Montgomery (Collegeville, MN: Liturgical, 1994).

7. Day, as quoted in "The Aims and Means of the Catholic Worker."

8. Ibid.

9. Ibid.

10. Father Thomas King, SJ, of Georgetown University asked this question in a sermon in 1989.

11. Day, *The Long Loneliness*, 282.

12. Ibid.

13. Ivan Illich, "Hospitality and Pain," McCormick Theological Seminary (Chicago, 1987), 3. The lecture can be found at www.davidtinapple.com/illich/1987_hospitality_and_pain.PDF.

14. Illich cites a letter of the Emperor Julian to his governors. Julian is giving directives on how to overcome Christianity. "Establish numerous hospices in every city... For it is disgraceful that not a single Jew is mendicant, and that the impious Galileans [Christians] maintain our poor in addition to their own, and that our needy are seen to lack assistance from us." Ibid., 8–9.

15. Dorothy Day, "Of Finances and Personal Initiative," *The Catholic Worker*, February 1938, 1–2. This article is found on www.catholicworker.org/dorothyday/reprint.cfm?TextID=145. The citation is listed on the online edition.

16. I take this insight from Brian J. Mahan, *Forgetting Ourselves on Purpose: Vocation and the Ethics of Ambition* (San Francisco: Jossey-Bass, 2002).

17. Dorothy Day, "More About Holy Poverty Which Is Voluntary Poverty," *The Catholic Worker*, February 1945, 1–2. The aricle is reprinted online: www.catholicworker.org/dorothyday/daytext.cfm?TextID=150&SearchTerm=catholic%20charity. In this article Day notes that families have a primary responsibility to their children *and* that they should also offer a Christ room.

18. See Juliet Schor, *The Overspent American* (New York: Basic Books, 1998).

Chapter 11 The Challenge of Religious Liberty

1. Out of respect for author Richard Buck, who does not use the holy name of G-d, the entire chapter, including quotations, uses the word "G-d."

2. This question is a version of the statement made famous by Pope Pius IX in his *Syllabus of Errors* (1864).

3. For a more detailed discussion of the distinction between the thesis and hypothesis of religious tolerance, see John Courtney Murray, "The Problem of Religious Freedom," in *Religious Liberty: Catholic Struggles with Pluralism*, ed. J. Leon Hooper (Louisville, KY: Westminster/John Knox, 1993), 131–32.

4. Ibid., 137–38.

5. Ibid., 138.

6. Ibid., 186.

7. For a history of *Dignitatis Humanae*, see Leslie Griffin, "Commentary on *Dignitatis Humanae*," in *Catholic Social Teaching: Commentaries and Interpretations*, ed. Kenneth R. Himes, OP and others. (Washington, DC: Georgetown University Press, 2005).

8. Of course, it is possible to manipulate people's beliefs, or to control what people think with the use of mind-altering drugs or less invasive measures like subliminal messages. But in such cases it is not correct to say that the person really believes what he or she has been manipulated into believing.

9. Vatican II, *Dignitatus Humanae* (1965), in *Vatican Council II: The Conciliar and Post Conciliar Documents*, ed. Austin Flannery, OP (Northport, NY: Costello Publishing, 1975), 801.

10. Ibid., 802–3, 805.

11. Ibid., 808–9.

12. United States Conference of Catholic Bishops, *Faithful Citizenship: A Call to Political Responsibility* (2003), www.usccb.org/faithfulcitizenship/bishopStatement.html.

13. United States Conference of Catholic Bishops, *Forming Consciences for Faithful Citizenship* (2007), 4, www.usccb.org/faithfulcitizenship/FCStatement.pdf.

14. Ibid.

15. Ibid., 6.

16. John Paul II, "Message of His Holiness Pope John Paul II For the Celebration of the Day of Peace" (January 1, 1980), www.vatican.va/holy_father/john_paul_ii/messages/peace/documents/hf_jp-ii_mes_19791208_xiii-world-day-for-peace_en.html.

17. John Paul II, *Centesimus Annus*, 4, www.vatican.va/holy_father/john_paul_ii/encyclicals/documents/hf_jp-ii_enc_01051991_centesimus-annus_en.html.

18. John Paul II, *Sollicitudo rei socialis*, 32, www.vatican.va/holy_father/john_paul_ii/encyclicals/documents/hf_jp-ii_enc_30121987_sollicitudo-rei-socialis_en.html.

19. Benedict XVI, Homily, Outdoor site of the Neue Messe, Munich (September 10, 2006), www.vatican.va/holy_father/benedict_xvi/homilies/2006/documents/hf_ben-xvi_hom_20060910_neue-messe-munich_en.html.

20. Out of respect for Richard Buck, who does not use the holy name of G-d, the quotation from Pope Benedict inserts [G-d] for Benedict's use of G-d's name.

21. Benedict XVI, Homily.

22. Vatican II, *Nostra aetate, Declaration on the Relation of the Church to Non-Christian Religions* (1965), in Flannery, ed. *Vatican Council II*, 738–41.

23. "'A Lesson of Value': A Joint Statement on Moral Education in the Public Schools," www.usccb.org/seia/moraleducation.shtml.

24. "Joint Statement on Pornography," www.usccb.org/seia/pornography.shtml.

25. "Joint Statement on Dealing with Holocaust Revisionism," www.usccb.org/seia/holocaust.shtml.

26. "National Jewish/Catholic Consultation in New Statement Urges End to the Death Penalty; Pledges Joint Efforts for Abolition," www.usccb.org/comm/archives/1999/99–288.shtml.

27. "Children and the Environment," www.usccb.org/seia/children.shtml.

28. "Joint Statement Condemning Acts of Religious Hatred," www.usccb.org/seia/hatred.shtml.

Chapter 12 Compassion and Hospitality

1. Martha Nusbaum, "Compassion: The Basic Social Emotion," *Social Philosophy and Policy* 13 (1966): 28.

2. World Synod of Catholic Bishops (1971), "Justice in the World," 3, 39, www.osjspm.org/majordoc_justicia_in_mundo_offical_test.aspx.

3. Vatican II, *Gaudium et Spes, Pastoral Constitution of the Church in the Modern World* (December 7, 1965), 21, www.vatican.va/archive/hist_councils/ii_vatican_council/documents/vat-ii_cons_19.

4. Philip Hallie, *Lest Innocent Blood Be Shed* (New York: Harper, 1994), 154.

5. Cardinal Joseph Ratzinger, *Truth and Tolerance* (San Francisco: Ignatius Press, 2003), 100.

6. Elaine Scarry, "The Difficulty of Imagining Other People," in *For Love of Country, Debating the Limits of Patriotism*, ed. Martha Nussbaum (Boston: Beacon Press, 1996).

7. Hans-Georg Gadamer, *Truth and Method*, 2nd ed., ed. J. Weinsheimer and D. G. Marshall (New York: Crossroad, 1989), 303n23.

8. Ratzinger, *Truth and Tolerance*, 60.

9. Aristotle, *Nicomachean Ethics*, Modern Library Edition, ed. Richard McKeon (New York: Random House, 1947), 22–23.

10. Jacques Derrida, *On Cosmopolitanism and Forgiveness*, trans. Mark Dooley and Richard Kearney (New York: Routledge, 2005), 16.

11. Derrida quoting Levinas in Derrida's speech at Levinas's funeral. *Adieu to Emmanuel Levinas* (Stanford: Stanford University Press, 1999), 72.

12. See John Paul II, *Veritatis Splendor* (1993), www.vatican.va/holy_father/john_paul_ii/encyclicals/documents/hf_jp-ii_enc_06081993_veritatis-splendor_en.html. John Paul II argues

that capital punishment is possible only in terms of a community's self-defense. Vengeance and retribution are excluded as legitimate reasons for the use of the death penalty. The pope holds that modern forms of incarceration are more than adequate to protect society; therefore, capital punishment should be abolished. In developed nations, it is no longer justifiable as self-defense.

13. Trudy Conway, "Moving Beyond Vengeance," Mount St. Mary's University's Calling Conference on Bearers of Hope and Healing (March 2007), 1–9.

14. Ibid., 1.

15. Ibid., 2.

16. Ibid., 4.

17. See www.usccb.org/sdwp/projects/socialteaching/excerpt.shtml.

Chapter 13 From Despot to Steward

1. John Paul II, "World Day of Peace" (January 1, 1990), 6, www.vatican.va/holy_father/john_paul_ii/messages/peace/documents/hf_jp-ii_mes_19891208_xxiii-world-day-for-peace_en.html.

2. Benedict XVI, "World Day of Peace" (January 1, 2008), 7, www.vatican.va/holy_father/benedict_xvi/messages/peace/documents/hf_ben-xvi_mes_20071208_xli-world-day-peace_en.html.

3. Lynn White Jr., "The Historical Roots of Our Ecologic Crisis," *Science* 155 (1967), 1205.

4. Ibid.

5. Ibid.

6. White acknowledges that Christianity is "a complex faith, and its consequences differ in differing contexts" (1206). He notes, for instance, that the Eastern church has historically fostered a very different attitude toward nature. He also recognizes the alternative view of the relationship between humans and nature presented by Saint Francis, whom he calls "the greatest spiritual revolutionary in Western history . . . [because] he tried to substitute the idea of the equality of all creatures, including man, for the idea of man's limitless rule of creation." The problem, White goes on to note, is that "he failed" (1207).

7. Ibid., 1206.

8. Ibid., 1207.

9. Anne M. Clifford, "Foundations for a Catholic Ecological Theology of God," in Drew Christiansen and Walter Grazer, *And God Saw that it was Good* (Washington, DC: United States Catholic Conference, 1996), 21.

10. Ibid., 24.

11. Ibid., 27.

12. Ibid.

13. Ibid., 33.

14. As the new *Catechism of the Catholic Church* notes, "*All* creatures bear a certain resemblance to God, most especially man, created in the likeness of God. The manifold perfections of creatures—their truth, their goodness, their beauty—all reflect the infinite perfection of God" (no. 41). (emphasis added)

15. Compare "*Finally, the aesthetic value of creation cannot be overlooked. Our very contact with nature has a deep restorative power; contemplation of its magnificence imparts peace and serenity. The Bible speaks again and again of the goodness and beauty of creation, which is called to glorify God (cf. Gen 1:4ff; Ps. 8:2; 104:1ff; Ws. 13:3–5; Sir. 39:16, 33; 43:1, 9).*" John Paul II, "World Day of Peace" (1990). (emphasis original)

16. As the U.S. bishops have noted, intense reflection on the truth, goodness, and beauty of nature reveals the sacramental aspect of creation. "For many people, the environmental movement has reawakened appreciation of the truth that, through the created gifts of nature, men

and women encounter their Creator. The Christian vision of a sacramental universe—a world that discloses the Creator's presence by visible and tangible signs—can contribute to making the earth a home for the family once again." "Renewing the Earth" in *And God Saw That it was Good*, 231.

17. Benedict XVI, "World Day of Peace" (2008), 7.

18. USCCB, "Environmental Justice Program: Caring for God's Creation," www.usccb.org/sdwp/ejp.

19. USCCB, "Renewing the Earth," 242.

20. Benedict XVI puts this point quite forcefully in his 2007 World Peace Day speech: "All this means that humanity, if it truly desires peace, must be increasingly conscious of the links between natural ecology, or respect for nature, and human ecology. Experience shows that *disregard for the environment always harms human coexistence*, and vice versa. It becomes more and more evident that there is an inseparable link between peace with creation and peace among men. Both of these presuppose peace with God," www.vatican.va/holy_father/benedict_xvi/messages/peace/documents/hf_ben-xvi_mes_20061208_xl-world-day-peace_en.html. (emphasis original)

21. Christiansen and Grazer, *And God Saw that it was Good*, 3.

22. USCCB, "Renewing the Earth," 225.

23. Compare "Modern society will find no solution to the ecological problem unless it *takes a serious look at its life style*. In many parts of the world society is given to instant gratification and consumerism while remaining indifferent to the damage which these cause. As I have already stated, the seriousness of the ecological issue lays bare the depth of man's moral crisis." John Paul II, "World Day of Peace" (1990), 13. (emphasis original)

24. As a starting point you might begin by calculating your ecological footprint or the magnitude of your resource use compared to others in the world. As a simple search will reveal, there are a number of different tools on the Internet to do this. For instance, visit www.earthday.ent/footprint.

25. Compare "*An education in ecological responsibility* is urgent: responsibility for oneself, for others, and for the earth. This education cannot be rooted in mere sentiment or empty wishes. . . . Instead, a true education in responsibility entails a genuine conversion in ways of thought and behaviour." John Paul II, "World Day of Peace" (1990). (emphasis original)

26. See the Graduation Pledge Alliance: www.graduationpledge.org/.

27. USCCB, "Renewing the Earth," 239.

28. Brian Henning and I had a discussion in relationship to his paper, "The Moral Efficacy of Beauty: A Kalocentric Approach to Global Climate Change," given at The Metaphysical Society of America, at University of Southern Maine, March 2008.

29. Paul M. Kellstedt, Sammy Zahran, and Arnold Vedlitz, "Personal Efficacy, the Information Environment, and Attitudes Toward Global Warming and Climate Change in the United States," *Risk Analysis* 28, no. 1 (February 2008), 113–26.

30. Ibid., 122.

31. Ibid., 121.

32. Ibid., 120n7.

Index